AF255150

The Path Toward Beauty
Through Texts and Works of Art

The Path Toward Beauty
Through Texts and Works of Art

By Francesca Weinmann

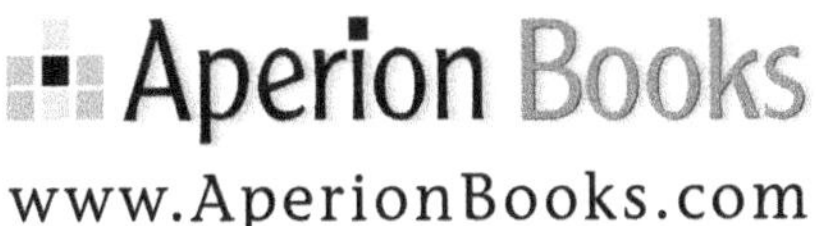

www.AperionBooks.com

APERION BOOKS™
1611 A South Melrose Dr #173
Vista, California 92081
www.AperionBooks.com

Copyright © 2012 by Francesca Weinmann

All rights reserved. No part of this book may be reproduced or transmitted in any form or by any means, electronic or mechanical, including photocopying, recordings, or by any information storage and retrieval system, without written permission from the publisher, except for the inclusion of a brief quotation in a review.

10 9 8 7 6 5 4 3 2
First Edition Published 2012
Printed in the United States of America on recycled paper

ISBN-10: 0-9829678-5-3
ISBN-13: 978-0-9829678-5-0
Library of Congress Catalog Card Number: 2012946155

Author photo by Diane Maroger
Cover & book design by CenterPointe Media
www.CenterPointeMedia.com

Disclaimer
Every effort has been made to identify the rightful copyright holders of material used in this publication and to secure permission, where applicable, for reuse of all such material. Credit, if and as available, has been provided for all borrowed material either on-page, on the copyright page, in an acknowledgment section, or in a list of illustrations. Errors or omissions in credit citations or failure to obtain permission if required by copyright law have been either unavoidable or unintentional. The author and publisher welcome any information that would allow them to correct future reprints.

Cover Image
The Cistercian Abbey of Fontenay was built between 1139 and 1147 in Burgundy France. Its beauty is based on unadorned stone, the play of light coming through grisaille windows, the absence of colored figurative windows, and, above all, the use of the most visible and simplest of proportions.

We do not admire work because of its past but because of its enduring present.
This surrender of oneself before beauty is for its eternity.
—Yanagi

Beauty is a slow discovery.
—Caillois

Table of Contents

PART III
The Artist and the Beholder

PART IV
Epilogue and Conclusion

    The Path Toward Beauty

Acknowledgements

Special thanks to Susan Gruenheck Taponier, without whom this book would never have come alive.

My gratitude to Jeanne and Bertram Salzman for coordinating the publication of this manuscript.

Publisher's Notes

Francesca Weinmann was an extraordinarily large-hearted and learned person. Her home was like a library; her books covered tables surrounded by easy chairs inviting friends to read, talk and learn together. She poured her knowledge into her teaching, especially her signature course on the history of aesthetics. She wished to convey this learning and the joy of her perceptions to a larger public and so aimed at a book-length project that she called "my life's work."

Sadly, Professor Weinmann died before the book could be published. Her friend and editor Susan Taponier played a significant role in making Francesca's manuscript accessible to a broad readership. Although Francesca identified all the authors and works she quotes, translates or interprets, as the footnotes and bibliography indicate, nonetheless, it has not always been possible to identify precisely the editions she used, especially when she made her own translations into English. In many cases, instead of referencing editions in their original languages, the editors have cited English translations, so that readers may pursue any author who arouses their interest, as Francesca would surely have wished.

Both Marie Bertrande Maroger and Lisa Baker Bulkley generously and affectionately supported the completion of *The Path Toward Beauty*, and we thank them for their valued support.

The assistance of those we've mentioned (and some who wish to remain anonymous) has made it possible to achieve Francesca's goal by publishing *The Path Toward Beauty*.

Foreword

Francesca Weinmann was a singularly gifted teacher who found herself with a devoted following. For art students like ourselves, her lectures were a revelation from the very first day of class; they were something we would never forget. She opened our eyes and invited us to ask essential questions about why human beings create. Through her profound love of the subject and her tireless dedication to teaching, she opened us to the possibility of bringing meaning and passion to whatever we did in our lives. She remained close friends with an exceptionally large number of her students until her death on March 4, 2011.

During study trips under her guidance, we discovered the route to Compostella, Romanesque churches in Burgundy, and Tuscan landscapes worthy of Italian quattrocento paintings. We were as moved by the art and what inspired it, as we were by the wonderful little restaurants she introduced us to and the meaningful discussions that often continued well into the night.

For those of us who have had the great fortune to visit her home in Italy, the experience represented the very essence of her teaching and character. The house, designed by an architect friend, inspired by medieval monastic architecture, sits on a hill among olive trees, oleanders and cypresses overlooking the beautiful Lake Como. Francesca, who was a natural gardener, would also cook delicious meals for us. We ate, drank, and talked for hours, utterly satiated with beauty.

We are grateful for her many gifts. She has helped us learn to look, to feel, and ultimately to love.

—Diane Maroger and Dorothea Naouai, Class of 1990

Introduction

The Common Thread

Beauty is an elusive, often misused word, whose meaning is constantly changing. Has it always been like this?

We live in the ephemeral and yearn for permanence; we experience chaos and search for an underlying universal order. Throughout human history, man has moved from the visible to the invisible, in search of permanence, in search of meaning, in search of truth and of beauty, as if these quests were all interrelated.

I have correlated the visual arts of various periods and civilizations with corresponding concepts of beauty. The examples mentioned in the following text are selective, however, and I have made no attempt to be exhaustive.

In reading philosophical texts, treatises on art, and artists' writings from the Pre-Socratic thinkers to Heidegger and from the earliest Greek texts to those of twentieth-century abstract artists, as well as the most ancient known Chinese and Hindu texts on the subject and those of an African Yoruba and a North American Navajo, we discover that before the eighteenth century in the West, beauty was not connected with a feeling of pleasure or related to a subjective judgment of taste. Until then, beauty was thought to be objective, along with aesthetic judgment, whereas pleasure, if it was taken into account at all, was on the contrary associated with the response of the individual. In most texts, beauty was viewed as distinct from loveliness and enjoyment, and pleasure was considered misleading.

Furthermore, only very rarely did artists produce works of art for the sake of formal beauty alone. In this respect, the naturalistic forms of art of ancient Greece and the Italian Renaissance (along with all later Western art that refers to them in one way or another) are exceptions and not the norm. Our own commonplace ideas about art and beauty seem to have been shaped by Western notions that, in fact, go no further back than the art theories of the second part of the sixteenth century, and concepts that date from the eighteenth century, when Aesthetics itself became a special branch of philosophy.

The concept of the artist as genius and the praise of imagination and creativity, in the sense of inventiveness, were not emphasized until the sixteenth century onward, and then only in the West, while the importance given to originality, in the sense of novelty and invention *ex nihilo*, begins in the eighteenth century and is especially associated with the twentieth century.

Let us thus go back and take another look at these concepts within a more universal context. How has beauty been conceived through the ages? Are there universal criteria of beauty? What has been the aim of art after all?

There is a common thread that runs through the infinite variety of artworks and the various treatises on art. The artist is urged to follow rules in compliance with imposed models and pre-established canons, not only so that the work will fulfil its spiritual, ritual or religious purpose, but also so that the artist can, after a long apprenticeship, free himself from the tyranny of the rules and acquire the ability to reveal the invisible through visible forms. Works of art were made to last; and, when they were meant to be destroyed, as in the case of Navajo, Indian or Tibetan sand paintings, there was always a ritual way of making them that had to survive. Survival is, in fact, the general aim not only of life, but also of art. Beauty seems to be one of the means for securing that survival.

Through the creative process, the artist learns his craft, with its technical, stylistic and iconographic rules and traditions. By following established criteria or aiming at the essential, the artist gradually forgets his own ego, and his artistic initiation becomes a spiritual one. The work of art has to incorporate life energy or the breath of life; the artist must be possessed by divine enthusiasm, be expert in vision, or be moved by the spirit. It is as if beauty could be attained only when all these conditions were fulfilled.

Synonyms have often been used for beauty, and the concept of beauty itself has changed over the ages, along with the criteria for it. The visible aspect and the meaning of art have changed as well, but neither can actually be understood outside the very general, human tendency to believe in the existence of invisible beauty that transcends human beings, which the artist tries to discover and bring forth through the beauty of forms.

Beauty has seldom been conceived as being in the eye of the beholder, as is commonly thought today. On the contrary, it was conceived as the attribute of a deity, as the "divine spark," if not as the secret of creation itself. The artist was believed to attain beauty by following rules that were often defined in terms of geometrical or mathematical proportions, but only insofar as those rules did not change and reflected the harmony of the world or a concept of the divinity, thereby connecting the microcosm to the macrocosm, the immanent to the transcendent.

There is a path towards beauty, just as there is a path towards that which transcends hu-

The Path Toward Beauty

man being, and there can be no beauty outside that path. While Plato's thought has dominated the Western philosophy of beauty, there are other non-Western traditions that have followed similar paths, and we shall attempt to explore them in the following text.

Some of the works of art we mention are illustrated here, and illustrations of the others are easily available. Yet beauty can only be fully captured when one is standing before, or within, the actual work of art, whether it be a plain rice bowl or a sacred building, as if the spirit was channelled through the artist's hands into matter, which he slowly transforms and brings to life.

The book is divided into three parts. The first, in the form of a prologue, uses disparate examples to raise some of the main issues. The second part begins by defining the terms most often used in relation to beauty and art, followed by a brief story of the main concepts of beauty, where special emphasis has been placed, in Western thought, on Platonic and Neo-Platonic philosophy and Kant. The third and final part returns to the general issues presented in the beginning, relating artist and beholder, outside any precise historical or cultural sequence.

The book is intended as a summary of the main approaches to beauty. The text itself is extremely succinct, as I preferred to allow the sources to speak for themselves rather than paraphrase them. It presupposes some previous reading and questioning and involves some re-reading and re-questioning. It also presupposes some knowledge of the history of art, and no doubt a love of art itself, as a reflection of the human quest for meaning, if not for truth and eternity.

The Path Toward Beauty

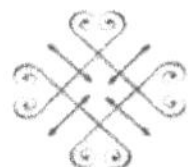

PART I
Prologue

Beauty is something that is perceived at the first glance, something which the soul names as from ancient knowledge and, recognizing, welcomes it, enters into unison with it.

—Plotinus, *Enneads*, I, 6, 2

A Metaphor for Beauty:
the Rose of *The Little Prince* and the Secret of the Fox

In *The Little Prince* of Antoine de Saint-Exupéry, we read about a rose, which did not look like any other flower on his planet; it was unique. The little prince observed how the rose prepared herself, how she worked at it with the greatest precision for days and days, to show herself, one day, at sunrise, in all her splendor, as if she had just barely awakened. The little prince exclaimed: "How beautiful you are." "Am I not?" the flower responded sweetly. "And I was born at the same moment as the sun." She had tamed him and he took care of her; she was so moving. After leaving his planet, the little prince landed on earth, where he discovered a garden full of roses that all looked exactly like his own. This made him very unhappy because he had thought that his rose was unique. Pursuing his journey on earth, however, he met a fox who taught him that these roses were in fact insignificant. He had not developed any ties with them as he had done with his rose, which therefore made *her* unique. The fox also taught him that we can truly know only what we love, implying that only what we love, and hence truly know, is unique and is beautiful.[1]

Just as the beauty of a flower is the result of millions of years of trial and error, and the

---

[1] Antoine de Saint-Exupéry, *The Little Prince*, trans. by Katherine Woods. New York, 1943, pp. 29-30.

beauty of any work of art is the result of a very long progression, so too the rose of the little prince had to work at it for days and days, even though her splendour would only appear suddenly one day, at sunrise. The little prince's exclamation: "How beautiful you are!" seems to express this sense of wonder.

Did the beauty of the rose lie in this uniqueness or in the fact that the little prince had come to know her well and love her?

When the little prince said goodbye to the fox, the fox told him another secret, which was very simple.

> "It is only with the heart that one can see rightly; what is essential is invisible to the eye. Men have forgotten this truth," said the fox. "But you must not forget it."[2]

A bit later in the story, the little prince says:

> "The stars are beautiful, because of a flower that cannot be seen." What makes the desert beautiful," said the little prince, "is that somewhere it hides a well . . ." "Yes, . . . what gives them their beauty is something that is invisible!"[3]

Throughout human history, man has moved from the visible to the invisible, in search of permanence, in search of meaning, in search of truth and of beauty, as if these quests were all interrelated. Beauty was connected to truth and both referred to transcendence.

The encounter with beauty may well be a mystery and may well precede any form of rational understanding, but the need for comprehension follows. The discovery of beauty is emotional and intuitive as well as intellectual, even though the beauty of some objects seems self-evident, as if they had been touched by grace.

Knowledge does not exclude emotion, nor does emotion exclude reason. When we exclaim in rapture: "How beautiful!," the emotion can be so intense that it seems forever incommunicable and beyond any knowledge, but it also provokes our curiosity and our thought. When we succeed in understanding the nature or reason for such emotion, it is like Archimedes' "Eureka!" and beauty becomes not only self-evident, but also intelligible.

Thanks to Saint-Exupéry, the rose of the little prince moves us but we can also understand the beauty of any rose through genetics or botany. Through these sciences we discover that each rose is, in fact, unique, not because it tamed anyone, but because no two living beings, not even identical twins, are ever exactly the same, anywhere, any time, while all of them have a common aim, which is to survive. Their elaborate architecture, their color and their forms all follow hidden universal rules and are indeed the result of millions of years of evolution, of trial and error.

---

[2] Ibid., p.70.
[3] Ibid., pp. 74-76.

Flowers are as they are in order to seduce insects that ensure pollination and fertilization, hence the perpetuation of life on earth. It is through what we call their beauty that flowers attract insects on whose work their survival depends.[4] Each flower is thus perfectly adapted to the sole aim of all forms of life—survival—not of the individual, whose life is ephemeral, but of the species, in other words, life itself.

Is the flower beautiful when it plays that role and do we find it beautiful because, as an integral part of nature, we too are in unison with these universal patterns? Roger Caillois affirmed as much when he wrote that man finds beautiful those forms that reflect him or in which he recognizes himself. Jean Guitton was to summarize the same thought when he wrote that: "the human mind reflects a world that reflects the human mind."[5]

Man is an integral part of nature, like a rose, but he is the most complex of all living beings, hence the result of further millions of years of evolution, but we are made of the same molecules as the flower, we are all made of the dust of stars. All inanimate and living matter thus obeys the same universal laws, which nevertheless leave room for innovations and chance, hence the infinite richness of forms and the absence of monotony which characterize both nature and art.

As far as we know, however, man is the only living creature with a reflexive consciousness, who is aware of his own destiny and hence of his mortality. Thus, he has proceeded to bury his dead, at least for the past 50,000-100,000 years, preparing their journey into an imaginary afterlife. He has done this with offerings and rituals, as well as by creating an imaginary world of signs and forms, hoping, thereby, to survive on his own terms. Imagination, as well as this poignant desire for immortality, are proper to man alone, and all forms of human creation appear to be a means of survival, acting as intermediaries between the here and the hereafter. We will try to find out whether beauty is also necessary for our survival, just as it is for the survival of the rose.

The beauty of the rose, of the desert and of the stars, as well as the secrets of the fox, are all metaphors with which this short story of beauty can now begin.

---

[4] C. Nurisdasany et M. Pérénnou, "Le Jeu de l'insecte et de la fleur," *Microcosmos. Le Peuple de l'herbe*, Paris, 1996, chapter 4, p. 111 ff.

[5] Roger Caillois, "Beauté," *Cohérences aventureuses. Esthètique généralisée*, Paris, 1973, p. 41; and Jean Guitton, Grichka and Igor Bogdanoff, *Dieu et la science*, 1991, p. 183.

Three Objects Through Three Different Approaches

Let us now take a look at three beautiful objects: an ordinary Korean food bowl, an Iranian dish from Samarqand or Nishapur, with Kufic inscriptions and a bird sculpted by Brancusi, to help us focus our discussion.

Korean pots were made during the Yi period (1392-1910) by very poor craftsmen for very poor people. They are unsigned and were not meant to be beautiful but merely to be used on a daily basis. One of them was owned during the sixteenth or seventeenth century, by a merchant called Kizaemon (fig.1). In 1631, it passed into the hands of Zen Tea-Masters, who came to consider it the most beautiful of all tea-bowls. In fact, it was the most ordinary of food bowls and the most common form of poor people's crockery. It is now exhibited with great care over the threshold of a temple in Kyoto.

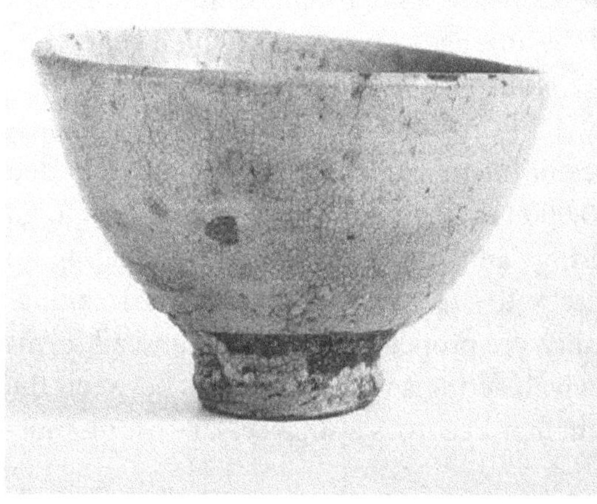

1 *Kizaemon Tea-Bowl*, from Korea.
Yi Dynasty, 16th century, Kyoto, Daitokuji

These bowls were the result of experience and wisdom accumulated over generations of potters. Their beauty was that of objects made by men who had abandoned themselves to the power of secular tradition. The bowls were produced rapidly and in great number, but the process of repetition itself led the craftsman to lose any notion of "I" and "it," or even of beauty and ugliness. Their beauty was not the result of any conscious effort or rational discourse, but rooted in an age-old tradition of pottery. Their beauty came all by itself.

The Kizaemon bowl is typical for its use, totally ordinary, made with clay that was easily available, with a glaze from the ash of the potter's hearth which ran over the foot. It was roughly turned on an uneven wheel, very quickly and with dirty hands, then carelessly fired, with sand remaining stuck to the bowl, thereby producing an irregular shape. This is the bowl that was to be considered, centuries later, as one of the most beautiful Zen Tea-Bowls ever made.

In a Zen Tea Ceremony, the participants used a very limited number of utensils of daily life, all of which had to be beautiful because beauty was an essential component of any Zen practice, leading to a meditative and contemplative state. Zen was always practiced in a world of beauty. The early Tea-Masters of the fifteenth and sixteenth centuries used traditional, unsigned, monochrome Korean food bowls because of their *shibusa*, which is a Japanese criterion of beauty.

The noun *shibusa,* or the adjective *shibui,* have been translated by terms such as "austere," "subdued," "restrained," "essential," "silent," "reserved," "humble" or "poor," although to a Japanese, the word seems more complex, suggesting "quietness," "depth," "simplicity" and "purity," in opposition to "showy," "gaudy," "boastful" and "vulgar." There is *shibusa* of form, of colour, of design.

When later Zen masters began to create their own tea-bowls with a conscious effort to make them beautiful, proudly signing them as well, something of this traditional *shibusa* was lost, to be replaced by a highly sophisticated approach to form, color and decoration, or by what could be called "boastful" virtuosity. *Shibusa* is, on the contrary, what characterizes the beauty of the Kizaemon bowl.

The Kizaemon bowl is also irregular and asymmetrical. Buddhists dislike perfection and symmetry, as if perfection did not admit of any freedom. The love for the irregular, which was not, however, to be deliberately opposed to regularity, also reflects the quest for freedom without which there can be no beauty.

For a Buddhist, beauty is timeless and the passage of time cannot affect an object that is truly beautiful. When an object is beautiful, it is undeniably beautiful, universally beautiful, independently of where, why, by whom or for whom, it was made. Beauty, in fact, eliminates all forms of dualism, of *now* and *then*, of subject and object, of what I see and what I know, of the perfect and the imperfect, or of the regular and the irregular.

> The opposition between the beautiful and the ugly is
> unknown in the land of Buddha.
> —Yanagi

Beauty lies beyond such distinctions because otherwise it would be only relative. The Buddhist notion of beauty is found in the absence of any dualism, which can only come about through grace, revealing a power that lies beneath the surface and of which the maker himself is totally unaware.

For Yanagi, beauty is thus an unending mystery, which cannot be apprehended through the intellect or be inspired by any theory of beauty. To perceive beauty, one must be able, first of all, to *see* an object, before trying to know anything about it: vision must always precede knowledge, or, at least, coincide with it.

The Tea-Masters who recognized the beauty of the Kizaemon bowl looked at it with "an unclouded intuitive perception," as if there had been an exchange of love between them and it, as if things of beauty were also things of truth.[6]

Beauty of form is the aim of all Islamic artists; to attain it involves an unending process. Art becomes, in Islam, a spiritual discipline.

> The poorest of the instruments is none other than that of the servant, while the beauty of the work can only be the reflection of the quality of the Lord. . . . Art is a laborious transformation of a relatively shapeless material into an object shaped according to an ideal model.[7]

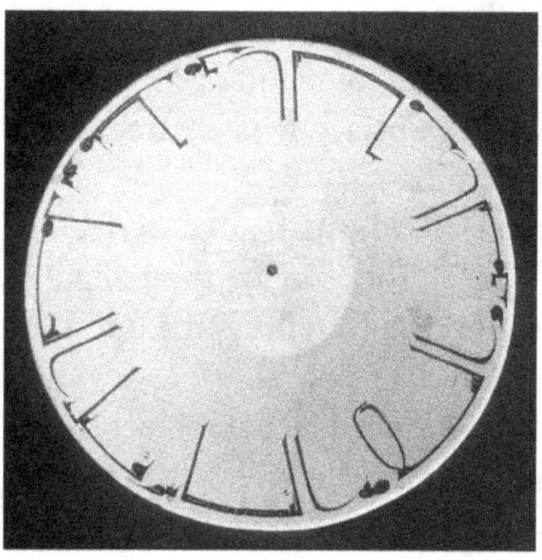

2 *Bowl with Kufic inscription*, from Nishapur, 10th century

We read in the *Quran*, that "God has ascribed *ihsan* (translated by terms such as perfection, beauty, wisdom) to all things" and in the Hadith that "God is beautiful, and He loves beauty."

Therefore, everything one does has to be done as perfectly as possible. This requires extraordinary discipline *and* love, thereby becoming also a ritual act and an offering to God. Contrary to the Buddhist, for an Islamic artist, perfection is not a form of captivity, but the ultimate end of an unending path (A carpet weaver will always leave something unfinished, because only God is perfect!).

In Islam, there is no difference between profane and sacred arts or between minor and major arts; all artists aim for perfection, be they carpet weavers, potters or architects (fig. 2). There is no hierarchy of the arts either, except calligraphy, which is considered the highest form of art because it transcribes the holy word of God as it was communicated to Mohamed. Islamic calligraphy, intertwined into arabesques, thus covers not only the Quran, but also all Islamic monuments. Like all Islamic art, it is based on very clearly defined geometrical rules and the absence of natural forms represented in any illusionistic style. In Islam, a work of art is beautiful insofar as it becomes an offering to God.

The same concept is found in the Hindu text of the *Bhagavad Gita,* chapter 18:

---

[6] Yanagi, "The Beauty of Irregularity" and "Buddhist Idea of Beauty," *The Unknown Craftsman*, London 1972 and 1989, pp. 119 -157.

[7] Titus Burckhardt, *L'Art de l'Islam, Langage et Signification,* Paris, 1985, p. 295.

     The Path Toward Beauty

When work is done for a reward, the work brings pleasure or pain or both in its
time; but when a man does work in eternity, eternity is his reward. . . . When the
work is done as a sacred work, unselfishly, with a peaceful mind, without lust or
hate, with no desire for reward, only then is the work pure. But when the work is
done with selfish desire, or feeling it is an effort, or thinking it is a sacrifice, then
the work is impure . . . . They [the craftsmen] all attain perfection when they find
joy in their work. Hear how a man attains perfection and finds joy in his work.
A man attains perfection when his work is worship of God from whom all things
come and who is in all.[8]

The Indian poet, Rabindranath Tagore, wrote:
We truly encounter God when we come to him with our offerings and not with
our needs, and the vehicle of these offerings is art.

Iranian pots were just as anonymous as Korean food bowls, but every potter ceaselessly
aimed for perfection, because God was conceived as perfection; in perfecting his craft, he
was also perfecting himself. In Iran, as in Korea and India, the name of the artist, i.e., his
individuality, should be absent; the artist was an instrument, not the maker. The Muslim is
not fascinated by the drama of individual artistic creation. Rather, he sees the reflection of a
cosmic order in everything, even in the artefacts which he makes. The artefacts are shaped
according to the nature of the object, by bringing forth the laws and the qualities, inherent
in the object itself. In pottery, the nature of the clay and the function of the pot called for a
given form and the potter worked at this form while he followed the rules that matter, craft
and tradition imposed upon him. The Iranian potter, like the Korean one, succeeded in
making a beautiful work when he had fully absorbed these rules, when they had been dis-
solved and forgotten in the work. When one perceives awkwardness or virtuosity in a work
of art, it is, in fact, because its author was not yet freed from them:
Whenever we encounter a work of quality, the rules yield to the metamorphosis
of the emotion which is its chrysalis.[9]

In a poem of Omar Khayyam, *Kuza-Numa*, we read about a potter's shop, where one
evening, at the end of Ramadan, as the moon was rising, the pots began to speak to each
other,
but only some could articulate, while others could not and, suddenly, one of the
pots, more impatient than the others, screamed: "Who is the Potter, pray, and
who the pot?"

---

[8] *The Bhagavad Gita* 1812, 23-24, 45-46, trans. Juan Mascaró, Penquin Classics, 1962, pp. 80-83.
[9] Alain Beltzung, *Le Traité du Regard*, Paris, 1998, p. 133.

In Iran, God was called the Potter of the universe, and the individual potter considered himself merely an instrument of God. However, some pots are articulate, and some are not, some are beautiful while others are not. The Islamic artist remained profoundly aware of the duality between the ugly and the beautiful, and between himself and God. Did the beauty of an "articulate" pot bridge the gap between the two?

Brancusi's *Bird in Space* exemplifies the approach of a Western artist of the twentieth century to art and beauty (fig. 3). It exists in multiple versions, on different pedestals, in different relations to other sculptures, in different materials, in different colors of the same material.

Brancusi sought to capture the sense of flight. "I am always working on it. I have not yet found it. It is not a bird, it is the meaning of flight. . . . It struggles . . . towards heaven. . . . All my life I have searched for the essence of flight. Flight, what a happiness!"

There has been a lot of writing and speculation about these *Birds in Space*, but scholarly work cannot substitute for standing in front of one of these sculptures, and still less for the transformation of matter into flight! Brancusi wrote:

> While carving stone, you discover the spirit of your material and the properties peculiar to it. Your hand thinks and follows the thought of the material.

> I have always looked for natural, primary and direct beauty, immediate and eternal. Do not look for obscure formulas or mysteries. I give you pure joy. Look at my work until you see them. Those who are closest to God have seen them.

> There are imbeciles that call my work abstract; that which they call abstract is the most realistic, because what is real is not the exterior form, but the idea, the essence of things.

> Sculptures are occasions for meditation.

> Simplicity is not a goal in art, but one arrives at simplicity in spite of oneself, by approaching the real sense of things.

> It is not difficult to make things, what is difficult is to reach the state in which we can make them.

> Once a bird came into my studio. When it wanted to leave, it could not find its way and threw itself against the walls and windows. Another bird came into the

The Path Toward Beauty

studio, rested for a while on a base, and flew off, easily finding its way to the sky. With artists, it is the same.

My last two birds are the ones closest to the right proportions, and I approached these proportions to the degree that I was able to rid myself of myself.

Whoever does not detach himself from the ego never attains the Absolute and never deciphers life.[10]

Brancusi also knew to what extent his experience had been that of other artists, over time, when he wrote: "My new 'I' comes from something very old."

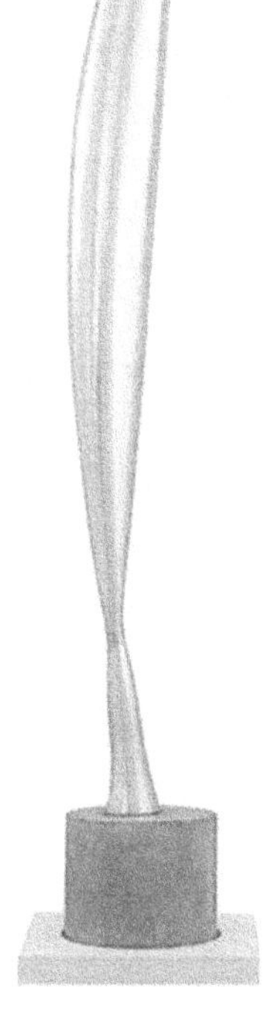

3 Constantin Brancusi, *Bird in Space,* c. 1930, New York, Guggenheim Museum

Brancusi's *Bird in Space* is as timeless and beautiful as certain Korean or Iranian bowls, and for exactly the same reasons as those evoked by the Little Prince: each one makes us aware of the invisible.

We are indeed struck by wonder when we are confronted by a beautiful landscape or with any beautiful form. This wonder forces us to move from the immediacy of the experience to an abstract world of thought and belief, as if beauty and faith in the existence of some eternal truth were, in fact, coinciding in the realm of human creations.

One can reach the absolute only through the faith implicit in the creative act. . . . Art works with the hieroglyphics of absolute truth. . . . He who cannot see truth, cannot see beauty.[11]

Like the rose of *The Little Prince,* these three objects are beautiful not because they please the changing tastes of their beholders, nor because they are valued by fluctuating

---

[10] Roger Lipsey, *An Art of Our Own. The Spiritual in Twentieth-Century Art,* Boston, 1988, pp. 225-246; and H. B. Chipp, *Theories of Modern Art, A Source Book by Artists and Critics,* Berkeley, 1968, pp. 364-365.
[11] Andrey Tarkovsky, *Sculpting in Time,* trans by Kitty Hunter-Blair, New York, 1987, Chapter 2.

markets, but because, as we said before, they seem to be touched by grace (figs. 1-3). Furthermore, each one creates a space of its own, which would not exist otherwise, just as their shadow brings out the object, and light exists only in relation to darkness, whilst the form, created out of formless matter, makes us aware of that which otherwise would have remained invisible. In the same manner, the immanent reveals what is beyond, and beauty lies in this mysterious interrelation.[12]

Some artists actually discovered that their art was a step by step path, slowly leading them to realize what they were actually aiming at, which was beyond the work itself and, when they became aware of it, it was also the end of their work. The Chinese story of the painter Wu Tao-tzu (d. 792) and the end of Dante's *Divine Comedy* illustrate this point.

The painter was finishing his last work for the imperial court, an immense landscape painted on a wall with woods, mountains, limitless sky, clouds and birds, and even men on the hill. He had worked at it for years, keeping the painting draped until it was completed. When the Emperor came for the unveiling and admired the painting in all its vastness and details, suddenly the painter pointed to the wall and said: "Look, here is a spirit in a mountain cave." He clapped his hands and the gate of the cave immediately opened. The artist stepped in, turned around and exclaimed: "The inside is even more beautiful. It is beyond words. Let me lead the way." Before the Emperor could follow or even begin to speak, the gate, the artist and the whole painting faded away. Before him remained a blank wall with no trace of any brushstrokes.[13]

At the end of his *Divine Comedy*, when Dante finally saw the light of God, his words also fell short. His poem did not disappear, but came to an end (*Paradise*, XXXIII, 121).

---

[12] Junichiro Tanizaki, *In Praise of Shadows*, New Haven, Conn., 1977.

[13] Chang Chung-Yuan, *Creativity and Taoism, a Study of Chinese Philosophy, Art and Poetry*, New York, 1963, p. 93. The same story about Wu Tao-tzu, painter of the T'ang dynasty, is cited in most texts on Chinese painting. His pictures were considered by later Chinese painters and critics as "divine things" because "a divine power worked through him." He was considered as having concentrated his breath of life, his vitality, his spiritual power and harmonized it with that working in Nature, rendering things through the power of his brush. He is also said to be the only painter to have possessed complete mastery of the Six Principles of Chinese Painting of which we will speak in the following chapter. Cf. O. Siren, *The Chinese on the Art of Painting*, New York, 1963, pp. 23-24, 31-32, etc.

  The Path Toward Beauty

PART II
A Brief Story of Beauty

What Are We Talking About?

Common Terms

While the definition of beauty itself remains elusive, we can try to give very general definitions of terms such as form, art, creation, aesthetic experience, aesthetic pleasure, symbolic reference, the holy or the sacred, absolute, relative, sublime, masterpiece and so on. All these terms are used in connection to beauty.

The following definitions could, I suppose, just as well appear in a preface or in footnotes, if each one did not also further our reflection. Plato taught that:

> There is one and only one way of beginning if one is to come to a sound conclusion; that is to know what it is that one is discussing; otherwise one is bound to miss the mark entirely. Now most people are unaware that they are ignorant of the essential nature of their subject, whatever it may be. Believing that they know it, they do not begin their discussion by agreeing about the use of terms, with the natural result that as they proceed, they fall into self-contradictions and misunderstandings. Do not let us make the mistake we find fault within others.[14]

The subject we are discussing is beauty as it is revealed through visible and tangible forms and as philosophers, artists and scientists, from very different periods and in very different places, have conceived it. Beauty is revealed through visible and audible *forms,*

---

[14] Plato, *Phaedrus,* 237, trans, by Walter Hamilton, *Phaedrus and the Seventh and Eight Letters,* London, Penguin, 1973.

and here we will be using the term in the general sense of shape. A work of art always has a given form and is always something made and transformed by man, thus it is "the creation of something emerging from non-existence into existence."

The word "form" comes from the Latin *forma*, hence *formositas*, which actually means beauty, as opposed to *deformitas*, which means absence of form and hence of beauty. It is through formal analysis, also called stylistic analysis, that one may grasp how beauty has been attained through specific forms, but only within a specific cultural context. One cannot analyze an African mask using Greek criteria of beauty or vice-versa, while both may nevertheless be beautiful.

A Chinese painter of the seventeenth century, Tshe-ao, had this to say about form: "The brush of the painter helps things to come out of chaos." And *chaos*, in Greek, is the opposite of *cosmos*—order—hence of the universe conceived as an ordered system. Pythagoras was the first Greek philosopher to conceive the order of the universe in terms of consonant numbers and a set of ideal proportions. This order was conceived as harmony, and harmony was conceived as beautiful. Pythagoras thought that the same ratios were found in the harmony of musical scales and vibrating strings, under equal tension, sounded together harmoniously if their lengths were in simple numerical ratios. Thus, in the sixth century before our era, Pythagoras established a profound correlation between the harmony of nature and the harmony of music and between certain mathematical ratios and beauty. This concept was to pervade all Greek art. For Aristotle, the chief characteristics of beauty were order, "symmetry" (from *sun metria*, meaning "with proper proportions of the parts to each other and to the whole") and definiteness. (*Metaphysics*, 1073 a 31 ff.)

In the third century of our own era, Plotinus wondered

> whether beauty was not something more than symmetry, whether symmetry itself did not owe its beauty to a more remote principle, and whether the primary nature of beauty was not, therefore, without form.[15]

For Heisenberg, the twentieth-century quantum physicist: "the discovery of Pythagoras is one of the most truly momentous discoveries in the history of mankind" and in a deeply moving essay on the "Meaning of Beauty in the Exact Sciences," Heisenberg writes that:

> Beauty is the proper conformity of the parts to one another and to the whole which touches the essence of what we may describe as beautiful: it applies equally to *King Lear,* the *Missa Solemnis* of Beethoven and the *Principia* of Newton.[16]

---

[15] Plotinus, *Enneads*, I, 6, 1-9 and VI, 6, 33. Translations of Plotinus are by Stephen Mackenna and B.S. Page. Chicago, 1952.

[16] W. Heisenberg, *Physics and Beyond: Encounters and Conversations*, New York, 1971, p. 61; E. Heisenberg, *Inner Exile: Recollections of a Life with Werner Heisenberg*, 1984, pp. 143-44, 157; S. Chandrasekhar, *Truth and Beauty. Aesthetics and Motivations in Science*, Chicago, 1987.

This movement from the visible forms of nature or of art to the invisible essence of beauty, from the sensible to the intelligible, is common to all concepts of formal beauty.

Panofsky defined a work of art "as a man-made object, demanding to be experienced aesthetically,"[17] but what did he mean and is such a general definition satisfactory?

"Art" comes from the Latin *ars,* and *ars* is the approximate translation of the Greek *techné.*[18] Within this strict etymological definition, a work of art is synonymous with an artefact and is thus any object made by man, using a given technique, hence it is any object artificially obtained and not forged by nature. To ask whether or not a work of art is truly art is not the right question, and therefore leads to a dead end.

When we see a stone or a branch that resembles a living form or any other figure fashioned by man, they are not in fact works of art, except in a metaphorical sense. They are the work of nature, but when Michelangelo saw a virtual figure in a rock and carved it out with his chisels, it became a work of art. When Picasso took a branch and transformed it into a bird by means of his imagination and his techniques, that branch too was transformed into a work of art. When a dancer imitates the flight of birds or a composer translates into music the sound of the wind in the grass, both have created works of art, each one using a different technique or art, while at the same time, at least in these precise examples, imitating nature's ways. Clay is a formless matter, but the potter brings forth a form by creating a pot with his art. He thus "creates" a pot just as Michelangelo created a statue, Mozart created a symphony, a carpenter made a barn, and an architect, a cathedral. Though works of art may be made for very different reasons and fulfil different functions, e.g., utilitarian, decorative, ritual or aesthetic, they are works of art all the same, regardless of their finality. In fact, in the West, no distinction was made between arts and crafts until the eighteenth century.

While *to create* simply means to make (from the Sanskrit *Kri*), it always implies the idea of a form emerging from nothingness, just as we imagine God creating the universe.[19] To create corresponds to the Greek *poïein.* Every created thing is literally poetry and Plato defines creation—*poësis*—as follows:

> By its original meaning, poetry [*poësis*] means simply creation, and creation, as you know, can take very various forms. Any action which is the cause of a thing emerging from non-existence into existence might be called poetry, and all the processes in all crafts are a kind of poetry, and all those engaged in it are poets.[20]

Works of art, as we mentioned above, were created for very different purposes and we

---

[17] Erwin Panofsky, "The History of Art as a Humanistic Discipline," *Meaning in the Visual Arts*, Penguin 1976, p. 37, New York, 1955.

[18] J. J. Pollitt, *The Ancient View on Greek Art*, New Haven, 1974, p. 27.

[19] George Steiner, *Grammars of Creation*, New Haven, 2001, pp. 16 ff. For Steiner: "No art form, it can be argued, comes out of nothing. Always, it comes *after*." (p. 23).

[20] Plato, *Symposium,* 205 b.

can naturally choose which of these we will take into consideration and which ones we will ignore when deciding to open a museum or simply reflecting on the common use of words and their changing meaning.

However we may choose, we should always bear in mind that man created nothing but tools for over two million years. When he began creating works of art with no immediate utilitarian end, it was for ritual purposes, and he continued doing so for at least another forty thousand years.

The earliest works of art were thus the first pebbles that our ancestors transformed into tools and, in retrospect, we might well ask ourselves if these were not the most important works of art ever made, thanks to which we were to emerge and very slowly evolve physically, mentally and spiritually. Man is man, in fact, because he is an artist.[21]

First, he became a constant toolmaker. Around a million years ago, however, a more evolved man (*homo erectus*) began making tools out of coloured stones, giving them forms and inventing the earliest symmetrical artefact—the bifacial tool (fig. 4). Did he do this for the sake of the beauty of form and colour, hence already for some aesthetic reason, or was it in view of greater efficiency? The question has not yet been resolved.

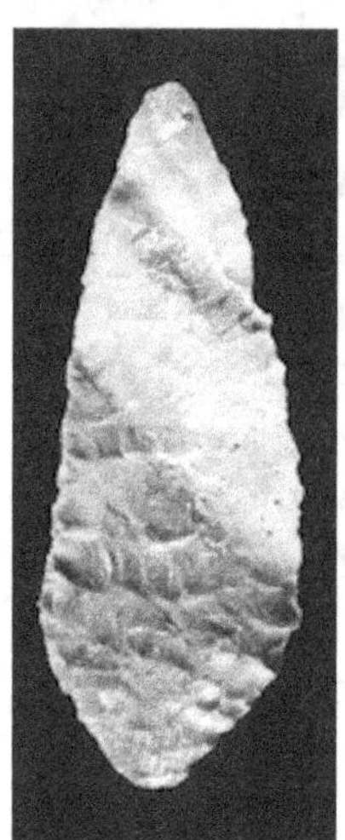

4 *Laurel Leaf, Feuille de laurier,* Solutrean stone tool, c. 19,000 B.P., Les Eyzies-de-Tayac, National Prehistoric Museum

Around 100,000 years ago, both Neanderthal man and modern man (*homo sapiens sapiens)* began burying their dead, and very gradually burial also became a human constant, reflecting a growing awareness of man's mortality as well as the need to believe in the existence of another world beyond death, however invisible.

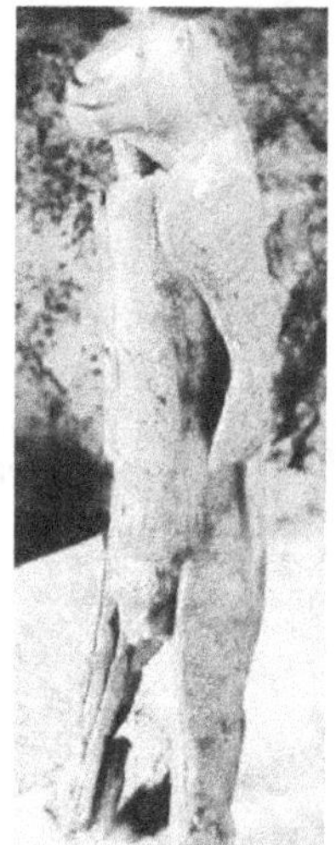

5 *Lion-headed Figurine,* from Hohlenstein-Stadel, Germany, c. 35,000-30,000 B.P., Ulmer Museum, Ulm, Germany

---

[21] Chimpanzees also transform natural elements into tools, but throw them away after use, and do not perfect them. They too have the aptitude of symbolic thought, even though it is more rudimentary; they too have complex social rules and, according to a very recent observation, even seem to follow some kind of funeral ritual, but they do not have any form of art that does not fulfil an immediate utilitarian purpose, except when trained by men in which case the result is chaotic. See E. Sue Savage-Rumbaugh, *Ape Language: From Conditional Response to Symbol,* New York, 1986; Claudine Cohen, *L'Homme des Origines, savoirs et fictions en préhistoire,* Paris, 1999; Pascal Pic, *Les Origines de l'Homme,* Paris, 2000.

   The Path Toward Beauty

Although the earliest traces of non-utilitarian art dating back roughly 50,000 years were found in Australia, the earliest figurines fashioned by man were found in a tomb in Sungir, Russia. Is it merely by chance that they were found in a tomb? Some 10,000 years later, other figurines were made and discovered in deep shelters in Stadel and Vogelherd (fig. 5).

They were followed by the earliest painted and decorated caves in southwestern France. Were these shelters and caves sacred places? These figurines and paintings all bear witness to man's need for, as well his capacity to create, an imaginary world of forms (fig. 6) and (fig. 7).[22] The experience of the sacred, on the contrary, is not an episode within human history, but an essential element of human consciousness, and it reveals itself through myths, rituals and symbols.

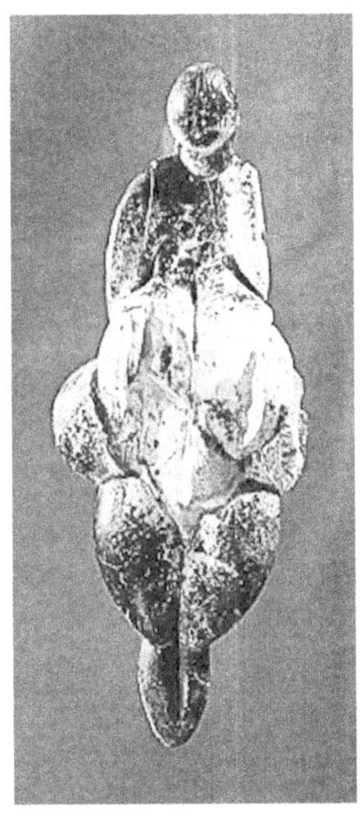

6 *Female Figurine of Lespugue*, 20,000 BP., Paris, Musée de l'Homme

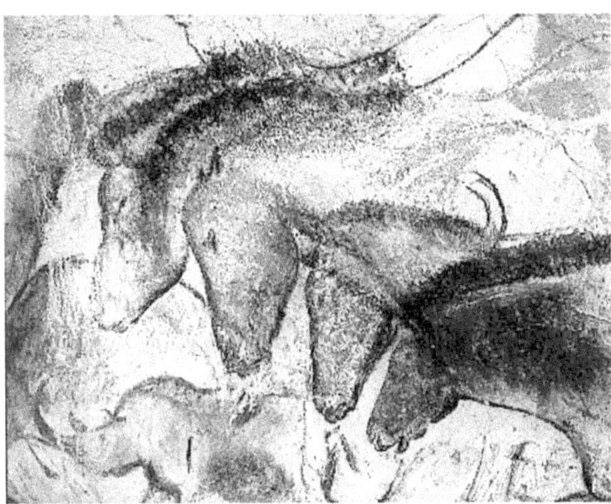

7 *Horses*, Wall painting, Chauvet Cave, c. 34,000 B.P., Vallon-Pont-d'Arc, Ardèche, France

However we interpret the earliest non-utilitarian artefacts discovered thus far, all of them were made by *homo sapiens* alone, and all were created with *a symbolic reference to a*

---

[22] Pascale Binant, *La Prehistoire de la Mort*, Paris, 1991. For the Tomb of Sungir, the shelters of Stadel and Vogelherd, cf. Gerhard Bosinsky, *Les Civilisations de la Préhistoire. Les chasseurs du Paléolithique supérieur—40,000—10,000* (av J. C.), Paris, 1990, pp. 42-77.

holy or sacred world. We will use *holy or sacred* in a very general way, as opposed to profane, referring also to Peter Brook's definition of holy theatre:

> Holy for short, but it could be called the Theatre of the Invisible-Made Visible. . . . Religious teaching asserts that this visible-invisible cannot be seen automatically, it can only be seen given certain conditions. The conditions can relate to certain states or to a certain understanding. In any event, to comprehend the visibility of the invisible is a life's work. Holy art is an aid to this. . . . The essential thing is to recognize that there is an invisible world, which needs to be made visible. . . . "Holy theatre" implies that there is something else in existence, below, around and above, another zone, even more invisible, even farther from the forms which we are capable of reading or recording, which contain extremely powerful sources of energy. In these little-known fields of energy exist impulses which guide us towards "quality." All human impulses towards what we call in an imprecise and clumsy manner "quality," come from a source whose true nature we entirely ignore but which we are perfectly capable of recognizing when it appears either in ourselves or in another person. It is not communicated through noise but through silence. Since one must use words, one calls it "sacred." The only question that matters is the following: Is the sacred a form?
>
> For thousands of years, man has realized that nothing is more terrible than cultivating idolatry, because an idol is only a piece of wood. The sacred is either present at all times, or doesn't exist. . . . So, in thousands of very unexpected forms, the invisible may appear. The quest for the sacred is thus a search. The invisible may appear in the most everyday objects. . . . The sacred is a transformation, in terms of quality, of that which is not sacred at the outset.[23]

Brook's definition of the holy, of the sacred, is related to theatre, but it is equally valid for every form of art and, in this text, we will use the term "sacred" rather than "religious," which could imply the idea of an institution and hence be associated with a given place or time in human history instead of being universal.[24]

The term *symbol* comes from the Greek *symbolon,* a "recognition token" that was divided in half and given to two people who did not know each other so they could recognize each other when the two separate pieces were put together, i.e., when the *symbolon* was unified once again. A symbolic work of art is, therefore, a work which makes us aware that

---

[23] Peter Brook, *The Open Door,* New York, 1993, pp. 69 ff. and for *spotha*: p. 60. See also his *Empty Space,* New York, 1968, pp. 42 ff.

[24] Mircea Eliade, *Patterns in Comparative Religion* (first edition in French, 1948) Lincoln, NB, 1996, chapter 1 and *The Sacred and the Profane, The Nature of Religion.* New York, 1968. Rudolf Otto, *The Idea of the Holy,* 2nd edition, New York, 1950.

The Path Toward Beauty

what is visible is only one part of the *symbolon*, and calls for another part, which remains invisible, which we must seek or at least understand. A symbolic act or artefact calls for a reunification of the visible with the invisible, that which appears with what it signifies. This reunification occurs through the work of art.

An important turning point in our humanization was, in fact, an increasing aptitude, as well as a need, for an abstract and symbolic form of communication. Human language consists of symbolic references, but words do not refer only to concrete objects, they also refer to memory, mental images, meaning, thoughts, complex associations and correspondences: "The problem of symbol discovery is to shift attention from the concrete to the abstract."[25]

This symbolic ability was fully developed only when the shape of the human brain changed, with the growth of the frontal lobe, which is also the seat of the human imagination. More complex symbolic forms could therefore be invented, and man was able to create an imaginary world of forms, to imagine the invisible through the visible, to have the experience of the sacred in a space, in front of objects or beings invested with symbolic meaning. With this new ability to create imaginary worlds, man also put order into the chaos of existence by giving it a meaning. Art fulfilled precisely this purpose, becoming a sign or a symbol of something else, acting as a means towards that end. In fact,

> as a species, we seem to be preoccupied with ends, in all senses of the word. . . . We organize our actions around imagined extrapolations of the consequences they will produce. We struggle in vain to comprehend the implications of our impending cessation of life. And we weave marvelously elaborate and beautifully obscure stories to fill our need to find purpose in the fabric of the universe. This fills no obvious adaptive need. Our evolution never included selection favouring anything like this intense and desperate drive. And yet it is so powerful. . . . If we are language savants, compared to other species, then the preoccupation with ends is the special exaggerated compulsion that complements our unique gift. . . . [26]

While an entire range of art and symbolic references has obviously not survived, as most media are perishable and gestures, sounds, movements and words leave no trace, those that have survived are among the greatest works of art ever made and none "demanded to be experienced aesthetically," such as the figurines of Vogelherd (fig. 5) or of Lespugue (fig. 6), and the paintings in the Chauvet cave (figs. 7 and 8) or Lascaux (fig. 9).

For another 30,000 years or more, man was to continue decorating ever deeper caves or isolated rock formations all over the world, representing a very limited range of animals

---

[25] Terrence Deacon, *The Symbolic Species. The Co-evolution of Language and of the Human Brain*, London, 1997, p. 402.
[26] Ibid., p. 3.

associated with each other and various abstract signs and handprints. We can only assume that these caves and rocks were sacred places, since no thick layer of ashes of any dwelling place was ever found there. We will never know which rituals were performed in the utter darkness of these deep, silent caves or in front of those rocks, but the recent hypothesis of Jean Clottes and David Lewis-Williams simply reiterates the conclusions that some type of shamanistic ritual did take place there, through which our ancestors communicated with the invisible world of the spirits.

8 *Lions,* Wall painting, Chauvet Cave,
c. 34,000 B.P., Vallon-Pont-d'Arc,
Ardèche, France

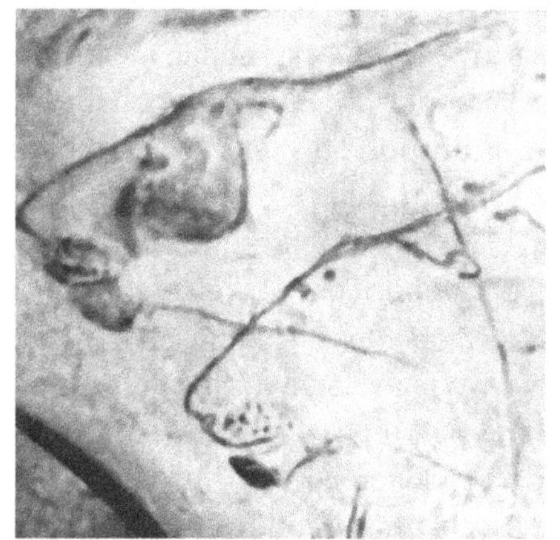

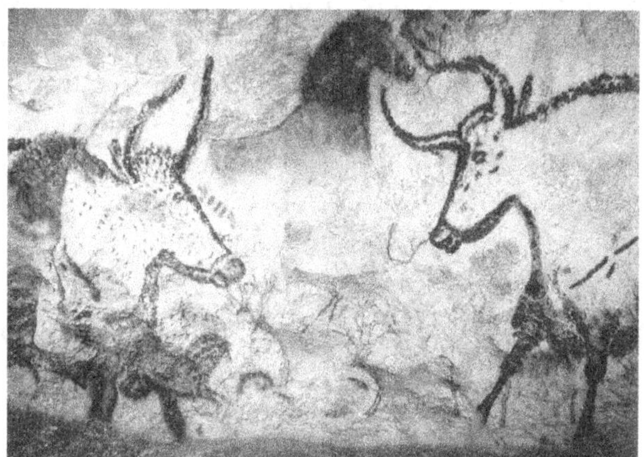

9 *Aurochs,* detail from the *Hall of Bulls,*
Lascaux Cave, c. 15,000 B.P., Dordogne France

According to Alain Beltzung:
> Art is precisely the act through which man penetrates the domain of mystery, whether it be the refined art of Mozart or that of the African blacksmith, half-craftsman, half-sorcerer.[27]

This power of creativity, as Paul Klee also underlined,
> remains ultimately mysterious. What does not shake us in our foundations is no mystery. Down to our finest particles we ourselves are charged with this power. We cannot formulate its essence but we can, in some measure, move towards its source. In any case we must reveal this power in its functions, just as it is revealed

---

[27] Beltzung, op. cit.

to us. . . . Creation lives as genesis invisibly under the surface of the work. . . .
Art does not reproduce the visible, but reveals the invisible, makes things visible
(*Notebooks*, 1922).

Indeed, as Peter Brook wrote:

All human impulses towards what we call in an imprecise and clumsy manner
"quality," come from a source whose true nature we entirely ignore.

As George Steiner stated as well:

Everything we recognize as being of compelling stature in literature, art, music
is of a religious inspiration or reference. . . . Referral and self-referral to a transcendent dimension, to that which is felt to reside either explicitly—this is to say
ritually, theologically, by force of revelation—or implicitly, outside immanent or
purely secular reach, does underwrite created forms from Homer and the *Ores-
teia* to the *Brothers Karamazov* and Kafka. It informs art from the cave of Lascaux
to Rembrandt and to Kandinsky.[28]

Because the main mystery of mankind has always been that of death, André Malraux
affirmed that art is antidestiny: "all life, created by the gods, is promised to death and what
has triumphed over death are the forms, the ideas, the gods themselves, all of them created
by man."

The earliest nonutilitarian works of art ever made were thus created to act as powerful
symbols referring to a transcendent dimension, as a visible means to an invisible end.

When we refer to *transcendence*, we understand this term in the most general sense, as
pertaining to a world outside, apart, or beyond physical appearances, which may or may not
imply belief in the existence of a God.[29]

In the context of this book, terms for what is invisible, such as "the spiritual" and "the
sacred" or the quest for the sacred, although by no means synonyms, are nevertheless correlated to that of "transcendence."

---

[28] George Steiner, *Real Presences,* Chicago, 1996, pp. 216 and 218.

[29] Louis Dupré, *Passage to Modernity. An Essay in the Hermeneutic of Nature and Culture,* New Haven,
1993, p. 162. This author shows how, after Kant, most philosophies of freedom, as well as those that
defended the principle of subjectivity in all forms of knowledge, rejected as incompatible any kind of
transcendence. In his conclusion, however, he writes that "The search for an adequate conception of
transcendence appears far from finished" (p. 253).

The meaning of the word "art" has changed throughout history, and we can trace these shifts, which seem to have been determined by a change of purpose, up to the second half of the eighteenth century.[30]

It was not until 1752, and only in the West, that the term *beaux-arts* was coined, hyphening art to beauty. Implicitly, a work of art thus became merely that which expressed an ideal of beauty. Art criticism emerged at the same time and a work of art was to be considered good if it was also aesthetically pleasing.[31] Subsequent museums of Fine Arts (*Beaux-Arts, Belle Arti*) became places in which only those works were exhibited that did not fulfil any immediate utilitarian purpose, but instead had to be aesthetically experienced as well as aesthetically pleasing. They were often, if not always, removed from their original context: an icon, however aesthetically experienced and pleasing, was never meant to be exhibited in a museum, but was made within a strictly religious context in support of contemplation. The connection of art to beauty was not new, however. It referred to the Greeks, who had been the first to aim self-consciously at making beautiful works of art. The earliest philosophical texts about beauty were, therefore, also Greek. It was, in fact, Plato who first discussed beauty, without ever connecting it to the sensuous world of art. Alone with Goodness and Truth, Beauty pertained to the unchanging, eternal and absolute realm of Being, which could only be grasped through the eye of reason.[32]

It was Alexander Baumgartner, in 1750, who was to call *Aesthetics* a new branch of

---

[30] In the *Petit Robert,* art has been defined as follows: 10th century: *art* was the knowledge of a given technique; 12th: there were liberal and mechanical arts, the liberal arts were intellectual disciplines such as grammar, rhetoric, dialectics, geometry, arithmetic, astronomy and music, whereas the mechanical or servile arts were all those subordinated to the use of matter and manual labour, such as the visual or plastic arts. 13th: art was applied knowledge and opposed to science, abstract knowledge, etc. Up to the 18th: art was defined as method, rules and aptitudes used to reach a certain goal or to make a given object: "the art of doing something." It is only in the 18th century that art became the expression of an aesthetic ideal in man-made works and that this term was used for all the creative activities of man that led to such an ideal.

[31] The term *beaux-arts* was coined by the *Dictionnaire de l'Académie*, in 1752, thus linking art to beauty for the first time and henceforth separating art from crafts. The criteria of beauty were established by the academies of fine arts and became standards of taste. Casts of Greco-Roman art and the works of the High Renaissance were proposed as models to the students. They were considered as standards of excellence, to be studied in class, hence "classical." Treatises were written in these academies in which the norms of art and of beauty were defined. Only works of architecture, painting, sculpture, music and literature were from then onward to be considered as beaux-arts. The Korean food-bowl or Palaeolithic tools, therefore, ceased to be considered as such by that new branch of philosophy called *Aesthetics*, after 1750 (Alexander Baumgartner, *Aesthetica*, 1750-58). Art criticism was also born at that time with the *Salons* of Diderot (1759-1781), in which the author judged contemporary art exhibitions and individual works, singling them out as either good or bad, not through traditional art theory, but in relation to his own subjective response to it.

[32] Plato, *Republic*, 505 ff. In this respect, it is also noteworthy that none of the nine Muses of Greek mythology is related to any handiwork.

philosophy, dealing with the sensuous understanding of art, considered as another form of knowledge. The term *aesthetics* is derived from the Greek *aisthetikos*, referring to any sensuous apprehension, with no particular reference either to art, knowledge, pleasure or beauty.

Since the early eighteenth century, philosophers had also recognized that the most important aim of art was to give pleasure,[33] hence to be *aesthetically pleasing*. For Immanuel Kant, but only in the very first part of his *Critique of Judgment*, the distinction between what was beautiful and what was not was related to the perceiving subject and to the feeling of pleasure or pain. Before then, works of art may well have been recognized as giving pleasure to the spectator, but, until the eighteenth century, that pleasure would not have been considered its main purpose.[34]

In the Middle Ages, the aim of art was to lead the mind of the beholder from the sensible physical beauty of the artefact "upward" or "inward" to the awareness of the invisible beauty of God. In Islam, abstract art, based on purely geometrical principles, was made to reflect the perfection and unity of God. In the Early Renaissance, its purpose was to discover the truth, through scientific knowledge, of the world or to discover the harmony of the universe as created by God while, in the Counter-Reformation, it aimed at stimulating strong religious experiences, and so on.

In most other civilizations, the purpose of art was not to give pleasure either, but to act as an intermediary. Beauty itself was to act as a *daimon*, as a Platonic mediator between man and the deity.[35] The beauty of the individual work of art could, therefore, only be *relative*, and it was beautiful only insofar as it partook of the *absolute beauty* of God, never to be confused with it (Plato, *Rep.* 476 c-d).

The *absolute* is that which exists independently of any relation to anything else, which exists unconditionally, which has no restrictions, which is a totality, which is perfect, and which is imagined such that nothing greater or more beautiful can be imagined. God was, therefore, conceived as being absolutely beautiful in most civilizations. So was truth.

In the Western world, this concept was to be shattered only at the end of the nineteenth century with Friedrich Nietzsche, for whom the word "truth" was a fable, an illusion, for whom nothing existed in itself or by itself, since there were no immutable truths but only multiple and different individual interpretations. Hence, there could be no absolute knowledge since there was no absolute thing in itself, nor was there such a thing as absolute beauty. With the Enlightenment, with David Hume and Kant, but especially with Nietzsche, relativism and individualism triumphed over Platonic idealism. There was no such thing as beauty in itself and art became a personal interpretation of the world.

---

[33] G.B. Vico, *Scienza Nuova*, 1725-1730; J.B. Dubos, *Réflexions critiques sur la poésie et la peinture*, 1719.

[34] Moshe Barasch, *Modern Theories of Art, 1. From Winkelmann to Baudelaire*, New York, 1990, chapters one and two (specifically: p. 23).

[35] Plato, *Symposium*, 203b-212c; Henri Michaux, *Un barbare en Asie*, Paris, 1933, p. 28; Oleg Grabar, *The Mediation of Ornament*, Paris, 1996, p. 33.

We have all become far more suspicious, if not plainly hostile, to any form of absolutism and dogmatism, because we link these notions to the political or religious totalitarianism and fanaticism of the past century, if not to present fundamentalism, but that has not always been the case.

Relative is the opposite of absolute; it is that which exists only in relation to something or to someone else. "Relative" implies a relation, which is interchangeable. In our discussion, the question is: has beauty always been considered as relative to taste, which is subjective, or, on the contrary, have artists and philosophers believed in the existence of absolute beauty?

In the *Will to Power*, Nietzsche wrote that there was not one world, but an infinite number of worlds, each one seen from an individual point of view, hence the result of individual interpretations and thus totally relative.

Today, we, too, wonder if there is anything at all which is absolute, eternal and unchanging, if there is such a thing as an initial divine plan, or if everything is not the result of pure chance, and, therefore, totally unpredictable. This has not always been the case. When reconsidering the issue of beauty, we are constantly reminded that in most texts the deity was imagined as absolutely beautiful and the formal beauty of works of art was thus believed to mediate the gap between men and the gods.

It is when the work of art actually ceased to be considered in this way that greater importance was also given to pleasure as well as to the aesthetic judgment of the individual spectator, to his intuitive knowledge, his sensitivity, hence to his taste. Gradually, from the second part of the sixteenth century onward, artists and critics alike were to exalt the artist's genius and power of creation as well as the subjective value of art and the importance of feelings and imagination.

It is in this same general context, but only during the second part of the eighteenth century, that Hume and Kant were the first philosophers to relate beauty and taste, stipulating that all *aesthetic judgment* was totally subjective and relative.

While recognizing that "the same Homer, who pleased at Athens and Rome two thousand years ago, is still pleasing at Paris and at London," Hume thought that one could not make a definite judgment about any work of art, or establish any true standard of beauty. Beauty, for Hume, was always related to feelings, however sound the understanding, and feelings were always subjective.

> Beauty is what one likes and there is no standard for it. . . . Beauty is no quality in things themselves: it exists merely in the mind, which contemplates them, and each mind perceives a different beauty. One person may even perceive deformity where another is sensitive of beauty, and every individual ought to acquiesce in his own sentiment, without pretending to regulate those of others.

The Path Toward Beauty

> To seek the real beauty or the real deformity is as fruitless an enquiry as to pre-
> tend to ascertain the real sweet or the real bitter; and the proverb has justly de-
> termined it to be fruitless to dispute concerning tastes.[36]

Kant's *Critique of Judgment*, and more precisely his *Analytic of the Beautiful*, begins with
the following sentence:

> In order to distinguish whether anything is beautiful or not, we refer the represen-
> tation, not by the understanding to the object for cognition, but by the imagina-
> tion (perhaps in conjunction with the understanding) to the subject and its feeling
> of pleasure or pain. The judgment of taste is, therefore, not a judgment of cogni-
> tion, and is consequently not logical but aesthetical, by which we understand that
> [its] determining ground can be [nothing] other than subjective.[37]

For Kant distinguishing whether anything is beautiful or not involves a judgment of
taste, related to a feeling of pleasure. It is not a judgment of cognition and is consequently of
a subjective and not objective nature. The Second Book of the *Critique of Judgment*, consists
of the *Analytic of the Sublime*, in which Kant writes more specifically, about the beautiful
arts. In the latter, Kant defines the genius as the maker of beaux-arts, "who quickens our understanding as well as our cognitive faculties" through the representation of images, leading
us, beyond any rational concept, to the awareness "of the suprasensible which underlies the
object and also the subject judging it (§ 57)." The "vehicle of communication" is the physical
beauty itself of the work of art which pleases us.

Although the reflection on beauty, as it is revealed through forms, began a very long
time ago, most of our own concepts of art and beauty date back only about two hundred
and fifty years, to the decade of 1757-1767, and Panofsky's definition of a work of art as
"a man-made object, demanding to be experienced aesthetically" can only be understood
within that precise eighteenth-century European context. His definition would make no
sense otherwise. Neither a Romanesque tympanum nor an African mask was ever made to
be experienced aesthetically and still less to be exhibited in a museum.

With the birth of aesthetics, philosophers also began referring more and more to the
beauty of the visible world of art rather than to the invisible beauty of God, whereas Plato,
like most other Western and Eastern philosophers, connected beauty essentially to God
or to the intelligible world of the mind. The very creation of aesthetics as the study of the
sensible reality of art works represented a break from Platonic philosophy. It also brought

---

[36] David Hume (1711-1776), "Of the Standards of Taste," in *Aesthetics* ed. by Jerome Stolnitz, 1965, pp.
86-97

[37] Immanuel Kant, *Critique of Judgment* (1790), ed. and trans. J. H. Bernard, New York, 1968, First Divi-
sion, First Book, First Moment, paragraph 1, p. 37. In 1764, Kant had written *Observations on the Feeling
of the Beautiful and of the Sublime*. For more on Kant, see below, pp. 121-136.

about a break with tradition, exalting the individual, and therefore, everything that was in-novative or original in a work of art. The latter was no longer conceived as a mirror of the world outside man, but as we mentioned above, as the expression of the individual and as a means of expressing individual feelings.[38]

In the nineteenth and twentieth centuries, the purpose of art changed again and with it, its meaning . The theory of *art for art's sake* emerged in the nineteenth century when Victor Cousin wrote in 1817 that "art is not an instrument, it is in itself its own end."[39] Friedrich Nietzsche was to reject this concept in the *Twilight of the Idols* (1888).[40]

> *L'art pour l'art. . . .* The fight against purpose in art is always a fight against the moralizing tendency in art, against its subordination to morality. *L'art pour l'art* means: "The devil take morality!" But even this hostility still betrays the overpow-ering force of the prejudice . . ., a worm chewing its own tail. "Rather no purpose at all than a moral purpose!" that is the talk of mere passion. A psychologist, on the other hand, asks: what does art do? does it not praise? glorify? choose? prefer? With all this it strengthens or weakens certain valuations. Is this only a "more-over?" an accident? something in which the artist's instinct had no share? Or is it not the very presupposition of the artist's ability? Does his basic instinct aim at art, or rather at the sense of art, at life? . . . Art is the great stimulus to life: how could one understand it as purposeless, as aimless, as *l'art pour l'art?* One ques-tion remains: art also makes apparent much that is ugly, hard and questionable in life, does it not thereby spoil life for us?

With the *Twilight of the Idols*, art could no longer act as a means of revelation or as mediator. For Nietzsche, in fact:

> "Beautiful in itself was a mere phrase, not even a concept . . . and nothing is more conditional—or let us say, narrower, than our feeling of beauty."[41]

Baudelaire distinguished "pure arts" from "philosophical arts," reacting very strongly against all forms of art that represented religious, historical or allegorical subjects.[42]

In the twentieth century, abstract painters reiterated once again the spiritual, if not reli-gious, nature of art. Thus, Kandinsky wrote:

---

[38] Barasch, *Modern Therories of Art, I. from Winkelmann to Baudelaire*, 1990, pp. 73 ff.

[39] Victor Cousin, *Du vrai, du beau et de l'utile*, 1817-18. Albert Cassagne, *La théorie de l'art pour l'art en France*, reprinted in Geneva, 1979.

[40] Friedrich Nietzsche, *Twilight of the Idols*, "Skirmishes of an Untimely Man," 1888 § 24 trans. by Walter Kaufmann, *The Portable Nietzsche*, New York, 1976 [1954], p. 529.

[41] Ibid., § 19; p. 525.

[42] Charles Baudelaire, *The Painter of Modern and Other Essays*, trans. J. Mayne, New York 1986.

                    The Path Toward Beauty

Each work of art originates just as does the cosmos, through catastrophes which, out of the chaotic din of instruments, ultimately create a symphony, the music of the spheres. The creation of works of art is the creation of the world. . . . Art is like religion in many respects. Its development does not consist of new discoveries which strike out the old truths and label them errors. . . . Its development consists of sudden illuminations, like lightning, or explosions, which burst like fireworks in the heavens . . . The trunk of the tree does not become superfluous because of a new branch, it makes the branch possible. . . . Abstract forms (lines, planes, dots, etc.) are not important in themselves, but only their inner sound, their life. . . . The world sounds. It is a cosmos of spiritually active beings. Even dead matter is living spirit.[43]

Paul Klee:
Everything passes, and what remains of former times, what remains of life, is the spiritual, the spiritual in art, or we might simply call it the artistic. In everything we do the claim of the absolute is unchanging.[44]

When Kazimir Malevich became an abstract painter, founding what he was to call *Suprematist art* (1913), he wrote:
The form becomes an allusion to space and the painting, an allusion to painting, revealing the essential, the supreme or essential being, a world without objects.[45]

The philosopher, Maurice Merleau-Ponty summarized:
The whole modern history of painting, its effort to free itself from illusionism and to acquire its own dimensions, has a metaphysical significance. (*L' Oeil et l' Esprit*, 1960, IV).

For millennia, everywhere, artworks thus seem to have been considered as means to an end and artists as instruments, as intermediaries between the visible and the invisible, or rather, to quote Merleau-Ponty, they have given visible existence to that which profane vision believed to be invisible. There is one exception, however: in ancient China, a painter

---

[43] Kandinsky, *Reminiscences*, quoted in *Modern Artists on Art*, 2nd edition, ed. by Robert L. Herbert, pp. 31, 35. See also Kandinsky, *Complete Writings on Art*, by Wassily Kandinsky, Kenneth C. Londsay, Peter Vergo, pp. 377-378, 250.
[44] Lipsey, op. cit., pp. 26, 42,188, 209, 216. See Lipsey's definition of "the spiritual" on p. 189, note 384.
[45] Ibid.

aimed particularly at capturing the vital breath of life (*ch'i*), at being in full harmony with nature, at living the Tao.[46]

Artists have always been obliged to conform to strict iconographic and stylistic traditions. Only by mastering these traditions could they transcend them and become instruments of the invisible.

When we are confronted with works of art that we would call beautiful, for lack of a better word, we often use other expressions (although none are really synonymous), and refer to them as "works of compelling stature," "of quality," or "*perfection*," as if we were aware, in fact, that their beauty was not related to the pleasure of the moment, but to a powerful, mysterious and timeless presence.

As Picasso stated:

> There is no past or future in art. If a work of art cannot live always in the present, it must not be considered at all. The art of the Greeks, of the Egyptians, of the great painters who lived in other times, is not an art of the past, perhaps it is more alive today than ever before.[47]

Perfection comes from the Latin *perficere*, which means to accomplish something, often in relation to a plan, or to a technique.

> [Perfection] is often a rhetorical term expressing the beholder's feeling of rightness, his conviction that everything in the work is as it should be, that nothing can be changed without spoiling the whole. . . . It is clear from continued experience and close study of works that judgement of perfection in art, as in nature, is a hypothesis, not a certitude. . . . [48]

---

[46] F. Cheng, *L'Espace du rêve. Mille ans de peinture chinoise*, Paris, 1980; G. Rowley, *Principles of Chinese Painting*, Princeton, 1974; M. M. Sze, *The Tao of Painting. A Study of the Ritual Disposition of Chinese Painting. With a Translation of the Chien tzu yuan hua chuan, or Mustard Seed Garden Manual of Painting*, 1679-1701. 2 vols., Bollingen Series, 49. New York, Pantheon Books, 1956, Vol. 1.

[47] Picasso quoted in Chipp, op. cit., p. 264.

[48] Meyer Shapiro, "On perfection. Coherence and unity of form and content", 1964, re-edited by B. Beckley and David Shapiro, in *Uncontrollable Beauty*, New York, 1998.

To designate the same idea of quality, the term "masterpiece" or *chef-d' œuvre* of medieval origin is often used (Boileau, *Livre des Metiers,*1261-1271).[49] The masterpiece was presented by the craftsman, at the end of his apprenticeship, to demonstrate his skills and excellence before a jury, which recognized his professional competence, qualified him as a master and thereby made him a member of a guild. The same term was used, however, during the same period in relation to God's creation of Adam and Eve, who were considered as the most magnificent of all "masterpieces." God was thus depicted with the compass in his hand in many representations of Genesis, just like any other contemporary master craftsman (*Bible Moralisée*, c. 1250, Vienna) (fig. 46). How much human beings have associated their own creativity to that of God, or vice versa, is also shown in most creation myths.

Masterpieces, in the original sense of the word, are no longer made in the Schools of Fine Arts nor taken into consideration in traditional museums, but they continue to be made by the *Compagnons du Devoir du Tour de France*, in the medieval tradition. One can still admire magnificent models of wooden staircases, locks and so on, at their school on the Place Saint Gervais in Paris. In Japan today, outstanding craftsmen, potters, embroiders, dyers and basketweavers are considered living national monuments.[50]

We have thus defined a number of terms very generally, except that of beauty itself, which continues to baffle us, although contemporary scientists do not hesitate to use it or to define it. Neurologists have been studying the effects of beauty on the human brain, trying to find out what attracts the eye to visual works of art, causing very complex interactions in the different parts of the brain and its neurons. These studies have analyzed the source and effects of aesthetic pleasure or of aesthetic emotion, however, rather than trying to understand the nature or common characteristics of beauty, if indeed they exist.[51]

Contemporary biologists and quantum and astrophysicists, on the other hand, draw

---

[49] Gradually, the term masterpiece came to be used to designate the Seven Wonders of the World, as well as contemporary monuments that had passed the test of time, considered as *mirabilia, merveilles* (Mont Saint Michel or Fontainebleau, designated as *"chef-d'oeuvres d'architecture"*). With the rise of the Academies, the original meaning of masterpiece was lost; the *chef-d'oeuvres* of Antiquity or the High Renaissance, architecture, but also painting and sculpture, became models and supreme standards for art. The artists of the seventeenth and eighteenth centuries were considered as liberal artists or intellectuals, and no longer as manual labourers or craftsmen; they were expected to do a *morceau de réception* for the Academy, and no longer a masterpiece in the medieval sense of the word. With the opening of the great European museums at the beginning of the nineteenth century, museums became the "temples" of "masterpieces" of the past, selected by juries that found it difficult to judge and select contemporary works because they were not modelled on Antiquity or the Renaissance, and hence did not comply with any of the Academic criteria or standards of taste. See Walter Cahn, *Masterpieces. Chapters on the History of an Idea*, Princeton, NJ. 1979.

[50] Itchiku Kubota, *Lumière Brodée*, Exhibition Catalogue, Paris, Palais de Tokio, 1990.

[51] Roger Vigouroux, *La Fabrique du Beau*, Paris 1992 (summarizing various other studies, especially those of Changeux).

---

frequent parallels between art and nature, where they have no trouble recognizing beauty. The astronomer Xuan Thuan begins his *Chaos et l'Harmonie* with a chapter on beauty and truth, stating that when a scientific theory is considered beautiful it is because it is inevitable, simple and in conformity with the whole. Heisenberg's definition of beauty is the same.[52] Mondrian, as a painter, draws a similar conclusion.

> People do not see why a painter should concern himself with the laws of life; they do not understand that the laws of life realize themselves perhaps more clearly in art.[53]

All of them would probably have agreed with Roger Caillois:

> Man does not oppose himself to nature, he is nature, living matter, subject to physical and biological laws that govern the universe. These laws penetrate him, organize him. Man coincides with these laws, or is, at least, inseparable from them, . . . these laws generate beauty, emanate beauty. . . .[54]

This concept of beauty is, in fact, very similar to that of Pythagoras, who, as mentioned earlier, was the first to conceive beauty as harmony, both of which are determined by geometrical ratios. Artists and philosophers continue to wonder with Plotinus whether beauty does not perhaps refer to a more remote principle, since unless the artist has an inner spark, he cannot ever recreate the beauty of a form, no matter how closely he may follow the same rules or the same order. Meyer Shapiro wrote this about order, but it could refer to beauty:

> Order in art is like logic in science, a built-in demand, but not enough to give a distinction of greatness.

Our discussion, we might recall, is about beauty as revealed by forms, and we have tried to define a few terms connected with this discussion, and at the same time we have become aware of how their meaning has shifted over time.

In the following chapters, we will analyze different examples of visual forms of art and some corresponding texts in order to grasp, if not understand, the nature of beauty, or sully this mysterious interrelation between the visible and the invisible, the immanent and the transcendent, matter and spirit, the namable and that which cannot be named,

> [but] which the soul names, as from ancient knowledge and, recognizing, welcomes it, enters into unison with it.[55]

---

[52] Heisenberg to Einstein, cited by Chandrasekhar, op. cit.
[53] Cited in H.L.C. Jaffé, *De Stijl*, 1956, p. 145.
[54] Roger Caillois, op. cit.
[55] Plotinus, *Enneads*, I, 6, 2.

In order to grasp more fully what is implicit in the concept of beauty as such on a more universal level, when related to works of art, we need to look at criteria[56] outside the Western philosophical and artistic tradition. We will look at the criteria of Yoruba African art, Chinese painting, Hindu art and North American Navajo.

Yoruba African Art

In the dialect spoken in parts of Senegal, the adjective "beautiful" does not exist, but there are equivalents, especially in relation to artefacts such as: "that which is suitable," or "that which is perfect." The poems, dances and masks that are "efficient," or "awaken emotions of sadness, joy, terror or laughter" are characterized as being "good" or "bringing a promise of happiness." A good action is often considered beautiful.[57]

In the Yoruba language, which is spoken by about twenty-five million people in Nigeria and Benin, the terms used to evaluate a work of art either correspond to those of our Western tradition, or, on the contrary, lead us to other, more universal concepts. What is perceived as beautiful among the Yoruba-speaking people? And do they ever use this term when they make a positive judgment about a work of art?

For the Yoruba, a work of art must first of all have vital energy (*ase*) in order to exist, to fulfil its function or to be ritually efficient, and the artist has to follow traditions (*àsà*) that always imply, however, a deliberate, constant choice (from the verb *sà*—to choose). The artists are itinerant, hence permanent strangers (*àrè*). They do not repeat, mindlessly, the unchanging ways of the ancients; tradition "entails creative imagination, exploration of a subject and/or medium, and innovation. . . . For the Yoruba, artistry is the exploration, an imaginative recreation of received ideas."[58]

In order to possess this vital power, hence to be judged as good, the work of art must reflect the essential nature of a thing (*iwà*) as well as the primeval order or the regulative principle of the universe (*ogége-a bayé-gun*). A carver has to have control of hand and mind (*ifarabalé*), and a sense of appropriateness with respect to the use of what is created (*yìye*). The artwork exists, in fact, only within a larger context of use and meaning, never for itself or in relation to any individual works or art collection. The artist must also have an inner

---

[56] The word "criterion" derives from the Greek verb "*krinein*," to choose, to discern, hence also to criticize.
[57] Léopold Senghor, cited in Jean-Pierre Barou, *L'œil pense, essai sur les arts primitifs contemporains*, Paris, 1996, p. 60.
[58] Olabiyi Babalola Yai, "In Praise of Metonymy: the Concepts of Tradition and Creativity in the Transmission of Yoruba Artistry over Time and Space" and John Pemberton III, "In Praise of Artistry," in *The Yoruba Artist*, ed. Rowland Abiodun, Henry J. Drewal, John Pemberton III, Washington, Smithonian Institution, 1994, pp. 107 ff. and 119 ff.

eye or insight (*ojù-inù*), as well as an eye for design and composition (*ojù-onù*), complete-ness and finished quality (*isé didan*).

A work of art is praised when it has all these qualities and therefore becomes enduring and lasting (*tìtò*), enlightening and shining (*tàn*), while also having depth (*ìnjìnlé*). The ulti-mate purpose of a work of art is to awaken the consciousness and deepen the understanding of the spectator and the user, both of whom are participants in every ritual manifestation. Their statues, altars, songs or dances are indeed conceived as means through which the invisible world is either merely evoked or made visible during the time of the sacred perfor-mance.

In the Yoruba scheme of things, the cosmos consists, in fact, of two distinct yet in-separable worlds, the invisible and spiritual realm of the ancestors, the gods and the spirits (*Orun*), and the visible and tangible realm of the living (*Aye*), in which the invisible forces nevertheless intervene, often and powerfully. The world in which we live is furthermore conceived as one through which we are merely passing, whereas the invisible one is our true home.[59]

This vital energy, which the work of art must receive and send forth, is that of life itself, of the gods, the ancestors and the spirits, as well as human beings, plants, minerals, streams, words, songs and prayers. It is that which is inherent in works of art that attracts the forces of the spiritual realm. (Is it because they are beautiful?)

To quote a Yoruba diviner, it is only if the artist has followed traditions—*asa*—and if this vital energy—*ase*—has penetrated into the work that

> the divinities do not come because of the representations; these come because of the divinities. . . . It is the idea of the sacred which matters, not the material object which attracts it. Art, like sacrifice, is conceived as a prayer or an offering. The presence and the visual power of an artwork enables an altar or a ritual to be efficient.[60]

As far as formal criteria are concerned, Frank Willett gives a summary of experiments involving comparative evaluations of sculptures among Africans and Westerners.[61] All the groups praised the moderate naturalism, or a balance between portraiture and abstrac-tion (although the same pieces would probably appear totally devoid of likeness to non-Africans), symmetry in relation to a central axis, hence the frontality and immobility of the

---

[59] Henry John Drewal, "Terre et Tonnerre: l'art yoruba destiné aux ancêtres et aux dieux," trans. Valerie Mortot, in *Arts d'Afrique*, Paris, Editions Gallimard, Musée Dapper, 2000, p. 51.
[60] Ibid., p. 54
[61] Frank Willett, *African Art*, London, Thames and Hudson, revised edition, 1997, pp. 207 ff.

 The Path Toward Beauty

statue, and the finished quality.[62]

It is obvious that the same criteria have been followed in producing an infinite variety of African styles and works; hence they can only serve as a very general framework, but in no way define the beauty of these works.

It is not, in fact, because the Yoruba sculptor obeys formal criteria, such as symmetry, likeness or finished quality, that his work will be considered "good." Skill alone does not suffice to give vital energy to his work, which has a very precise meaning and is made for a specific purpose, which is clear to the Yoruba sculptor, but not always to a foreign spectator. The Yoruba sculptor indeed belongs to a world of beliefs and ideas and the knowledge of the meaning and function of any work of art is also a vital part of how we perceive it. One perceives only what one has learned to perceive.

For example, if we look at a Yoruba dancing staff (fig. 10), which is topped by a naked, kneeling female devotee, with patterns of scarification on her disproportional large head,

---

[62] Ibid., p. 210 ff.: Hans Himmelheber noted that the artists, customers and others within the Guru people (Ivory Coast), to whom he had shown a number of sculptures, all chose the same three pieces for no clear reason except that of an intended and obtained likeness, although these same pieces seemed totally devoid of likeness to non-Africans. To P. J. L. Vanden houte, the Dan informants (Ivory Coast) justified their choice through the criteria of symmetry in relation to a central vertical axis of balance, rhythm and harmony among the various masses, surfaces and lines, but they expressed their choice through gestures rather than words, holding the pieces upside down or backwards, at arm's length. African sculptors do not do sketches before starting their work, but work directly in the wood. According to E. Fischer, the Dan artists (northeastern Liberia) added the criteria of the finished quality in the polish and the color, and for masks that of being comfortable to wear, hence the finished quality both outside and inside. Robert Thompson carried out an experiment amongst a hundred Yoruba, recording their comments, the criteria mentioned and their frequency. Among the nineteen most frequently used criteria were: moderate naturalism (*jijora*), which was always pointed out; symmetry of pose, which is a basic African characteristic (*gigun*); the portrayal of human figures in their prime of life (*odo*); the careful finish of all details and the clear visibility of the various parts of the sculpture (*ifarahon*); the luminosity, or the shining smoothness of surface, offering a play of light and shade (*didon*) and the criterion of composure, or of absence of violence, in facial expression or gesture. This unemotional quality also reflects a moral ideal of self-control(*tutu*). Leon Siroto showed thirty nine photographs of BaKwele masks to a number of BaKwele informants, selected for their experience in making or using masks, and to Yale art students and critics. He noticed that there was "substantial overall agreement between the BaKwele and the New Haven judgments", except for two photographs, showing "fierce" masks used to exercise social control, the meaning of which was known only to the BaKwele and not to the Yale critics, who judged them, therefore, only by their appearances, hence the disagreement. Fernandez asked some of his Fang informants which of twelve figures they liked best and why. Their answers referred to technical qualities, such as the smoothness of surface and the completeness of the figure, but they also stressed the importance of balance (*bibwe*), the symmetry in relation to a central vertical axis, because without this balance "the figure would not be a real one, it would have no life or vitality within it." Furthermore, he noticed that no Fang informant would ever have made a judgment on any sculpture used on reliquary boxes of ancestral bones because of a religious awe which "placed them beyond the reach of everyday aesthetic judgment."

supporting a double axe on which we see the same patterns, how can we judge its quality, except aesthetically, without understanding its meaning and purpose? The staff was, in fact, held during ceremonial dances performed in honor of Shongo, the god of thunder, to the abrupt rhythm of a drum, imitating the thunder itself. It was either raised above the head of the dancers or suddenly lowered, like lightening, to the ground. The double axe was the visible sign of the presence of Shongo. The engraved patterns repeat the scarification of the devotee's face, suggesting the humanity of the god. They also suggest that the god had entered the head of the devotee during the trance, and that the devotee had become one with the god. The realm of the invisible world of the gods—*orun*—had become one with the visible tangible world—*aye*—of the dancer. The woman carried the ritual object to the dancers or held it during the ceremony, and her nakedness and kneeling position were a sign of respect and of ritual purity, whereas the double axe was the symbol of the divinity. The head was increased in size, usually by one fifth to one third in proportion to the body, because it was considered the seat of the vital energy—*ase*—of any individual, as well as of inner qualities such as serenity, self-control and patience. Furthermore, the head was also the link between the visible world of the individual and the invisible one of the god, becoming the receptacle of the vital energy of the divinity itself during the time of the trance. The Yoruba staff thus partook fully in the ritual for which it was made.

Was its beauty a major element of its ritual efficiency or would any staff, provided of course we imbued it with our own imagination, have fulfilled the same purpose?[63] This question is at the root of most image-making.

In fact, no work seems to be considered "good" by any true Yoruba judge, if it does not first of all fulfil its specific ritual purpose by having that vital energy (*ase*), which could only be obtained by the artist, who had followed traditions (*àsà*), as well as all other criteria such as *iwà*—the essential nature of a thing—*ogége-a bayé-gun*—primeval order or regulative principles of the universe—*yiye*—sense of appropriateness with respect to what is created—through *ifarabal*—the control of hand and mind—as well as all the formal criteria of symmetry and likeness and so on.

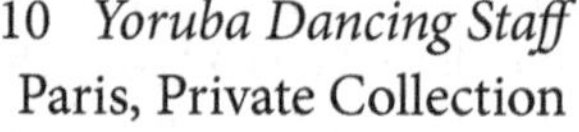

10 *Yoruba Dancing Staff*
Paris, Private Collection

---

[63] Drewal, op. cit., pp. 54, 60, 63-65 and E. Gombrich, "Meditations on a Hobby Horse or the Root of Artistic Form," *Meditations on a Hobby Horse and Other Essays on the Theory of Art*, London, second edition, 1971, pp. 1-11.

To take a further African example, why do Fang reliquary statues represent the ancestors in the shape of an infant with short, bent legs? Because the ancestors are in charge of fertility and growth, and their representation is thus related to the desire to give birth. In most African countries, death is not conceived as an end, but only as part of a cycle that guarantees life and the survival of the family or society. Therefore, the ancestors are worshipped through their representations, their masks or statues, and are present at all great ceremonies; they are consulted and feared because they are an integral part of life.[64] In both of these examples, the meaning of the object determined the form.

The ideal mathematical ratios used by the Greek and the Renaissance sculptors to make beautiful statues were also supposed to reflect the beauty of the gods, imagined as ideal young men, who were furthermore thought to have created men in their own image.
It is therefore indispensable to know the meaning of a work of art before we can judge its "goodness," which is the most frequently used synonym of beauty.

It would seem, in fact, that the beauty of a given work could not be defined through the knowledge of formal criteria alone or by the mere understanding of its original meaning and function. The knowledge of both widens our perception and therefore leads us from what is tangible and visible to what is intangible, invisible, indefinable and yet undeniable.

We have chosen these examples though we could have taken others from any major civilization (figs. 11 a and b), including our own. There are those, however, for whom this beauty would have been self-evident. Picasso recognized this:

> [The] sublime beauty of African statues and how these works were passionately religious and rigorously logic, belonging to the most powerful and to the most beautiful of what human imagination had produced, whereas Matisse characterized their formal beauty by a single word: *simplification*.[65]

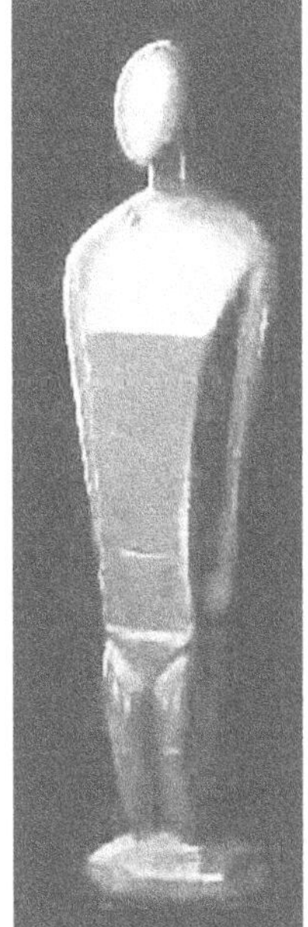

11 a *Figurine representing a divinity,*
Caroline Archipelago, Nukuoro Atoll, Micronesia

---

[64] James W. Fernandez, "Principles of Opposition and Vitality in Fang Aesthetics," *The Journal of Aesthetics and Art Criticism,* 25, 1 (1966), 53-64.
[65] Charles H. Caffin, *Camera Work,* 25.

Henry Moore, referring to works of African art, wrote:

> A work must have a vitality of its own . . . When a work has this powerful vitality, we do not connect the word Beauty with it . . . Beauty comes by the way and can never be an end in itself. . . . [66]

These two requirements, namely that a work of art must incorporate the vitality of life itself, and that in order to do so the artist must follow traditional canons, are found in many civilizations, Western and Eastern, for example in China, India, and amongst the Navajo Indians of America.

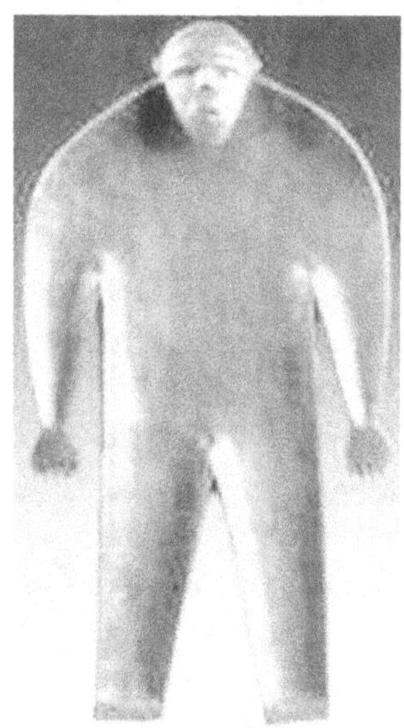

11 b *Spoon,* from the Fiji Islands, Geneva, Barbier-Mueller Museum

Chinese Painting

The Chinese painters refer to vital energy or *Ch'i* (or *qi),* the breath of Tao, the life-breath that pervades and gives form to everything in the universe, in the sky and on earth, day and night, mountain and water, man and beast, tree and rock, summer and winter. The Chinese painter had to capture this breath of life in each one of his brush strokes. *Ch'i*[67] was actually the first of the Six Principles of Chinese Painting, and is a term that cannot be understood outside Chinese life and thought, especially Taoism.

Through a few Taoist quotes, we may be able to grasp, more intuitively than rationally, the meaning of Tao (*Dao),* generally translated as the Way.

> There was something formless, yet complete, that existed before heaven and earth, without sound, without substance, dependent on nothing, unchanging, all-pervading, unfailing. One might think of it as mother of all things under heaven. Its true name we do not know. Tao is the name that we give it.[68]

---

[66] Robert Herbert, *Modern Artists on Art,* Englewood Cliffs, N.J. 1965, pp. 138-144.

[67] For various translations of this essential Chinese concept, see note 56 in Sze, op. cit., vol. 2, p. 19, 6. For its character, or pictograph see p. 614. Cf. also all other texts mentioned below, and the seventeenth century manual: Shitao, *Les Propos sur la peinture du moine Citrouille-amére,* ed. and trans. by Pierre Ryckmans, Paris, Hermann, 1984.

[68] G. Rowley, *Principles of Chinese Painting,* Princeton, 1974, p. 5.

                    The Path Toward Beauty

The Tao of the origins is also conceived as the supreme void, from which the One emerged, which gave birth to the two complementary breaths of *yin* and *yang*. The association, correspondence, complementary nature and interaction of both animate all creation.[69]

The pictograph of Tao consist of a left foot—*ch'o*—taking a step, and a head—*shou*—implying the choice taken by the head. The combination of head and foot symbolizes the idea of wholeness, of spiritual and physical step by step growth. The notion of Tao thus implies more the idea of knowing how to walk than that of reaching a goal.

In all Chinese treatises, one reads about the painter who worked in the spirit of the Tao, evoking the creative power of nature and partaking of it, showing the vital breath of nature in operation. The *Ch'i* (or the *Qi)* was the manifestation of the Tao. As Lin Tao, a painter of the Sung period, said, the action of the *Ch'i* and the powerful brush stroke go together. For the painter Shih-t'ao (or Tao-chì) the *Ch'i* had to be captured with "a single stroke of the brush," which is at the root of all representation.[70]

In Chinese Taoist thought there is neither a concept for "being" nor for "truth," which are, on the contrary, at the root of all Greek and Western philosophy. Everything is conceived in constant transformation.[71] Both painter and beholder have to learn to live in harmony with nature, hence conform to that which is in constant motion.

The mind of the perfect man is like a mirror. It does not move with things nor does it anticipate them. It responds to things, but does not retain them. Therefore, he is able to deal successfully with things but is not affected (Chuang-tzù).[72]

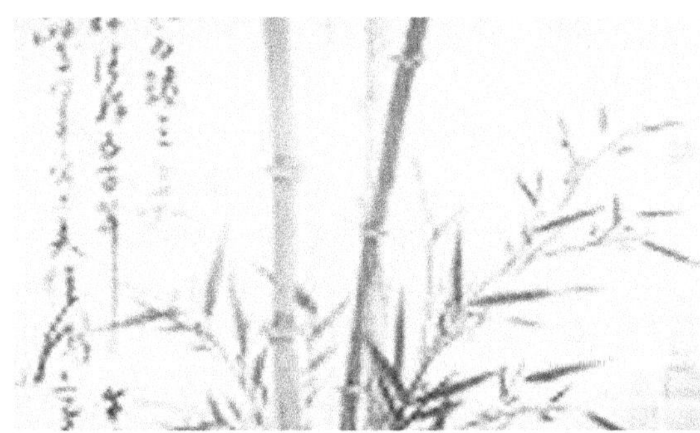

12 Wu Zhen (1280-1354), *Study of Bamboo, detail, Taipei*, National Palace Museum

---

[69] Anne Cheng, *Histoire de la Pensée Chinoise*, Paris, 1997, Chapter 7 § 10; François Cheng, *L'Espace du rêve, mille ans de peinture chinoise*, Paris, 1980, p. 30; F. Cheng, *Vide et Plein, le langage pictural chinoi*; Paris, 1979 and *Souffle-Esprit, textes théoriques chinois sur l'art pictural*, Paris, 1989.

[70] Shitao, op. cit., notes of pp. 14-18, where the editor examines the technical, aesthetic and philosophical meaning of this "single stroke of the brush." In the latter sense, this single stroke stands also for the One and the Absolute, that which preceded all forms of Creation, the Tao itself.

[71] Sze, op. cit., vol. 2, p. 610; Cheng, op. cit., Introduction; François Jullien, *Un Sage est sans idée*, Paris, 1998, pp. 95 ff. Instead of "truth," we find, however, the concepts of *li*, of the underlying principle, and of *hsing*, the nature of things: "Observe things in the light of their own principles."

[72] Sze, op. cit., vol. 1, the whole introduction.

The Tao is the way, but also the nameless, the source of life, the whole, a total interpenetrating of man and nature. Everything is, in fact, formed and permeated by the same vital breath of Tao, hence by the interaction of *yin* and *yang*. Tao is said to be "one time *yin* and one time *yang*." *Yin* cannot exist outside *yang*; both exist only in relation to each other, and never as effect or cause of the other. To live the Tao is to fully understand these two principles that lead back to the unity of the Tao: void and solid, mountain and water, sky and earth, male and female, breath and structure, heart and desire, life and death, light and dark,

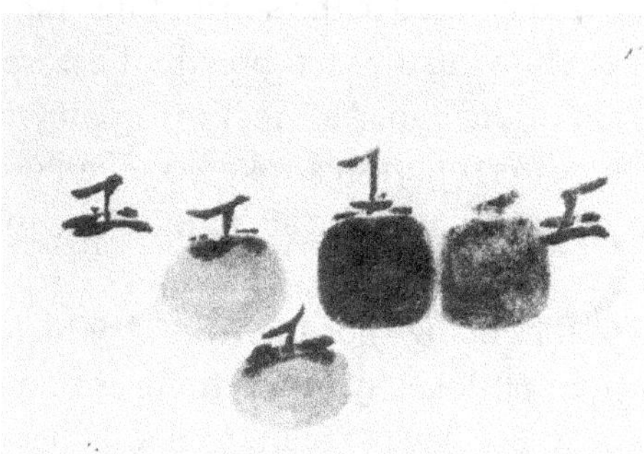

brush and ink, the solid and empty part of the same bamboo branch, and so on. The Chinese considered themselves an integral part of the universe, neither more nor less than a butterfly, and not as the crown of creation. Hence, to understand the significance of a thing, one must become that thing: a mountain, a bamboo, a cloud, or a lotus flower, live with it for years, know its dreams, and so on (fig. 12).

13 Muqi, *Six Persimmons*, second half of the
13th century, Kyoto Ryokoin, Daitokuji (detail)

Look at things from the point of view of the things and you will see their real nature, look at things from your point of view and you will only see your feelings, because nature is neutral and evident, whereas your feelings are only prejudices and obscurities [73] (fig. 13).

In China, a landscape painting is called a mountain-water picture. The mountain is *yang* and the water is *yin*, the empty space of the canvas, of the paper or of the wall, is *yin*, and the full solid forms are *yang*. The harmony of both is Tao, the unity of spirit and matter, Heaven and Earth (fig. 14).

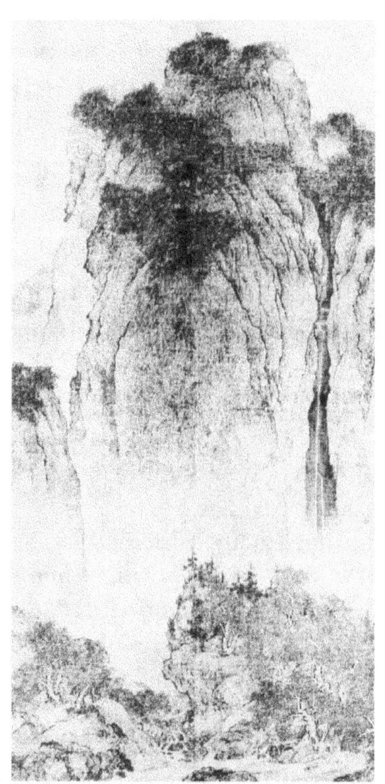

14 Fan K'uan (active late 10th to early 11th century),
Travelers amid Mountains and Gorges,
Taipei, National Palace Museum

---

[73] Shao Yong, 11th c., cited in A.K. Coomraswamy, *Transformation of Nature into Art*, New York, 1956.

The breath of life (Ch'i), has no form, but it is through the objects that it takes form . . . the painter tries to capture that breath of life or to collaborate with the work of creation. . . . The play of the brush must be dominated by the breath of life, and when that breath of life exists, the vital energy is present and it is then that the brush brings forth the divine . . .

In another text, a disciple asks the master:

"Painting is to make beautiful things and the important point is to obtain their true likeness, is it not?" The master answers: "It is not. Painting is to paint, to estimate the shapes of things, to really obtain them; to estimate the beauty of things, to reach it; to estimate the significance of things and to grasp it. One should not take outward beauty for reality. He who does not understand this mystery will not obtain truth, even though his pictures may contain likeness." The disciple asked: "What is likeness and what is truth?" The old painter answered: "Likeness can be obtained by shapes without breath of life (Ch'i,), but when truth is reached, both breath of life and substance is fully expressed. He who tries to convey breath of life through ornamental beauty will make dead things."[74]

If the Tao is achieved, the artist is said to be divine, because he has captured the breath of life itself, and:

When one approaches the wonderful, one knows not whether art is the Tao or Tao is art.

To capture *Ch'i*, to participate in the dynamic energies of creation, was the real aim of any Chinese painter but in order to do so, like the Yoruba sculptor, he had to follow the other five Principles of Painting, which are primarily technical: the structure of the brush stroke, the likeness, hence the intelligibility of the forms that have to be easily recognizable,

---

[74] Siren, op. cit., p. 39 and Appendix IV, but also II and III. See also: Wen C. Fong, *Images of the Mind*, Princeton, 1984.

the application of colors, the composition and the copying of old masters.[75]

In the introduction to the seventeenth century *Mustard Seed Garden*, we read, however, that:

> You must learn first to observe the rules faithfully; afterwards, modify them according to your intelligence and capacity. The end of all method is to seem to have no method, … if you aim to dispense with method, learn method. If you aim at facility, work hard. If you aim for simplicity, master complexity.[76]

And, according to the editor of that treatise:

> All, but the First Principle, could be learned and practiced to the point of accomplishment, but the possessing of the Ch'i or the being attuned to it was an aspect of the soul, something one was born with, one does not know how, yet it is there.

According to Confucius:

> He who is in harmony with Nature hits the mark without effort and apprehends the truth without thinking. (Confucius, cited in Sze., vol. 2).

Since the eighth century, Chinese painters have been divided into three classes: divine (*shên*), wonderful (*miao*) and skillful (*néng, ch'iao or ching*). Painting was considered divine when it was self-existent or self-evident, when the indefinable breath of life, the manifestation of Tao, was captured, when:

---

[75] The Six Principles of Chinese Painting (*Lu Fa*) are presented, with translation and comments, in all the texts we have mentioned. They were first defined by Hsieh Ho's, in 500 C.E. According to Soper's translation: the first is "animation through the spirit consonance;" the second is "structural method in use of the brush;" the third is "fidelity to the object in portraying forms;" the fourth is "conformity to kind in applying colors;" the fifth is "proper planning (of elements);" the sixth is "transmission (of the experience of the past) in making copies" (*The Art and Architecture of China*, Pelican History of Art, 1978 p. 133). According to Chin Hao, a Confucian scholar who became a hermit and a painter after the fall of the T'ang dynasty (900-930), the Six Essentials for Landscape Paintings are: *Ch' i* (or *Qi*, the breath of life) as the heart responds and the brush moves forward, forms are seized without hesitation; *Yün* (resonance or harmony) consists in establishing correct and perfect forms, which are not conventional; *Ssù* (thought) causes you to deduct and detach essentials and concentrate on the forms of things; *Ching* (scenery) established by observing the laws of seasons, by looking for the wonderful and finding the true landscape; *Pi* (brush-work) means to follow the rules, the basic methods, but to be at the same time free and flexible in movement, so that everything seems to fly and to be in constant motion; *Mo* (ink wash) should be high and low, thick and diluted, according to the depth and shallowness of various things, high and low peaks are described by a light ink wash, which also makes objects stand out clearly either in shallow or deep recession, so natural that they do not seem to be made by a brush: Siren, op. cit. pp. 39-40 and Wen Fong, *Summer Mountains. The Timeless Landscape*, New York, Metropolitan Museum, 1975.
[76] Sze, op. cit. vol. 2, pp. 17, 19.

    The Path Toward Beauty

One does not get tired by looking at it a whole day. By concentrating the spirit and far-reaching meditation one realizes the self-existent; both the painted thing and oneself are forgotten; the realization is separated from the form; the body becomes like dry wood and the mind like dead ashes. He reaches the mysterious fitness (miao li), which may be called the Tao of painting.[77]

This same "mysterious fitness" was also used to describe the secret of a wheelwright who knew how to coordinate mind and hand and mastered his art, which could not, however, be transmitted by words or mechanical skill.

A painting is said to be divine:
> When a painter makes no effort of his own, his hand moves spontaneously. This "self-existence" or "self-evidence," that which is beyond all definition (tsù-jan) and this effortlessness [reflect], in fact, the harmony of the artist with the universal breath of life, and that he did grasp the natural without effort.[78]

The only painter, cited by most Chinese treatises as having mastered all Six Principles and as being divine is Wu Tao-tzu, who:
> had exhausted completely the creative power of nature, and the resonance of the vital breath was so overwhelmingly strong in his works that it hardly could be confined to the silk, . . . a divine power worked through him.

We have seen what happened to him: he discovered the door through his painting, saw that what lay beyond it was far more beautiful, went through the door and disappeared, while his painting faded away. In fact, "When painting has reached divinity, there is an end to the matter."[79]

The main principle of Chinese painting, which suggests more than it defines, is: *ch'i yün shêng tung. Ch'i,* breath of heaven, vital force, breath of life; *yün,* to turn, revolve, rhythm, harmony; *shêng tung,* life-movement. Siren translated the whole formula as: "resonance or vibration of the vitalizing spirit and movement of life," but the same principle is discussed in every treatise of Chinese painting.[80]
> The Ch'i yün shêng tung is a principle of Heaven. When it is operating through the painter, the effect of his picture is beyond definition, and the painter may be said to belong to the shên (divine) class. [81]

---

[77] Siren, op. cit., pp. 90, pp. 26-27, 33.
[78] Rowley, op. cit., p. 35 and Siren, op. cit., p. 26.
[79] Siren, op. cit., p. 23 and Coomaraswamy, *Transformation,* p. 22 and note 21 on p. 189.
[80] Siren, op. cit., *Appendix.* See also: Sze, op. cit., vol. 2 and Shitao, op. cit., note 60. For the explanation of the different terms and their various combinations, cf. Cheng, op. cit.
[81] Sze, op. cit. vol. 2, p. 22.

If to paint was to live the Tao, to look at a painting was also to live the Tao. Thus, paintings were never framed—a frame would have arrested the freedom of thought and imprisoned the breath of life—and they were never permanently displayed. They were painted on long, horizontal or vertical scrolls, and were unrolled partially or entirely, unrolled for meditation and contemplation.[82]

The Chinese never speak of the beauty of a painting, but always of *Ch'i*.[83] A painting should be vital in its breath, harmonious, alive and full of motion in its execution. A painting is praised when it has "density of soul" (*I-ching*) and "divine resonance," divine harmony or rhythm (*shen-yun*)[84], which goes far beyond all notions of beauty.

The Chinese painter partakes in the perpetual re-creation and transformation of nature.[85]

Hindu Art

The equivalent of the Chinese *Ch'i*, of the Yoruba *ase*, is the Hindu *prana*, the life energy, identified with life itself and with Brahman (the Absolute). The rules to be followed are those of the *sastra-mana*, the canonical standards, and of the *pramana*, the criterion of truth, which finds expression in rules or canons of proportions.[86]

> Only an image made in accordance with the canon—talamana or pramana—can
> be called beautiful; some may think that beautiful which corresponds to
> their own fancy, but that not in accordance with the canon is unlovely to the
> discerning eye.[87]

---

[82] Ibid., and Siren, op. cit.

[83] Rowley, op. cit., p. 32.

[84] François Cheng, *Souffle-Esprit*, Paris, 1989, pp. 141-145: "The ultimate aim of Chinese art, beyond all notions of the beautiful, is the *I-ching* (density of soul) and the *shen-yun* (divine resonance)." *Shen*, meaning soul, spirit, spiritual/divine power /essence, and *yun*, resonance, rhythm and harmony. Cf. Also Anne Cheng, op. cit., p.127; pp. 118-120; F. Cheng, *Toute beauté est singulière. Peintre chinois de la voie excentrique*, Paris, 2004, pp. 42-43.

[85] The subject matter of Chinese painting is limited to different sets of classification that overlap but follow established conventions: Landscape; Man and Things; Birds and Flowers; Grasses and Insects. See the classification in: *The Mustard Seed Garden Manual of Painting*, Ed. by Mai-Mai Sze: Book of Trees; Book of Rocks; Book of People and Things; Book of Orchid; Book of Bamboos; Book of Plum; Book of Chrysanthemum; Book of Grasses, Insects and Flowering Plants; Book of Feathers and Fur and Flowering Plants. All subjects have furthermore a symbolic significance.

[86] Coomaraswamy, *Transformation*, pp. 16-18, 167ff, 187. He refers to Indian treatises in Sanskrit, especially to the medieval treatise of *Sukranitisara* by Sukrâcarya, chapter 4. The proportions are expressed in terms of basic units, the Indian measure is that of the "face-length" from the forehead to the chin, and the canons are therefore designed Ten-face, Nine–face, etc.

[87] Ibid., p. 167.

The Path Toward Beauty

The artist also has to be expert in vision and in no other way, certainly not in the presence of a model, can the work be accomplished.[88]

The meaning of tradition, or of canonical proportions, must not, however, be understood as being constraining or as conducive to mindless repetition of one and the same model.

In Hindu civilization, tradition has its roots in a belief of a metaphysical order: "Stretching back into the past and reaching forward into the future," related to discipline, itself conditioned by belief and by formal as well as iconographic prescriptions. These prescriptions, nevertheless, allow extraordinary freedom of expression. One has only to look at the great variety of interpretation in a single subject of Hindu art, such as the image of the dancing Shiva. To understand that tradition could produce works of individual creative power (figs. 15 and 16).[89]

15 *Sculpture of Shiva Dancing the Lalitam*, interior of Hindu Ravan ka khai Cave (Cave 14), Ellora. Photographer: Johnston, © The British Library Board

16 *Shiva as Lord of Dance (Nataraja)*, Chola period, (880-1279), late 12th-early 13th century, New York, Metropolitan Museum of Art (detail)

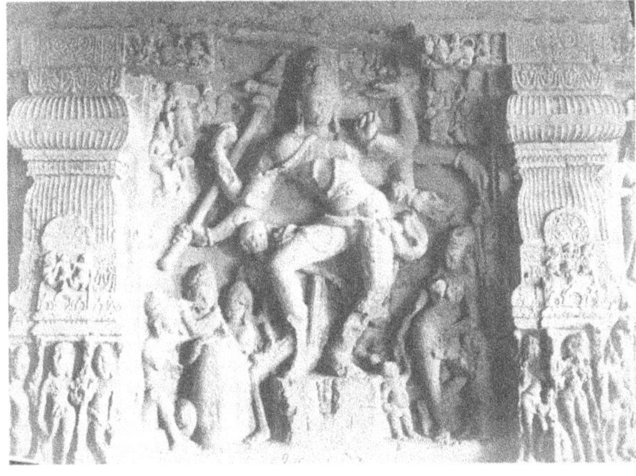

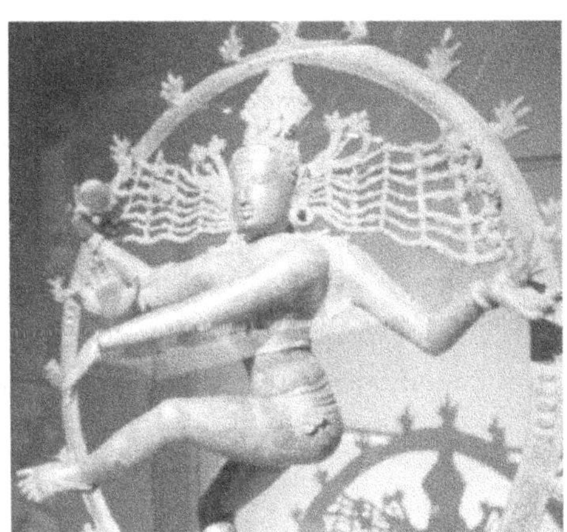

---

[88] Ibid., p. 126.
[89] Ibid.

The correctness of the iconography, hence a clear understanding of the meaning of the artwork, was also considered in India to be a prerequisite of any form of judgment and one of the criteria was, therefore, always that of clear intelligibility.[90]

A work of art was said to be worth looking at (*darsaniya*) or delighting the mind or the heart (*manohara*), and an entire Hindu literature, mostly related to poetry, theatre and dance, referred to flavor/savor (*rasa*), and to the "tasting" of art, that is to the aesthetic experience of *rasa* (*rasâsvadana*), in relation to seven or nine emotions, the most important of which is love.[91] This experience is not determined, however, only by the vital energy of the artwork, but also by that of the spectator. It is accessible only to the knowledgeable and the competent, arising from the identification of the spectator with dance, theatre, poetry or a visual work of art:

> *Rasa*[92] is not an object, nor an emotion, nor a concept; it is an immediate experience … which relishes its own essence when it communes with the other—actor or poet. It is simple, like the taste of a complex dish . . . It compels an act of union between the actor (or poet), the represented heroes and the audience. It does not exist beyond the perception of it. . . . We know it only by savouring it. . . . Amazement and expansion of the spirit, created by contact with a reality superior to this world, is the principle of all savour (*rasa*) and is found in all true poetry.[93]

According to one Hindu treatise (*Sahitya Darpana*, III, 2-3):

> Pure aesthetic experience is born of one mother with the vision of God, its life is like a flash of blinding light of transmondane origin, impossible to analyze and yet in the image of our own being.

In the same treatise (V, 1, Commentary) we read:

> All expressions, human or revealed, are directed to one end beyond themselves, and if not so determined are thereby comparable only to the utterances of a madman.

---

[90] Benjamin Rowland, *The Art and Architecture of India, Buddhist, Hindu, Jain,* Pelican History of Art, 1977, p. 25.

[91] Coomaraswamy, *Transformation*, p. 26.

[92] Ibid., pp. 47 ff. and pp. 99 ff.

[93] The theory of *rasa* is based on a text of the first century of our era, the *Nayta Shastras* by Bharata, related to dance, music and theatre, but applied to all forms of art. The translations, from Sanskrit into English, at least in the Exhibition Catalogue of 1986, are those of Manomohan Ghosh.

　　　　The Path Toward Beauty

To conclude:

> The work of art itself serves as the stimulus to the release of the spirit from all in-
> hibitions of vision and can only exist as a thing ordered to specific ends. Heaven
> and Earth are united in the analogy of art. . . .[94]

In Sanskrit there are a number of synonyms for beauty, such as *ramya*, lovely, *sadhu*, what is good in a work of art, while others designate natural beauty and incidental embellishments only. The value of a work of art is, in fact, only expressed by its conformity to the prescribed canons (*pramana*) and the value of poetry through its richness of *rasa*.[95]

A goddess of beauty and plenty exists, however, in the Hindu mythology and she is called *Lakshmi*. No canonical rule can define her.

> When the sage Shukracharyya was tackling the mystery of beauty with his scales
> and measures, perhaps Beauty herself (the goddess Lakshmi), in the form of an
> image, violating all the Shilpa Sastras (texts of canonical rules given to the art-
> ists)—strange creation of some rebellious spirit—appeared before him and de-
> manded his attention. The great teacher must have seen her and understood, and
> it is his understanding that prompts him to say:

> "These, Lakshmi, are not for thee, these laws that I lay down, these fine analyses
> of what an image should be, are for those images that are made to order, for
> people who would worship them. Endless are thy forms, no sastra can define
> thee, and nothing can appraise thee. . . . By chance, one in a million has perfect
> form, perfect beauty. So only that image is perfect which conforms to the stan-
> dard of beauty laid down in the Sastra. Nothing can be called perfect which has
> not the sanction of the Sastra, this the learned would say. Others would insist that
> to which your heart clings becomes perfect, becomes beautiful."[96]

North American Navajo Culture

Beauty and art are not at all related to each other in the Navajo culture of North America, where there is, in fact, no word for art, and where the equivalent of beauty—*hozho*—refers to the notion of health, balance and harmony, to the order of nature, the cycle of the seasons, the sunrise and its setting, the night which follows the day and so on. The Navajo stresses the unity of man and nature, like the Yoruban, the Chinese or the Hindu. Scientists

---

[94] René Duval, *Rasa, or Knowledge of the Self*, Toronto, 1982, pp. 17 (note 26), 41, 106.
[95] Coomaraswamy, *Transformation*.
[96] Duval, op. cit., p. 16 (note 14).

today would speak of man sharing the same particles with the universe. For the Navajo,[97] a man loses *hozho* when he becomes sick, when harmony is broken, within himself, his social group and the universe.

It is only the so-called medicine-man who can re-establish the lost equilibrium. He can heal through sacred, ancestral, traditional ceremonies that consist of songs and sand paintings. *Hozho* is also the name given to the entire process of healing and of educating. The ceremonies commemorate the history and myths of the Navajo, from their origins to today.

Throughout the ceremony, the person being healed repeats: "with, or in me, there is beauty," or: "beauty shines through me." *Hozoh* is a gift of the ancestors, who are called the Twelve Sacred Beings, and who have fixed, once and for all, the healing ceremonies, and have given to men the songs, the prayers and the dances, while tracing the sand paintings on the clouds, the mist, and spiderwebs. These sand paintings are to be traced on the floor of a round, octagonal, or square ceremonial hut—the *hogan*—which also marks the centre of the universe.

Sickness is primarily the consequence of a behavior which disregards the Navajo concept of order. The "dreamer" who has stopped hunting, the gambler, who gambles even the insignia of his father, he who is interested only in material goods, the woman who is only fascinated by her own appearance, are all considered as being sick and have thus lost their beauty.

The colors used for the sand paintings are of natural origin and refer to the moments of the day: white for dawn, yellow-orange for daytime, blue for evening and black for night. The ceremony includes dozens of sand paintings, drawn by the medicine man with utmost precision, but gradually destroyed or given back to the earth every night, and hence ephemeral. While he draws the ritual forms and sings the ritual songs, in empathy with his patient, utter concentration is required, hence a total detachment from all outer thoughts. The same concentration is required from the patient, who focuses on a special basket, woven clockwise by a woman and decorated with twelve points that refer to the Twelve Sacred Beings, around an inner circle representing the rainbow, which symbolizes the pact of the Sacred Beings with man. This is how harmony, order, health and, therefore, beauty are recovered. It is the way towards beauty. When the cure is finished, the song of beauty is sung:

> In beauty I walk, . . . with beauty in front of me I walk, . . . with beauty behind
> me I walk, . . . with beauty above me I walk. . . . Beauty has returned.

What counts is, therefore, the healing process, the ritual itself, hence the return of beauty. It requires knowledge, concentration, detachment, respect for traditions and its unchanging rules. What is important is not the finished artwork, since the sand paintings are destroyed. In this case, the tradition is also a guarantee of success (fig. 17).

---

[97] Sylvie Crossman and Pierre Barou, *Peintures de sable indiens navajo, la voie de la beauté*, Paris, 1996.

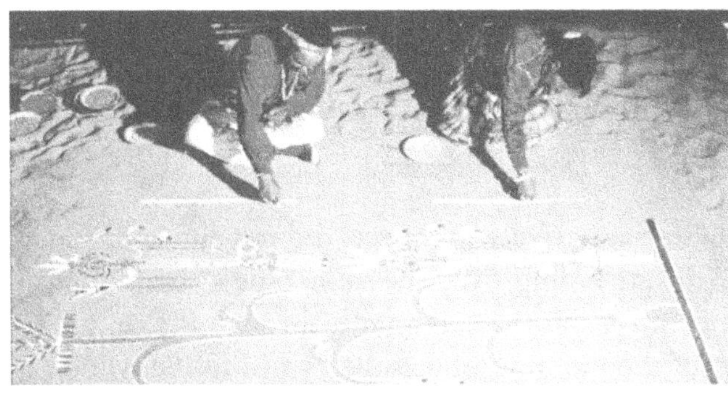

17 Navajo Indians engaged in sand painting

Beyond this recurrent concept of prescribed rules there is, in fact, a belief in the existence of a divine order, a metaphysical principle of life as well as art. Their existence seems to be a confirmation of the immutability of the divine order itself. Thus, when this belief ceases to exist, art moves away from tradition, which becomes totally emptied of meaning. No tradition was followed, however, without the creative impact of the artist. He never mechanically copied any established model. How else could a Yoruban, Chinese or Hindu work have such vital energy, and how else could a Navajo ritual succeed?

For, as far as beauty is concerned, we are still tackling its mystery because, as we have seen, Lakshmi, the goddess of Beauty, violates all rules.

Major Greek and Western Criteria

Ancient Greece is at the origin of all Western criteria of beauty as well as its critical terminology, and philosophers and artists have used the same terminology, accepting it or reacting against it, up to today. Pythagoras, or the Pythagoreans, tried to define mathematically the harmony of the universe, thus establishing the concept of *symmetria*, from the Greek *sun metron*, meaning "with correct proportions," which is one of the most deeply rooted and omnipresent features of ancient Greek thought.[98] In the *Timaeus* (27c ff.; 34c-36c), when Plato describes the Demiurge creating the world according to an ideally beautiful model, he refers to Pythagorean proportions the beauty of, forms being found in measures and proportion. (*Philebus,* 64 e and 65 d)

According to Aristotle, this concept had, in fact

> [Originated] among the Pythagoreans, who devoted themselves to mathematics
> . . . and thought that its principles were the principle of all things. . . . They sup-
> posed the whole universe to be a musical scale and a number (*Metaphysics*, 985
> b23-986 b8 and 1090a23 ff.).

---

[98] Pollitt, *The Ancient View of Greek Art*, pp. 15 ff.

The qualities of numbers exist in musical scale (harmonia), in the heaven, and in many other things." (Ibid., 1090 a 23)
The entire universe was thus seen as a harmony of consonant numbers (Ibid., 986a5).

This concept of *symmetria* underlies all Greek art. Greek architects did not aim at originality, but at perfection (figs. 18 and 19). Thus, they improved the same type of building, the main features of which were the fluted column and the colonnade, through the centuries, perfecting the relationship of each part of the building to the others and to the whole, as well as establishing the architectural orders.[99]

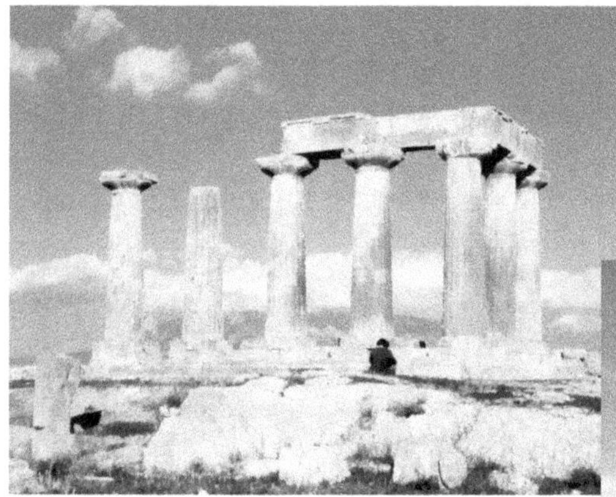

18 *Doric Temple of Apollo* Corinth, c. 550 B.C.E.

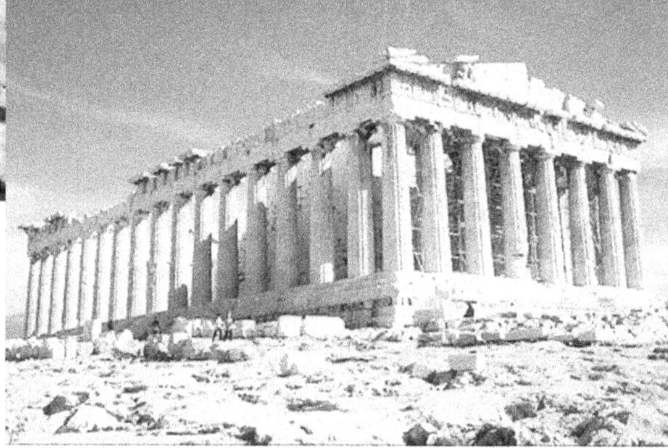

19 The Parthenon, 447-432 B.C.E., Acropolis, Athens

Greek sculptors and painters were the earliest artists in world history to attempt to represent the human body by matching the appearances of the visible world, that is of human anatomy, rather than of any imposed grid system or established formulae as in Mesopotamia or Egypt. They introduced an art based on the observation of nature, but once they mastered the representation of human anatomy and were able to represent bodies capable of motion, they aimed, above all, at making beautiful statues. Their concept of beauty, like that of the Greek philosophers, architects and musicians, was related to the principle of

---

[99] E. Panofsky, "The History of the Theory of Human Proportions as a Reflection of the History of Styles." *Meaning in the Visual Arts*, New York 1955. H. Schaefer, *Principles of Egyptian Art*, Oxford, 1974.

The Path Toward Beauty

symmetria, through which they were to achieve "the beautiful"—*tò kallòn*.

When we look at the canonically "beautiful" statues of the fifth and fourth centuries B.C.E., we are faced, however, with bodies that go far beyond any form of naturalism.[100] Naturalism and idealism do, in fact, merge in classical Greek art, as they were to merge again in the Italian Renaissance.

Furthermore, the fascination for the beauty of the young male body was also linked to a real cult of male beauty, attested by the importance given to gymnastics in Greek education of the sixth and fifth centuries B.C.E.,[101] to beauty contests held at religious festivals such as in the Panathenaic Games of Athens, and the inscriptions found in Greek gymnasia.[102]

No treatises on art have come down to us from antiquity, except for the *Ten Books on Architecture* by Vitruvius, from the late first century B.C.E., and allusions to *The Canon* (the Rule) of Polykleitos in a passage from a medical treatise by Galen, in which the sculptor, active around 430 B.C.E., is said to have underlined the relation:

> [Of] the finger to the finger, and of all the fingers to the metacarpus, and the wrist, and of all of these to the forearm, and of the forearm to the arm, in fact of everything to everything, as it is written in the Canon of Polycleitos. For having taught us in that treatise all the symmetriae of the body, Polycleitos supported his treatise with a work, having made the statue of a man according to the tenets of his treatise, and having called the statue itself, like the treatise, the Canon.

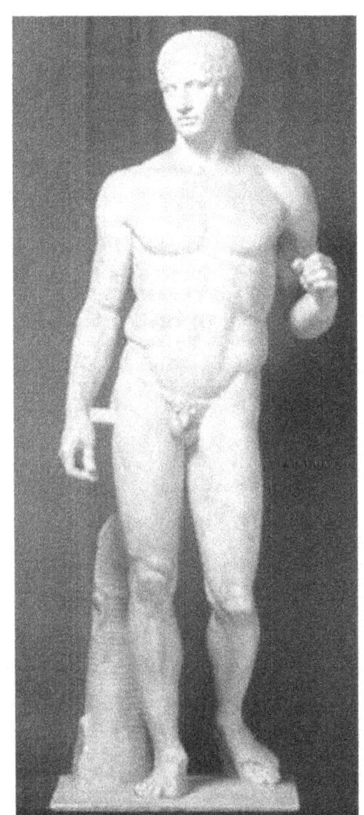

The statue that illustrated this treatise seems to have been Polykleitos' *Doryphoros* or Spear-Carrier (fig. 20.), some Roman copies of which have survived. Polykleitos is also supposed to have written:

> [That] beauty comes about little by little, through many numbers.

20 Polykleitos, *Spear Bearer (Doryphoros)*, Roman copy after the original bronze of c. 440 B.C.E., Naples, National Archaeological Museum

---

[100] N. Spivey, *Understanding Greek Sculpture. Ancient Meaning, Modern Reading*, London, 1997, p. 39.
[101] M.I. Marrou, *Histoire de l'éducation dans l'Antiqité*, Vol. 1: Le monde grec, 1948.
[102] Spivey, op. cit., pp. 36 ff.

The aim of the sculptor was indeed to achieve beauty, which was conceived within the Pythagorean mathematical and philosophical tradition.

> Transforming the visual arts into a medium in which beauty is realized was largely the intellectual achievement of the artists themselves, and they propounded a major theme in European thought. We know too little to account for the forces that motivated this specific development of the workshop, but it is clear that beauty itself was conceived as symmetry, as a system of harmonious, balanced proportions.[103]

"The Greek Revolution"[104] was contemporaneous with, although not totally parallel to, Greek philosophy, which analyzed beauty and tried to define it. In order to understand what beauty may have meant for the Greeks, however, we will try to understand what constituted beauty in the visual arts, and how beauty was conceived in the abstract, by philosophers, that is, unrelated to art or to any other physical phenomenon.

"The Greek Revolution"

During the years between about 600 and 480 B.C.E., Greek artists moved from the conceptual art of the Egyptians and Mesopotamians towards an increasingly naturalistic or illusionistic form of art. Relief sculptors and painters not only had to master the representation of the human body, but also to tell a story or recount the actions of men through images, in other words, find a new narrative technique that no longer consisted of superimposed registers but of a unified space. Thus, they invented the first tricks of foreshortening and of perspective, to give the illusion of the three-dimensional world on a two-dimensional surface. Perhaps they were trying to 'match' through visual means the epic poems of Homer or the famous tragedies of the period, thereby involving the beholder as closely as possible. (figs. 21, 22)

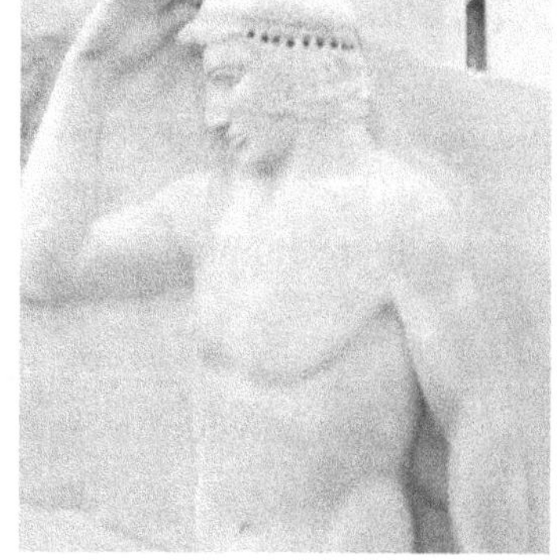

21 *Athlete Crowning Himself*,
relief from Sounion, Attica, c. 460 B.C.E.,
Athens, National Archaeological Museum

---

[103] Barasch, *Modern Theories of Art*, 1, p. 17.
[104] Ernst Gombrich, "The Greek Revolution," *Art and Illusion*, 1972, pp. 99 ff.; and Spivey, op. cit., chapter 2.

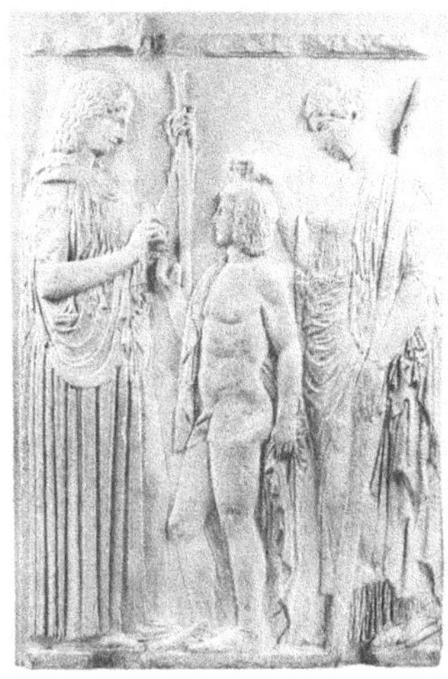

In Egypt, a grid system underlined all relief sculpture and painting (fig. 23 a); there was no foreshortening, but a frontal-profile view (fig. 23 b). The approach to narrative was through superimposed registers and not through a unified space (fig. 23 c).

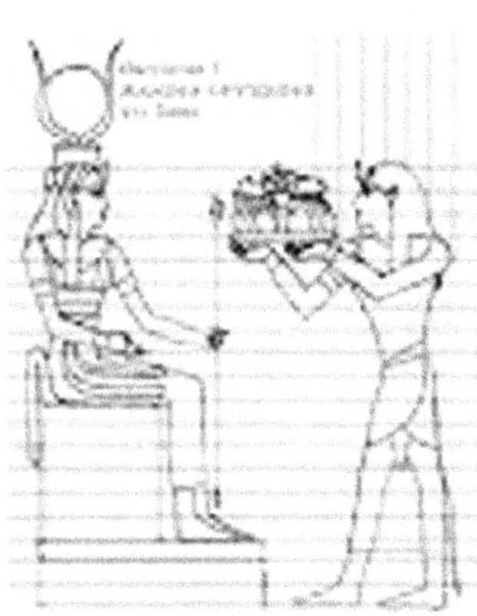

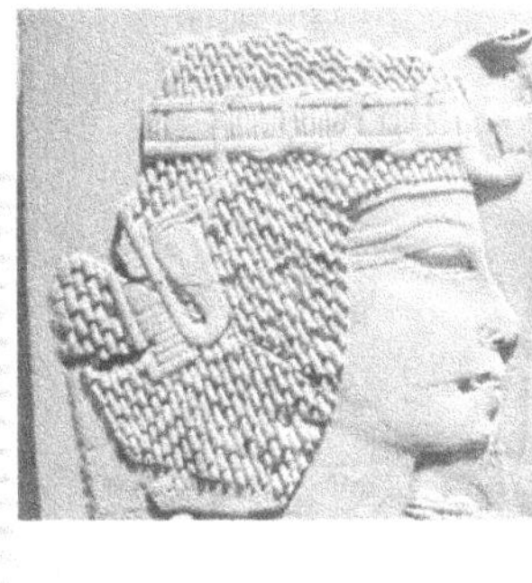

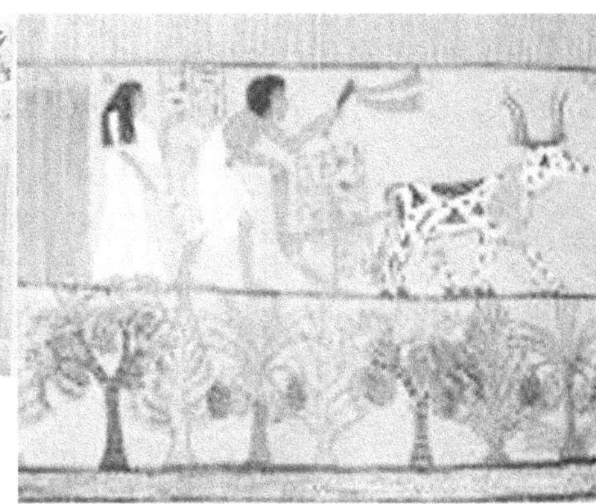

23 a   Drawing reconstructing the grid system of Egyptian art in the relief of *Seti I making offering to Isis*, 19th Dynasty, Abydos
23 b   *Amenhotep III*, detail, 18th Dynasty, c. 1370 B.C.E., Berlin, Altes Museum
23 c   Wall painting in the Tomb of Sennedjem, 19th Dynasty, 13th century B.C.E., Deir el-Medina, Theban Necropolis

Greek sculptors, on the other hand, first had to master the representation of human anatomy, which they did by 480 B.C.E. Then they had to abandon the age-old law of frontality, and hence the immobility of cubic Egyptian and cylindrical Mesopotamian statuary (figs. 24-25) in order to represent bodies in a relaxed, standing posture—in *contrapposto*—or in motion, before they also subordinated all these separate observations to a general ideal of beauty, through the increasingly harmonious proportions of all the parts of a statue to one another and to the whole (figs. 20, 26 and 27).[105]

---

[105] Pollitt, *The Ancient View of Greek Art*, pp. 14 ff., 160 ff.

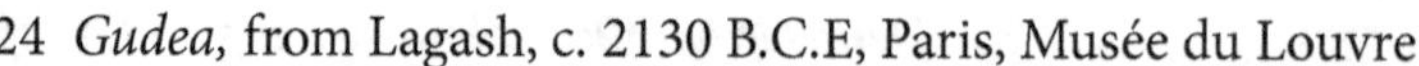

24 *Gudea,* from Lagash, c. 2130 B.C.E, Paris, Musée du Louvre

In the Mesopotamian and Egyptian civilisations, the human figures were, on the contrary, represented according to the strictest law of frontality, hence with bodies that were not susceptible of movement, which were represented for ritual purposes immobile for all eternity. The Mesopotamian statue took the place of the mortal king and was put in a temple, where it offered prayers for all eternity, whereas most Egyptian statues were put in tombs as the eternal support of their *ka,* or of what makes any man unique and never dies, provided it has this support.

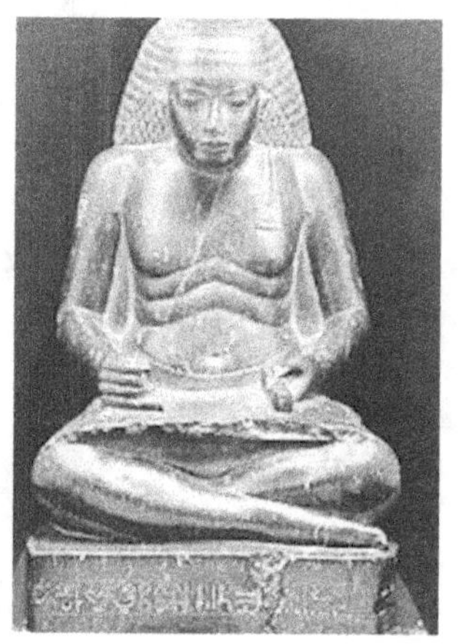

25 *Amenhotep, son of Hapu, as scribe,* 18th Dynasty, 14th century B.C.E., Cairo, Egyptian Museum

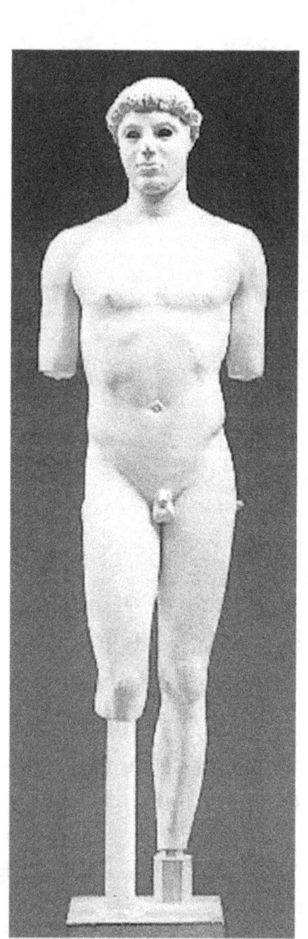

26 *Kritios Boy,* c. 480 B.C.E., Athens, Acropolis Museum

With the *Kritios Boy* (fig. 26), the Greek sculptors abandoned the Mesopotamian and Egyptian law of frontality. They represented a body susceptible of motion. This statue was found on the Acropolis of Athens, where it was probably offered as a token of thanks to Athena for a victory obtained.

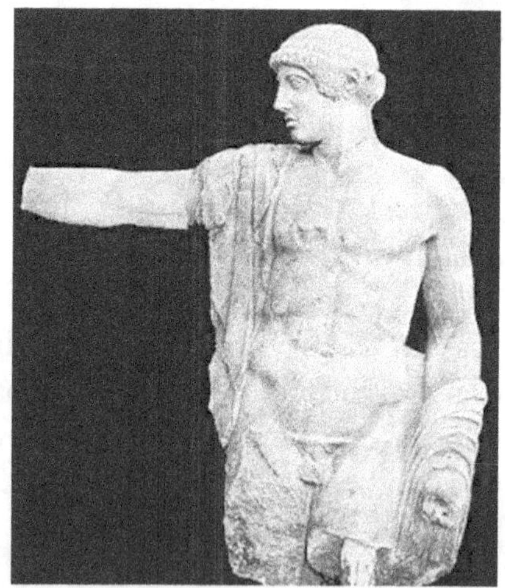

27 *Apollo Granting Victory to the Lapiths,* detail from the west pediment of the Temple of Zeus at Olympia, c. 470-456 B.C.E., Olympia Museum, Greece

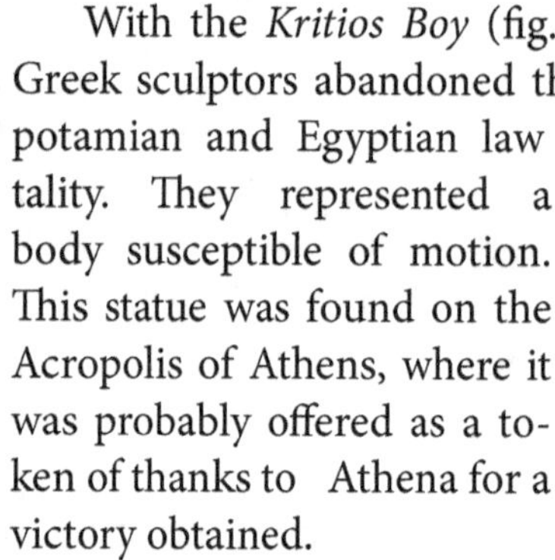

The Path Toward Beauty

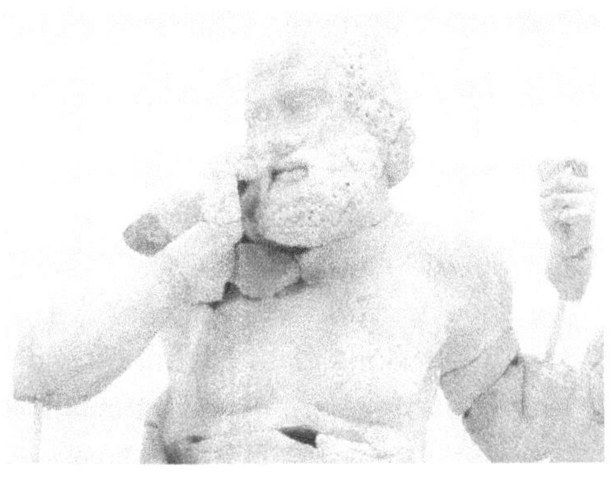

28 *The Seer,* detail from the east pediment of the Temple of Zeus at Olympia, c. 470-456 B.C.E., Olympia Museum, Greece

30 *Battle of the Gods and Giants (Gigantomachy),* detail of the Altar of Zeus from Pergamon, c. 175 B.C.E., Berlin, Staatliche Museen zu Berlin, Antiken Sammlungen, Pergamonmuseum

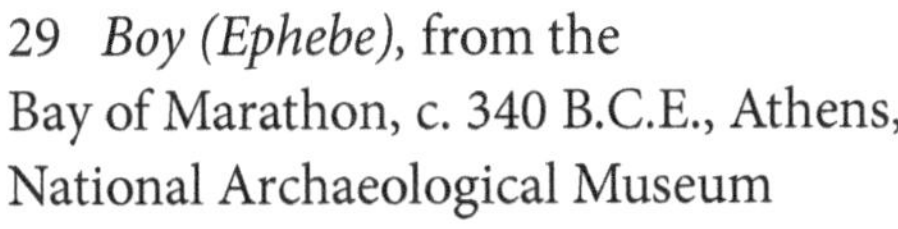

29 *Boy (Ephebe),* from the Bay of Marathon, c. 340 B.C.E., Athens, National Archaeological Museum

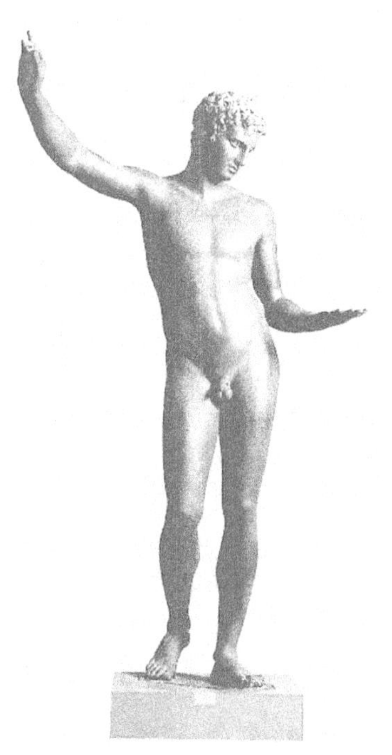

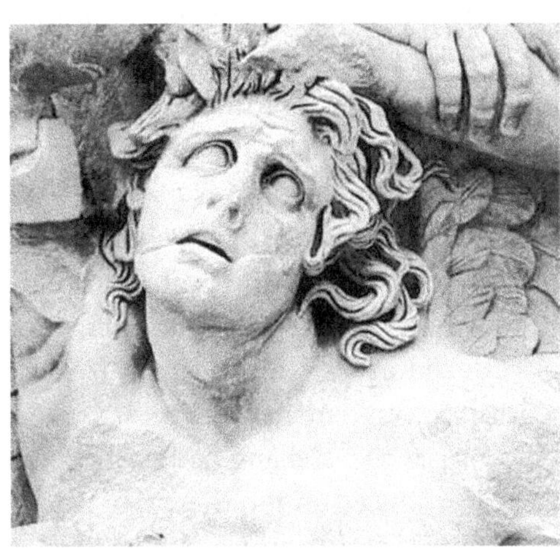

The two male figures (figs. 27 and 29) were produced during two successive periods of Greek Art, and correspond to two different ideals of beauty, or to two different sets of proportions. The two reliefs, three centuries apart (figs. 28 and 30), reflect two different ways of expressing emotions, the fully self-controlled *ethos* in the *Old Seer* of Olympia and the uncontrolled *pathos* in the *Giant.* The latter conveyed by the facial features, the thrown back head, the eyes turned upward, the wild curls, the posture of the body and the bulging muscles (see also figs. 96 and 97).

It was the first time in history that works of art were actually made for the sake of beauty, rather than in view of ritual or funerary purposes, which had been the case in Egypt or Mesopotamia. Nature itself was perceived as beautiful, especially the human body. It was represented with its joints in their natural place, based on observations taken from nature, and not reconstructed according to established, unchanging codes, or in the shape of a cylindar or a cube, and with a grid system, as in Egypt. It was nevertheless mathematically perceived, according to a set of ideally beautiful ratios (recall Polycleitos' *Canon*, illustrated by the *Doryphorous*) (fig. 20).[106]

In so doing, Greek sculptors and painters invented an art based on what Plato and Aristotle were to call *mimesis,* or imitation, which they considered to be the origin of all visual and non-visual forms of art. For them all art forms were, in fact, mimetic.[107] Of course, the artist did not imitate the appearances of nature, as Plato and Aristotle claimed, but the way things came into being in nature, since art is, in fact, a mental thing, and never a mechanical reproduction. Nature cannot be imitated or "transcribed" without first being taken apart and put together again.[108] The naturalistic representation of anatomy, drapery, space, and so on, followed a formal development that implied a diversity of styles, and therefore a slow but constant change through time. Art ceased to reflect an unchanging truth through a set of unchanging rules.

Through the centuries of Greek, Hellenistic and Roman art, the subject matter of *mimesis* became increasingly varied, although it remained centred on the representation of the human body, to the exclusion of almost all other subjects. As Greek religion was anthropomorphic, the statues of gods had to seem "life-like." When landscape painting was introduced in Hellenistic times, it was, in fact, not at all "life-like," but made according to workshop conventions.

During the Hellenistic period, concepts such as that of *phantasia* (*visiones* in Latin) were introduced in the theory of art, and art itself was no longer considered merely as an imitation of nature, however idealized and mathematically "corrected," but also as an image of the mind, hence as a work of imagination.[109]

The ideal of beauty, which was always related to the principle of *symmetria*, varied from one generation of artists to the next and from one artist to another, within the same generation (figs. 20, 26, 27 and 29). Thus, the proportions between the length of the torso and its width, between the size of the head and the overall height of the body, and so on, differed, although they were always measurable and precise.[110]

By the third century C.E., Plotinus rejected this principle as the only formal criterion of beauty, and slowly replaced it with others. For him the beauty of a work of art could not

---

[106] Panofsky, "The History of the Theory of Human Proportions," *Meaning in the Visual Arts;* H. Schaefer, *Principles of Egyptian Art*, Oxford, 1974.

[107] Barasch, *Theories, The Ancient View,* chapter 1, pp. 4 ff.; Pollitt, *The Ancient View,* pp. 37 ff.

[108] Ernst Gombrich, op. cit., p. 121.

[109] Pollitt, *The Ancient View,* pp. 52 ff.

[110] Compare the *Ephebe of Marathon*, 340 B.C.E. (fig. 29) to the earlier statue of Polykleitos (fig. 23) of about 430 B.C.E., while also understanding the contemporary changes that occurred throughout Greek culture: J. J. Pollitt, *Art and Experience in Classical Greece,* Cambridge, 1972.

consist solely of the harmony of its parts, and hence could not be based on the principle of *symmetria:*

> Can we doubt that beauty is something more than symmetry, that symmetry itself owes its beauty to a remoter Principle? (*Enneads*, I, 6, 1).

Beauty, for Plotinus, resided first in the mind of the artist, itself a spark of the divine mind. The artist had to have the vision of the divine form before starting his work, which was only beautiful if it was a reflection of that vision.[111] And vision, for Plotinus, was "for those only who see with the Soul's sight."[112]

Plotinus, however, lived at a time when the Greek, Hellenistic and Roman naturalistic trend of art had slowly been replaced, once again, by a non-naturalistic one, which was to characterize the art of the Middle Ages, as it had and would continue to characterize the art of most other civilizations throughout time. Art was no longer based on *mimesis*. Plotinus was the first commentator of Plato's dialogues, hence at the origin of Neo-Platonism, which was to have preponderant influence on all later philosophy of beauty.

Greek Philosophy of Beauty: Plato, Aristotle and Plotinus

Plato (427 – 347 B.C.E.)

The scope of this book does not allow for a detailed analysis of Plato's discussion on the nature of beauty and arts,[113] but all his concepts are summarized in his general Theory of Knowledge and his *Myth of the Cave* in the *Republic*.[114] For Plato, there are different realms of reality and different forms of knowledge. On one hand, there is the sensible reality which we perceive (Plato calls it "the aesthetic," *to aistheton)* and which appears to our senses (*to phainomenon)*, and on the other, the intelligible reality (*to noeton),* which we can only apprehend with our minds, through our intelligence, which is knowledge of ultimate truth, or of "that which is" (*to on, ousia)*. Sensible reality is made up of shadows and mirror images, of the reflections of things in water as well as of all works of art and their models (plants, animals, human beings or manufactured objects). All of these are, in fact, nothing but reflections of eternal and unchanging forms, of ideas (*eidon)* and knowledge of them leads only to common sense beliefs, and sense experience, to statements based on observations made obsolete by new observations, and to variable opinions, hence to obscurity and ignorance. For Plato, if we trust our experience of sensible reality, our souls will fall asleep.

---

[111] Plotinus, *Enneads*, I.6 and V.9. Cf. Barasch, *Theories,* pp. 14 ff. and Pollitt, *The Ancient View*, pp. 56 ff.

[112] Hofstadter, op. cit., p.145.

[113] *Hippias Major, Symposium, Phaedrus, Republic*, Book II, III and X and some paragraphs of the *Sophist, Philebus, Theaetetus, Timaeus, Ion* and *Laws.*

[114] *Republic*, 505 ff., and 514 ff.

There are different forms of knowledge. On one hand, there is knowledge based on beliefs and illusions, which leads to changeable opinions, and on the other, there is knowledge based on mathematical reasoning and the dialectical reasoning of philosophy, which leads to knowledge of truth, which is unchangeable. Knowledge of intelligible reality is acquired not through sense perception alone, but through rational operations, proceeding through various, consistent steps, which are used in mathematics, astronomy and music: "The real object of their investigation is invisible, except for the eye of reason, this type of thing I called intelligible."

The last step in the world of intelligible reality is the Good, the first principle, or "that which is" (*to on, ousia*). Plato compares it to the Sun, which makes everything else visible. Knowledge of truth can only be attained through dialectical reasoning, which means philosophy. Furthermore, Plato uses the image of an ascent from the lowest form of knowledge to the highest, thereby introducing a hierarchy of knowledge. Knowledge acquired through works of art is at the lowest level, while that which we attain through philosophy is at the highest. In the *Phaedrus* (248-249), he reiterates the idea of hierarchy, again putting "the seeker after wisdom or beauty or a follower of the Muses" at the highest level, and a poet or a practitioner of some other imitative art almost at the bottom.

The *Myth of the Cave* explains this theory (*Republic*, 514 ff.). Plato describes prisoners chained in a dark cave. A fire located behind the backs of the prisoners lights up the cave. People carrying things move between the backs of the prisoners and the fire, which casts their shadows on the opposite wall facing the prisoners, who take these shadows for real things. When one of the prisoners is freed and moves towards the exit of the cave, he discovers that what he had taken for real things were, in fact, only shadows. Then, when he emerges from the cave, he cannot look immediately at the objects in the bright light of the sun. Instead he has to adjust his sight very slowly to the outside world. First, he looks at things during the night and in reflections, and then, only very gradually, will he be able to look at the sensible world in broad daylight. At last he will be able to gaze at the Sun itself, without which, nothing would be visible at all. The Sun, for Plato, becomes an allegory of the Good, and both are synonyms of truth and beauty.

For Plato, as we said above, all forms of art imitate the sensible world (art is based on *mimesis*), further deceiving our senses, because they make us take for real things that are, in fact, only painted or sculpted. Thus, works of art lead us into a kind of daydream rather than to knowledge of truth. In the *Republic* (597-598 c), we read about the ideal form of a couch, the carpenter who makes a copy of that ideal model and finally the painter copies the appearance of that same couch, representing it through foreshortening, hence only from one point of view, and therefore incomplete.

Hence, the painter is twice removed from the ideal form of the bed, which, for Plato, is the only real bed and the only one worth knowing. The Greek painter created an illusion.

Shall we not say that we make an actual house with the art of building and with

the art of painting that we make another house which is a kind of man-made
dream for people who are wide awake? (*Sophist*, 266 c).

The painter appeals to the emotions, not to the rational part of the soul and even
destroys reason, painting things of which he has no knowledge, just as the writer
writes about things he does not know (*Republic*, 605 b).

Both are magicians and creators of illusion of reality (*Sophist*, 234-235).

It is only within this general theory of knowledge that we can understand Plato's attitude
towards art and, more specifically, towards painting, which he uses, in fact, throughout his
dialogues as a metaphor for the phenomenal world.[115]

Because Plato advocated the study of geometry and mathematics for the training of the
mind, he also referred to the art of architecture as a way of attaining knowledge of truth,
because:

[It] makes use of a great number of measures and instruments. [It] is the most
scientific of all arts because it uses the ruler, the compass, the string. It is precise.
. . . What I am looking for is not which art or science is better or greater, or more
useful, but which is searching for clarity, precision and supreme truth, small or
great (*Philebus*, 56 b and 58 c).

Through mathematics, which Plato advocated for the training of the mind, one studies,
forms that are measurable, precise, unchanging, hence true and, therefore, also beautiful.

I do not mean the beauty of human figures or of paintings, I mean the straight
line or the circle, the plane and solid figures, formed by means of compass, ruler,
square, because I say that these figures are not, as the others, beautiful in some
way, but they are always beautiful by themselves, They give us pleasure that
belongs to them and have nothing to do with the pleasure given by tickling.
. . . There are also pure colors or unmixed colors and pure notes that are not
relatively beautiful, but absolutely beautiful . . . not based on appearances, not
deceiving . . . belonging to a world that can be defined, finite, limited, measurable (*Philebus*, 51 c).

Among these unchanging forms are equilateral triangles which make up all the geometrical bodies that can be inscribed in a circle, the latter being the most beautiful of all
forms. These unchanging forms include also the perfect geometrical proportions of squares

---

[115] Eve Keuls, *Plato and Greek Painting*, Leiden, 1978, and Bernhard Schweitzer, *Platon und die bildende
Kunst der Griechen*, Tuebingen, 1953.

and cubes, and numbers that never change (*Timaeus*, 53 c, and 54 c ff.). There was no doubt for Plato that "the objects of geometrical knowledge are eternal. Geomentry tends to draw the mind to the truth and direct the philosopher's reason upward" (*Republic*, 527 b-c).

Greek painters and sculptors, on the contrary, imitated the perpetually changing world of appearances, altering natural proportions to create optical illusions, thus producing fantastic imitations (*phantastike)* that did not even correspond to sensible reality (*Sophist*, 235 e, 236 a, 266 e - 266 e, 268 c-d).[116] Consequently, art could never lead to the knowledge of truth, except for Egyptian art, in which for thousands of years (10,000 according to Plato) "the beautiful schemata had undergone no change" (*Laws*, 656 d-e).

For Plato, as Pollitt writes

> if the artist . . . could apprehend that which is real (*to on*), permanent, behind the changing appearances of sense experience, the object would be truly beautiful, kalòn, . . . an analogue of a divine model like Plato's ideal state. . . . The result is a kind of spiritual mimesis in which the artist becomes a visionary and his work, an emanation of the (eternal) forms themselves.[117]

Indeed, this was precisely the aim of twentieth century abstract artists, such as Mondrian (fig. 102) and Malevich, as it had once been the aim of Irish and Islamic aniconic art. Mondrian wrote:

> We must carefully distinguish between two forms of reality, one which has an individual and one which has a universal appearance, . . . the latter, through neutral forms and colors. Pure abstract art aims at creating universal realities, pure and complete in its beauty. . . . It has always been only one struggle, . . . to create universal beauty, . . . the universal—as the mathematical—is the essence of all feelings of beauty.[118]

Malevich gave up representing what he called "things," "the verisimilitude of the illusion," "the virtuosity of the objective representation," "the dearly loved reality of the public" in order to create an art of purely geometrical forms, such as the *Black Square* (fig. 65) or the *White Square on the White Background* (fig. 101)

> where the form becomes an allusion to space and the painting an allusion to painting, revealing the essential, the supreme or essential being, a world without objects.[119]

---

[116] Pollitt, *The Ancient View*, p. 28 and 46 ff. Plato referred to the sculptures of the Parthenon when he wrote about an optical illusion and "fantastic" proportions.

[117] Pollitt, *The Ancient View*, 1974, p. 47

[118] *The New Art-The New Life: The Collected Writings of Piet Mondrian*, ed. and trans. Harry Holzman and Martin James, London, 1986, p. 35.

[119] Lipsey, op. cit., p. 90.

The Path Toward Beauty

The Irish (fig. 31) and Islamic arts (figs. 2, 83-84) were aniconic, since God had forbidden the representation of any living being. Their art was also entirely based on geometrical principles that brought forth an infinite number of patterns, all drawn with a compass. These principles were, in fact, unchanging, thus reflecting the unchanging truth and beauty of the Good, hence of God, while obeying his command.

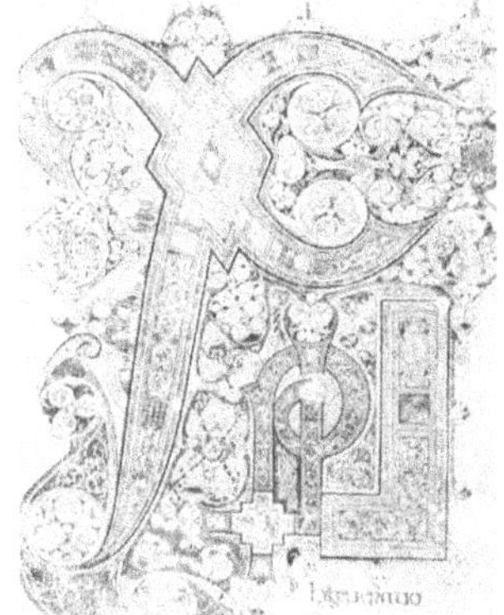

31   *Chi Rho Iota Page*, *Book of Kells*, late 8th or early 9th century. Dublin, Board of Trinity College (Ms. 58, fol. 34 v)

Plato never referred to inspired painters or sculptors. In Greek mythology, there was, in fact, no Muse that inspired an artist who used his hands to create and was despised as a manual labourer, an attitude towards the artist that endured until the sixteenth century.[120] He does, on the contrary, refer to the inspired poets. In the *Phaedrus*, for example, Plato compared the inspired and blind poet Stesichorus to the uninspired Sophist Lysias, to show that technique alone was not enough to make a good poet. A good poet also had to be possessed by the Muses or by a god-sent madness (*maniké, manìa Mousòn*), hence be inspired. We will come back to this concept of inspiration.

Aristotle (384 – 322 B.C.E.)
Within his general law of four-fold causality, Aristotle (Plato's pupil) related the artist, whom he defines as the efficient cause, to the art work or formal cause, to the material used constituting the material cause, and to the goal, the purpose, or the final cause of the work. If one of these four causes was eliminated, the object would simply cease to exist. A work of art was therefore inconceivable without a final cause. He also wondered who was moving the hands of the artist:

> Watching the carpenter at work, we see that the wood he works on is moved by his tools, and that the tools are moved by his hands. But, one cannot help asking, who moves the hands?

---

[120] For Plato and the visual arts, see Pollitt, *The Ancient View*, and Barasch, *Theories*, as well as Keuls, op.cit. and Erwin Panofsky, *Idea. A Concept of Art Theory*, New York, Icon, 1968. For the status of the artists in Greece; R. Mondolfo, "The Greek Attitude to Manual Labour," *Past and Present*, 6 (1954),1-5. For the Renaissance, Anthony Blunt, "The Social Position of the Artist," *Artistic Theory in Italy 1450-1600*, Oxford, 1975, chapter IV.

Aristotle's answer was ambiguous:

> It is his knowledge of his art and his soul in which is the form that moves his hands (*Generation of Animals*, 730 b, 15).

Elsewhere, he stated that "the soul is the place of forms" (*On the Soul*, 429 a, 15-28 ff.) and that the place within the soul, in which the forms dwell, is "the thinking place of the soul," as if the origin of the creative process was, in fact, the mind, and not the imitated object. The work of art was becoming not only a far-removed copy of some ideal model, as Plato had said, but the result of a creative process.[121]

Michelangelo may have been referring to this passage when he asserted that the beautiful form does not come from the imitation of nature, but from within the artist's mind, from the *concetto* or concept.

For Aristotle, nevertheless, as for Plato:

> The chief forms of beauty are order and symmetry and definiteness which the mathematical sciences demonstrate in a special degree (*Metaphysics*, 1078 b, 1-3).

Symmetria, for Aristotle, was a condition of formal beauty and anything which was not clearly defined produced horror (in our own time, we would probably say that the undetermined, or the boundless, produces anguish), while disorder produced monsters, which Nature herself eliminates when it produces them:

> To be beautiful, a living creature and every whole, made up of parts, must not only present a certain order in its arrangement of parts, but also be of a certain definite magnitude. Beauty is a matter of size and order (*Poetics*, 1450 b, 34-37).

How Did Plato Conceive of Beauty?

If we have understood that Plato's ultimate aim is knowledge of "that which is" (*to on*, *ousia*), of eternal and unchanging truth, and that truth is synonymous with the Good and the Beautiful, then we can see why for him, the particular beauty of any particular object can only be relative and a thing is beautiful only insofar as it shares in beauty itself:

> "What about the man who recognizes the existence of beautiful things but does not believe in beauty itself, and is incapable of following anyone who wants to lead him to a knowledge of it? Is he awake or merely dreaming? Look, isn't dreaming simply the confusion between resemblance and the reality that it resembles, whether the dreamer is asleep or awake?"
>
> "He is dreaming."

---

[121] Barasch, *Theories*, p. 11 and Bernard Schweitzer, *Zur Kunst der Antike*, Tübingen, 1963, I, pp. 11-104.

"Then what about the man who, on the contrary, believes in beauty itself and can see both it and the particular things that share in it, and does not confuse particular things and that in which they share? Do you think he is awake or dreaming?"

"He is very much awake" (*Republic*, 476 c-d).

If he is "awake," the beauty of a particular object can nevertheless become the first step towards the recognition of the existence of beauty itself.

In the *Myth of the Cave*, it is the philosopher who takes the prisoner out of the utter darkness of the cave into the full light of day, whereas in the *Symposium*, it is Eros or Love, conceived as an intermediary between man and god—as a *daimon*—who leads us upward, from the beauty of the sensible world to that of the intelligible world, and to the revelation of absolute beauty, and it is Diotima, an inspired priestess, who guides us.

In the *Hippias Major*, Plato raised some very general, though important, questions about what "beautiful," considered only as an attribute, might be. He has not yet analyzed what beauty might be in itself, or the driving force that leads to our awareness of it. Hence he does not yet relate beauty to love. Instead he wonders if there are different levels of beauty, if beauty is a quality which, when added to an object, would make it beautiful. He thereby raises the issue of the analogy between what is suitable and adequate (we may say functional) and that which is beautiful. He also wonders if one can call "beautiful" that which conceals the ugly, if one can call "beautiful" that which is only related to the present and to a particular place, or if the beautiful is only that which is timeless and universal. Can the beautiful be confused with the good? Is the beautiful that which is pleasurable? He concludes, not without irony, that "difficult are beautiful things," and opens the way to the following two dialogues.

In the *Symposium*, the debate is about love (Eros or Love is always, in Plato, the active force of the lover) but love of what? Love of beauty, but to what end?

"The object of love, Socrates, is not, as you think, beauty, . . . Its object is to procreate and bring forth in beauty, . . . Now why is procreation the object of love? Because procreation is the nearest thing to perpetuity and immortality that a mortal being can attain. . . . Mortal nature seeks, as far as it may be, to perpetuate itself and become immortal. The only way in which it can achieve this is by procreation . . . because procreation is endowed with a touch of immortality."

When one procreates, *kalloné*—a name invented by Plato, derived from *tò kalòn*, the beautiful—one presides over birth. To procreate is, in fact, something divine. As the gods are beautiful by definition, one can only procreate in, or with, what is beautiful. Beauty is the means, but the aim is to come closer to the immortality of the gods through physical or spiritual procreation.

Among the spiritual begetters are:

> those who long to beget spiritually, not physically, the progeny which it is the nature of the soul to create and bring to birth. If you ask what that progeny is, it is wisdom and virtue in general. Of this all poets and such craftsmen as have found out some new thing may be said to be begetters. . . . Everyone would prefer children such as these to children after the flesh. Take Homer, for example, and Hesiod and the good poets, who would not envy them the children that they left behind, children whose quality have won immortal fame and glory to their parents (*Symposium*, 209 a-d).

But what is love? Socrates and the priestess Diotima initiate us to its mystery. Love is not a god, as most of the previous speakers at the *Symposium*, except Aristophanes, asserted. It seeks eternal beauty and immortality that only gods possess. It is not "the name for the desire and the pursuit of the whole," the longing for a lost unity "each part yearning for the half he or she has lost," as Aristophanes stated. Love is a *daimon*, neither man nor god, but an intermediary between the two, taking the beloved, hence all of us, step by step, from the love for the physical beauty of one particular object or being, to the revelation of beauty itself, that is, the divinity.

There are four steps in this ascent. It begins with the love of one beautiful physical object and the discovery that physical beauty is shared by many. Hence, it moves from the particular to the universal. From the love of physical beauty it goes on to love of the soul, of activities and institutions, to the point where "physical beauties taken as a whole" are considered "a poor thing in comparison." Then, it rises from spiritual and moral beauty to that of the sciences. One who would pursue this goal must find beauties

> [and] contemplate their beauty, so that having his eyes fixed upon beauty in the widest sense, he may no longer be a slave of a base and mean-spirited devotion to an individual example of beauty, whether the object of his love be a boy or a man or an activity, but gazing upon the vast ocean of beauty to which his attention is now turned, may bring forth, in the abundance of his love of wisdom, many beautiful and magnificent sentiments and ideas, until, at last, strengthened and increased in stature by the experience, he catches sight of one unique science whose object is the beauty of which Diotima will now speak (Ibid., 210-211).

Finally, when man has been guided thus far in the mysteries of love and beauty, he will have a sudden revelation of beauty itself:

> This beauty is first of all eternal, it neither comes into being nor passes away; neither waxes nor wanes; next, it is not beautiful in part and ugly in part, nor beautiful at one time and ugly at another, nor beautiful in this relation and ugly

The Path Toward Beauty

in that, nor beautiful here and ugly there, as varying according to his beholder; nor again will this beauty appear to him like the beauty of a face or hands or anything corporeal, or like the beauty of a thought or science or like beauty which has its seat in something other than itself, be it a living thing or the earth or the sky or anything else whatever, he will see it as absolute, existing alone with itself, unique, eternal, and all other beautiful things as partaking of it, yet in such a manner that, while they come into being and pass away, it neither undergoes any increase or diminution nor suffers any change (Ibid., 210-211).

Once you have seen it, you will not value it in terms of gold or rich clothing or of beauty of boys or young men. What do you suppose to be the felicity of the man who sees absolute beauty in its essence, pure and unalloyed, who, instead of a beauty tainted of human flesh and color and a mass of perishable rubbish, is able to apprehend divine beauty where it exists apart and alone. . . . Do you not see that in that region alone where he sees beauty with the faculty capable of seeing it, will he be able to bring forth not mere reflected images of goodness [goodness has again replaced beauty] but true goodness, because he will be in contact not with a reflection, but with the truth? And having brought forth and nurtured true goodness he will have the privilege of being loved by God and becoming, if ever man can, immortal himself (Ibid., 211-212).

Plato has again substituted goodness for beauty and has made both of them synonyms of truth and, ultimately, synonyms of the love of the divinity, or of Love itself.

In the Indian philosophy, *sundara*, which means beauty, is also conceived as one aspect of the divinity, along with truth, goodness and wisdom, and it was to be the same in Christian and Islamic philosophy.

Thus, in the *Symposium,* love is love of beauty in view of immortality, granted only to the gods, and which man can only reach through physical and spiritual procreation. The artist is a spiritual begetter. Beauty presides, as Plato emphasizes, over everything that is divine, hence over any form of procreation.

If a human being "has directed his thought towards examples of beauty in due and orderly succession," and arrives at the highest level, he will have the sudden revelation of absolute beauty, goodness and truth and will become, thereby, the beloved of the divinity. When the lover actually becomes the beloved, it is, however, the end of the process, just as the *Divine Comedy* came to an end when Dante had the ultimate vision of God, or as the Chinese painter Wu Tao-tzu disappeared into the wall and his painting faded away, as soon as he discovered that what was beyond it was far more beautiful.

What seems relevant to our own reflection in relation to the visual arts is that there can be no beauty, at any stage, without love; neither can there be love of beauty if we fail to move beyond the particular beauty of a particular object, however beautiful it might be.

Let us recall that only he "who believes in beauty itself and can see both it and the particular things that share in it, and does not confuse particular things and that in which they share" is awake (*Republic*, 476 d).

In the *Phaedrus*, love is also linked to beauty, even though the subject of the dialogue is education, "which opens the soul to the search for truth" and not to "that which gives you the technique of how to make things seem plausible or true." In the *Phaedrus*, love is a god-sent madness (*maniké*), in which we do not obey only the desire to possess the beloved immediately and to share the immediate physical pleasures of love, but allow reason and wisdom to take over. Love is *maniké* only when it is subject to self-control, measure and virtue.

In this dialogue, the beauty of the beloved acts as a reminder of eternal beauty, that which was ours to contemplate, once upon a time, when, as Plato writes, our immortal soul had not yet lost its wings and fallen into the prison of our mortal body. Through love, we have the feeling that our wings are growing back; the beauty of the beloved is a reminder of the absolute beauty of the gods. The beloved, too, can be made aware of that beauty, because he sees himself in the love of the lover, as in a mirror. "He sees himself reflected in the lover as in a glass and his soul is filled with love" (*Phaedrus*, 255 d). Thus, he, too, can be led back to the contemplation of eternal beauty.

At the end of the *Phaedrus*, Socrates turns "his heart to the love of wisdom"(Ibid., 257 b). Because he is the teacher, he knows the nature of his disciple's soul, and his love can open it up to the search for truth. At the end of the dialogue, Socrates compares the teacher, who sows a seed of truth in the soul of his disciple, to a gardener sowing in a suitable soil, and then:

> The fruits can defend themselves as well as the man who planted them, they are not sterile but contain a seed from which fresh truths spring up in other minds, in this way they secure immortality for it (Ibid., 277 a).

Once more, immortality is secured.

Socrates is physically ugly, according to Alcibiades' description at the end of the *Symposium*, and he does not love his disciples physically because he is chaste. He is compared to those containers shaped like satyrs that are hollow inside but filled with beautiful statuettes of gods. Moreover, Socrates is himself a *daimon*, possessed by a god-sent madness. He is ignorant, but he is aware of it and he leads his disciples to the same awareness. This is the first step in the search for that which we lack, namely the knowledge of truth, beauty, goodness and wisdom (all of them synonyms) which, for Plato, can never be relative. Skeptics, remember, were not yet born.

Immortality is not allotted to man; it is through children of the flesh or, better still, through deeds and works of art that we can come closer to attaining it. If love for the beauty of any particular object acts as a reminder of that which we cannot see, such as the absolute beauty of the divinity, can we not say that love may also reunite the *symbolon*, the Greek recognition piece, of which we see only the visible part? Every particular beautiful object shares in beauty itself, insofar as love inspired the artist and guided his hand. If that does not occur, does it mean that the work is simply not beautiful, or that the beholder is not yet ready to recognize it?

Could we not, in spite of Plato's distrust for the art of his own time, equate Plato's lover to the artist, and draw a parallel between the beloved and the work of art itself? Is not a beautiful work of art also a mirror image in which we, as beholders, can see ourselves, provided we, too, love and have grown in awareness and knowledge?

We have already noted that in many, if not all, civilizations, a work of art was not considered beautiful in itself, but only insofar as it was an offering to the deity, a reminder of the invisible beauty, or of the vitality, of a divinity, a way to live the *tao*. A work of art was deemed beautiful when it led the worshiper, the beholder, and above all the artist, to transcend the object which then became a reflection of their own faith and longing.

In the history of the visual arts and in that of the philosophy of beauty, no artwork has ever been considered universally beautiful, unless it was made by a highly skilled artist, inspired by a *maniké* and the *manìa Mousòn* (*Phaedrus*, 245 a) or a *daimon*, which, at times, implied total abnegation of the artist's ego. If, on the contrary, a work of art does not reveal immaterial beauty, or does not take the beholder further on the own path towards transcendence, is it for a lack of love, and on whose part, the artist's or the beholder's?

In the *Phaedo* (100 d), Plato uses yet another concept, participation (*methexis*), whereby he describes the relationship between the universal and the particular. The latter is never identical to the former, but takes part in it. It is the same concept, which we already brought out in the *Republic* "about beauty itself and the particular things that share in it." Plotinus was to develop this concept of participation, but it was to be used above all by the defenders of images during the Byzantine iconoclastic period (726-843). For them, a representation of Christ could only be made if it was not considered identical to the model, but only as participating in the archetype, suggesting the invisible, and becoming, in fact, its symbol.[122]

----

[122] Barasch, *Theories*, pp. 56 ff.

Plotinus and the Neo-Platonic Approach

In the Greco-Roman world, by the third century of our era, the visual arts had ceased to be based on *mimesis.*

A few quotes from the *Enneads* of Plotinus (205-270) best summarize the thought of the first Neo-Platonic philosopher.

> When one looks down upon the arts because they are concerned with imitating nature, it must first be replied that also the things of nature imitate other things; then you must know that artists do not simply reproduce the visible, but they go back to the principles in which nature itself had found its origin; and further, that they on their own part achieve and add much, whenever something is missing, for they are in possession of beauty. Phidias produced his Zeus according to nothing visible (*Enneads*, V, 8, 1),[123] but he made him such as Zeus himself would appear should he wish to reveal himself to our eyes. . . . The artist must have an inner vision, the image that he will create will be an emanation of God, hence an image of beauty. He creates a second cosmos and copies at every point the archetype . . . and has beauty as springing from the divine world. Beauty is of the divine and comes thence only (*Enneads*, V, 8, 12).

How can the beholder recognize that beauty?

> To any vision must be brought an eye adapted to what has to be seen, and having some likeness to it, never did eye the see the sun unless it has first become sun–like, and never can the soul have vision of the First Beauty unless it itself be beautiful (Ibid., 1, 6).

For Plotinus, the artist is no longer primarily interested in matching the visible appearance of nature. Although convinced that physical beauty was only "an image and a vestige and a shadow," Plotinus nevertheless tries to show that a work of art contains an idea or a vision. He conceived beauty not only through the principle of *symmetria*, but as an emanation of God, which shines through the work of art. Hence, artists are also "holders of beauty" (Ibid., V. 8. 1).

> Beauty addresses itself chiefly to sight. The secret of beauty there is in all that derives from the soul. . . . Almost everyone declares that symmetry . . . with, besides, a certain charm of color, constitutes the beauty recognized by the eye, that in visible things, as indeed in all else, universally, the beautiful thing is essentially symmetrical, patterned. But think what this means. Can we doubt that beauty is something more than symmetry, that symmetry itself owes its beauty to a remoter principle? . . . Undoubtedly, this principle exists, it is something that is perceived

---

[123] For Phidias' Zeus: P. Clayton and M. Price, *The Seven Wonders of the Ancient World*, London, 1988.

at the first glance, something which the soul names as from ancient knowledge and, recognizing, welcomes it, enters into unison with it. But let the soul fall in with the ugly and at once it shrinks within itself, denies the thing, turns away from it, not accordant, resenting it. . . . The material thing becomes beautiful by communicating in the thought that flows from the Divine (Ibid., I. 6. 1-2).

According to Plotinus, the particular beauty of a particular work of art participates in the universal idea. Plotinus also gives great importance to the splendour of colors, to the beauty of shimmering light. This emphasis on light was to be picked up by Dionysus the Pseudo-Aeropagite,[124] for whom God is "superessential Light" or "the Father of the lights." The analogy between the supreme divinity and light is a human constant, especially in the Old and New Testaments.

Plato's and Plotinus' philosophies of beauty provide the background for Medieval and Renaissance philosophy, even though, as Panofsky wrote, Plato accuses the arts of continually limiting man's inner vision to the realm of sensory images and obstructing his contemplation of the world of Ideas. Plotinus defends works of art, but, as Panofsky observed, "condemns the arts to the tragic fate of eternally driving man's inner eye beyond these sensory images, that is, of opening to him the prospect of the world of Ideas but at the same time veiling the view."[125] In Plotinus, works of art reveal the Ideas but are not sufficient in themselves.

Greek Origin of Medieval and Renaissance Criteria of Beauty

Medieval Criteria

When Christianity was given freedom of cult, after 313 A.D., and finally triumphed, the question about the making of images arose. In the Old Testament, God had, in fact, prohibited any form of representation:

---

[124] *De Hierarchia Coelestis*, a Greek text written by a monk named Dionysius around 500 A.D. One manuscript of this text was given to the Abbey of Saint Denis and translated around 800 from Greek into Latin by John Scotus Erigena. The author was thought to be Dionysus the Aeropagite, first Bishop of Athens, who was believed to be the same person as Saint Denis, the martyr, whose relics were venerated in the Abbey of Saint Denis itself. This text was very influential. It promoted the mystique of light, hence also the creation of stained glass windows by Suger, Abbot of Saint Denis in the early twentieth century and his entire upward-leading or anagogical approach to beauty. English Translation. *Mystical Theology and the Celestial Hierarchies*, Shrine of Wisdom, Fintry, 1965.
[125] E. Panofsky, *Idea*, 2nd ed, pp. 31-32.

You shall not have gods except me, you shall not make yourself a carved image
of any likeness of anything in heaven or on earth, beneath the waters, under the
earth, you shall not bow down to them or serve them (Exodus 20:4 and Deuter-
onomy 5:8).

The Jewish God, or Yahweh, is not only unique, but also invisible; the concept of the absolute transcendence of God was born on Mount Sinai during the second millennium before our era. The prohibition against making images was, in fact, against worshipping lifeless idols and also implied the idea, or the dread, that artists compete with the Creator, the "Artificer," "the very source of beauty" (*Wisdom* 13:3).

Christians, however, believe that Jesus is the Messiah, the Son of God, hence that God had made Himself visible through the Incarnation. The nature of Jesus Christ is both divine and human. His divinity is, by definition, invisible: "God, that is the only true God, is perceived not by the senses, but by the mind" (Clement of Alexandria).

Through his humanity, however, he had become visible. This visibility became the Christian justification for image-making. How, then, could Jesus be represented in any material work of art without fear of idolatry? This was also to be the great dilemma of the Iconoclastic Controversy, which was finally solved by invoking the Platonic *methexis*, the participation of the particular in the universal.

By 750, in the midst of the iconoclastic debate, John of Damascus wrote:

An image is a likeness and cannot be endowed with the spiritual faculty, it is
indicative of something which is hidden. . . . Every image is declarative and indicative of something hidden. I mean the following: in as much as a man has no
direct knowledge of the invisible, . . . the image has been invented for the sake of
guiding knowledge and manifesting publicly that which is concealed.[126]

Ernst Kitzinger shows how the icon stood "in a transcendental relationship to the holy person it represented, . . . a reflection of its prototype, a link with the invisible and the supernatural, a vehicle of transmission for divine forms." [127] In order to become that vehicle, the painter had to follow very strict iconographic and stylistic rules, imposed after the end of Iconoclasm, in 843, by the Church of Byzantium. No naturalistic portraiture or innovations of any kind were allowed. Paul Evdokimov underlines that the role of the icon is to make us aware of the invisible through forms, leading to a revelation and becoming a means of communication with God, who remains invisible.[128]

---

[126] C. Mango, *The Art of the Byzantine Empire, 312-1453. Sources and Documents,* Englewood Cliffs, NJ, 1972, pp. 169-172.

[127] E. Kitzinger, *Byzantine Art in the Making,* Cambridge, MA, 1980, pp. 107 ff.,

[128] Paul Evdokimov, *The Art of the Icon: A Theology of Beauty,* trans. by Steven Bigham, Redondo Beach, CA, 1990, 1972.

This obviously does not occur with all icons, such as those reproduced mechanically, for example, that one finds in most monastery shops in Greece today, where the mysterious wedding of mind and matter has been lost . Even the most beautiful ones, such as the earliest existing icon of Christ, in the monastery of Saint Catherine, at the foot of Mount Sinai, do not have the same effect on every beholder (fig. 32).

Again, no stylistic or iconographic rule can explain this mystery. Who or what guided the hand of the artist? How did the icon become a reminder of the beauty of the prototype? We are back to Plato's *Phaedrus* and the *Symposium*, as well as to the *Enneads* of Plotinus.

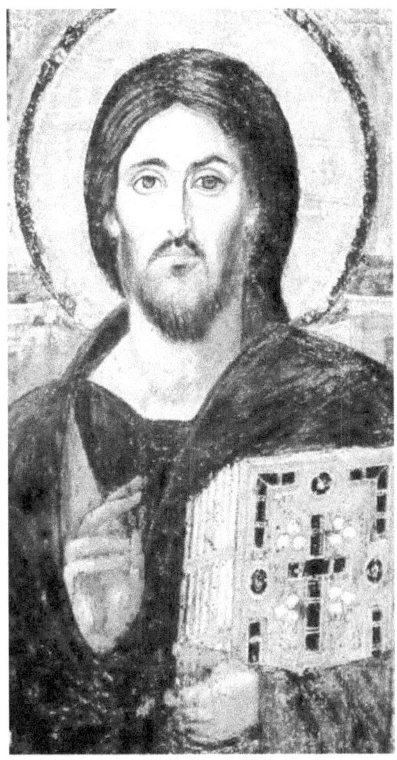

32 *Portrait of Christ*, Icon, 6th or 7th centuries, Monastery of Saint Catherine, Mount Sinai, Egypt

When Suger, the Abbot of Saint-Denis, rebuilt his abbey (1130-1144), he followed the anagogical (*anagogus mos)*, or upward-leading, approach to beauty of Dionysus the Pseudo-Aeropagite.[129] Suger thought that, through the perception of the material beauty of an art work, anything that glittered and shone such as gold, stained-glass windows, jewelled crosses, bronze doors, and so on, the beholder would be led upward to the awareness of the invisible beauty and "superessential light" of God (fig. 33). A work of art was considered beautiful only if it succeeded in doing so, thanks to the skill of the artists, the materials used and their symbolic meaning, which were all intrinsically interrelated:

> The beauty of the house of God must give to the faithful as a foretaste of the beauty of heaven. The joy of material beauty such as that of colored stones and windows can transport us, with the help of God, to the spiritual delectations of a superior beauty, . . . the beauty of the pure radiance of God. (Suger)

---

[129] E. Panofsky, *Abbot Suger. On the Abbey of Saint Denis and its Art Treasures*, Princeton University Press, Second Edition, 1979; M. M. Davy, *Initiation à la symbolique romane*, Paris, 1977; idem, "La lumière dans le christianisme," in *Le Thème de la lumière*, Paris, 1976.

The same approach had been that of Hypatius of Ephesus, writing in the mid-sixth century, justifying probably the magnificence of the Hagia Sophia, built under Justinian, in Constantinople (figs. 80 c-d):

> We, too, permit material adornment in the sanctuaries, not because God considers gold and silver, silken vestments and vessels encrusted with gems to be precious and holy, but because we allow every order of the faithful to be guided in a suitable manner and to be led up to Godhead, inasmuch as some men are guided even by such things towards an intelligible beauty, and from the abundant light of the sanctuaries to the intelligible and immaterial light.[130]

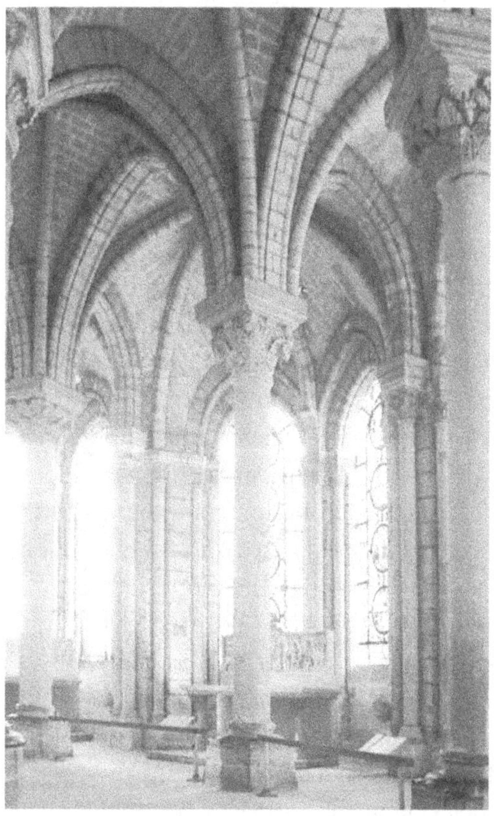

33 Ambulatory, 1140-1144, abbey church of Saint-Denis, France

God was, in fact, conceived, throughout Christian medieval philosophy either as light, referring to the Sun of Plato's *Myth of the Cave*, or the flood of light through which God appeared to Moses (Exodus 33:20), or as order and harmony, because "God has ordered everything in measure and number and weight" (Wisdom 11:21), and we are reminded once again of Pythagoras.

The builders of Byzantine churches, such as Hagia Sophia in Istanbul (figs. 80 c-d), San Vitale in Ravenna, sixth century (fig. 34), or the Church of the Dormition in Daphni, Greece (figs. 49-50) as well as Gothic cathedrals, such as the ambulatory of Saint Denis, consecrated in 1144 (fig. 33) or the cathedral of Chartres, 1194-1220 (figs. 35 and 82), all attempted, through the technical means at their disposal or

---

[130] Mango, op. cit., p. 117. If the justification of such magnificence and luxury was that nothing could ever be beautiful enough to celebrate the absolute but invisible beauty of God, it did not say to what extent architecture and all the magnificence of art were also powerful symbols of earthly power. Legend has it that Justinian compared his accomplishment with that of the legendary builder of the First Temple in Jerusalem, saying, "Solomon, I have outdone you." Suger affirmed that his new church, which was also that of the French Royalty, had to be as beautiful as the Hagia Sophia, the church of the Byzantine Emperor.

through technical inventions, to materialize the concept of God as light, while those of Cistercian monastic churches, such as Fontenay (figs. 36, 98 and cover), in Burgundy, underlined that of order and harmony.

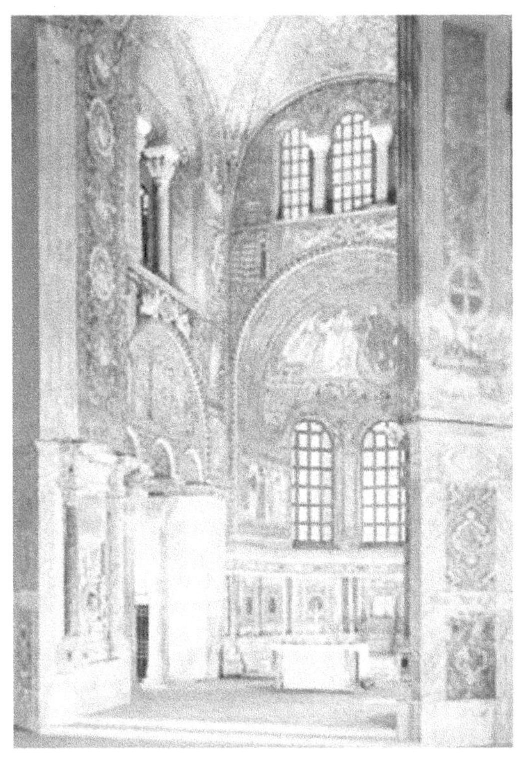

34 Interior view into the chancel and apse, 6ᵗʰ century, San Vitale, Ravenna, Italy

Through the Byzantine golden mosaics, reflecting the pure light of the sun, through the filtered light and iconography of Gothic stained-glass windows, through the sculpted doors, the golden jewel-incrusted vessels and embroidered ecclesiastic vestments, and finally through the overall visible magnificence of the place and the liturgy, one could only be led upward towards the awareness of the pure light of God that no human eye could ever face without being blinded, from the perception of material and relative beauty of individual works upward towards the invisible and absolute beauty of God (figs. 34, 50, 54, 80c).

The harmony of a Cistercian church (figs. 36 and 98) was, on the contrary, obtained through the use of the square, the simplest of geometrical shapes, which was the unit of measure, and through the clearest of Pythagorean ratios, such as 1:1 or 1:2, which were not only those advocated by Plato, but also those imposed by God Himself for the construction of Noah's Ark (Genesis 4:14-16) or of the Ark of Alliance (Exodus 25 ff. and 35-38) and the Holy Jerusalem (Revelation). The typical Cistercian church, devoid of decoration and glitter, was thought to be conducive to finding God, not outside, above or beyond oneself, but within oneself. The light, which still enters through grisaille, non-figurative windows, was also supposed to lead the monk to an interior light.

For Saint Bernard, the spiritual leader of the Cistercians in the early twelfth century, the beauty of the Abbey of Saint-Denis was reprehensible, at least in a monastic institution.

> Tell me, you who made the vow of poverty, what has gold to do in your sanctuary? In short, everywhere so plentiful and astonishing a variety of contradictory forms is seen that one would rather read in the marble than in the books, and

spend the whole day gawking at every single one of them than in meditating on the law of God. "Good God! If one is not ashamed of the absurdity, why is one not at least troubled by the expense.[131]

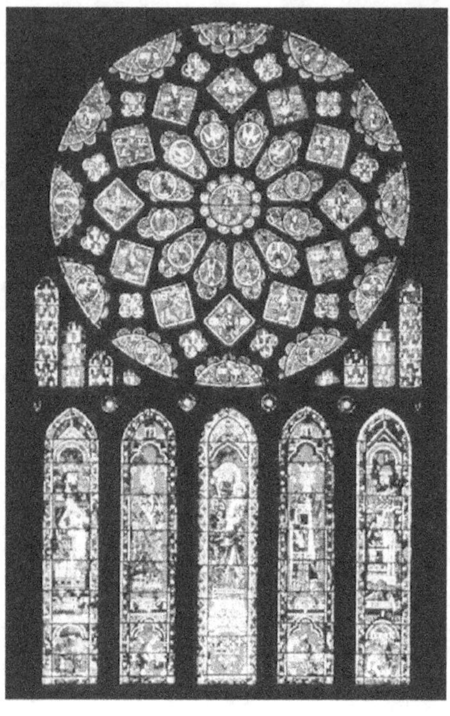

35   Rose Window, North Transept, c. 1220, Chartres Cathedral

36   View towards the east, 1139-41, Cistercian Abbey Church of Notre-Dame Fontenay

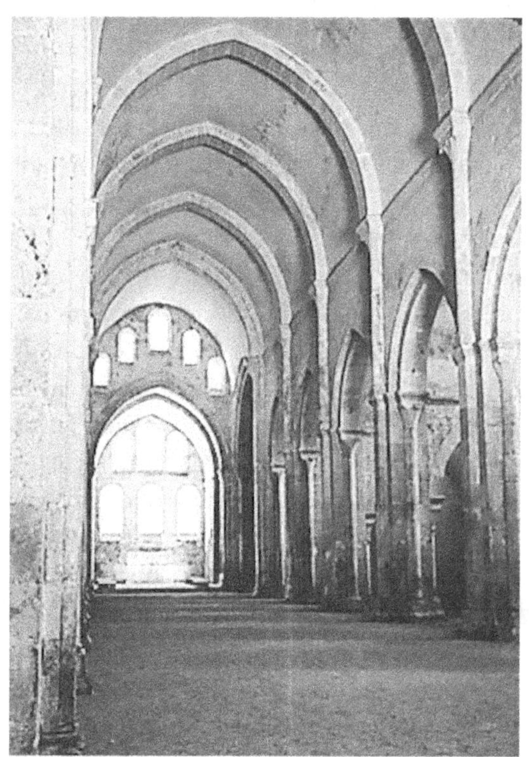

For Saint Augustine (354-430), the path to God goes from the beauty of the world, created by God, to the knowledge of the unchanging rules that God used in His Creation and that the mind discerns in geometry and music:

> Beautiful things please by proportion and number. These rules reflect the eternity and the beauty of God whom the soul is seeking.[132]

---

[131] *Letter to William*, cited in D. Menozzi, *Les Images. L'Eglise et les arts visuels*, Paris 1991, pp. 117 ff.

[132] Saint Augustine, *De Ordine*; *De Musica*, also *Confessions* and *City of God*. Excerpts in *Philosophies of Art and Beauty. Selected Readings in Aesthetics from Plato to Heidegger*. Ed. A. Hofstadter and R. Kuhns. The Modern Library, New York, 1964, pp. 203-238; K Swodoba, *L'Esthétique de Saint Augustin et ses sources*, Brno, 1933; Barasch, *Theories*, pp. 60 ff.; Umberto Eco, *Art and Beauty in the Middle Ages*, New Haven, 1987; and Edgar de Bruyne, *Etudes d'Esthétique Mediévale*, Bruges 1947, vol. 2.

   The Path Toward Beauty

Augustine asks the earth, the sea and its abyss, the living beings, the wind, the sky, the sun, the stars, etc. if they knew who God was, after all. All of them answered that he had to look beyond. Then he asked if they could at least tell him something about God, and all of them exclaimed: It is He who created us I had only to contemplate them and their answer was their beauty (*Confessions* X, 6).

These medieval concepts of beauty are of Greek origin. Plato's *Timaeus* and the *Ten Books of Architecture* by Vitruvius were in most medieval monastic libraries, but so were the Neo-Platonic texts of the Pseudo-Aeropagite, or those of Saint Augustine and of other Neo-Platonic thinkers. All of them stressed the importance of the symbolic and allegorical meaning of each liturgical act, gesture, or work of art.[133] The function of the symbol and of its understanding is always to reveal the invisible and to establish communication between man and God.

Renaissance Criteria

This Platonic or Neo-Platonic approach was also to be that of the Platonic Academy of Florence, founded at the end of the fifteenth century by Ficino[134] who translated Plato's Symposium, as well as Plotinus's comments to which he added his own.[135]

> "Beauty," for Ficino, "is the splendour of God, whose rays come down to earth" and "a kind of force, or light shining from Him through everything,"[136] hence also through works of art.

Ficino's teaching had a profound influence on Michelangelo (1475-1564). During the artist's youth, he conceived the physical beauty of the human body as a reflection of divine beauty and the beauty of a work of art was intended to make one long for its origin. For him, as for Plato, it was through love that one could be led back to the origin, which he expressed in sonnets written from 1530 onward (fig. 37).

---

[133] H. de Lubac, *Exégèse Médiévale. Les Quatre Sens de l'Ecriture*, 4 vols, Paris, 1961.

[134] N. A. Robb, "Neoplatonism and the Arts," *Neoplatonism of the Italian Renaissance*, London 1935, pp. 212-238; Andre Chastel, *Marcel Ficin et les arts*, Lille and Geneva, 1954; R. J. Clemens, *Michelangelo's Theory of Art*, New York, 1961; and Panofsky, *Idea* 1968, chapters 4 and 7.

[135] Chastel, op. cit.

[136] Hofstadter and Kuhns, op. cit., pp. 203-238.

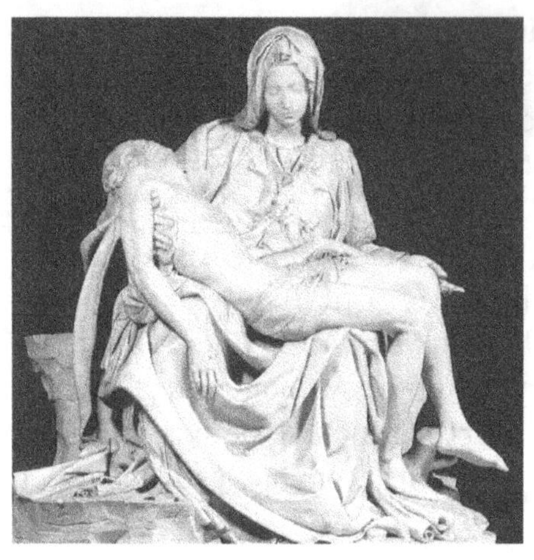

37 Michelangelo, *Pietà*, c. 1500, Saint Peter's, Vatican, Rome

At the end of his life, however, at the age of eighty, under the influence of the Counter-Reformation, he rejected all standards of physical beauty (fig. 38).

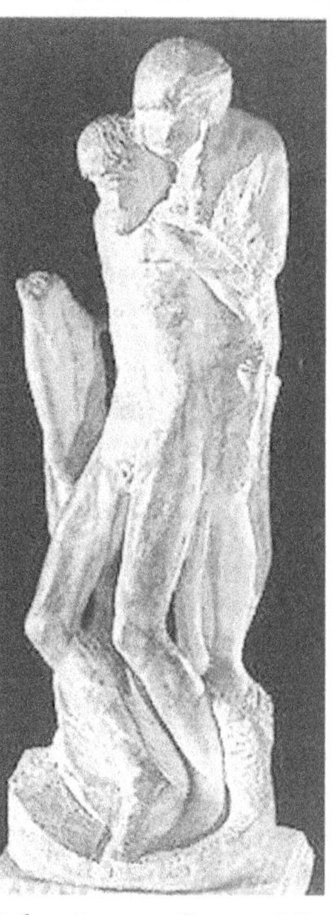

38 Michelangelo, *Rondanini Pietà*, 1555-1564, Milan, Civiche Raccolte d'Arte del Castello Sforzesco

He ceased to see a reflection of divine beauty in the beauty of the human body, and thought instead that physical beauty had kept him from God. In a sonnet of 1554, fearing his impending death, he wrote:

> Thus, I now know how fraught with error was the fond imagination which made Art my idol and my king, and how mistaken that earthly love which all men seek in their own despite. . . . No brush, no chisel will quieten the soul, once it is turned to the divine love of Him, who, upon the Cross, outstretched His arms to take us to Himself.[137]

In 1555, he repeated: "I have let the vanities of the world rob me of the time for the contemplation of God."[138] This is obviously reminiscent of the *Symposium*, even though Plato, as a pagan, wrote about Absolute Beauty, Truth, Goodness and Love rather than about Salvation or Grace. We are also reminded of biblical texts, such a Wisdom 13:3:

> If charmed by their beauty, they have taken these [statues] for gods, let them know how much the Master of these excels them since he was the very source of beauty that created them.

Michelangelo was reacting against the concept of beauty of Leon Battista Alberti, for whom the lasting value of any work of art was its beauty, i.e. its physical, not metaphysical, beauty. For Alberti (1404-1472), architect and theoretician of the Earlier Renaissance,

---

[137] A. Blunt, *Artistic Theory in Italy, 1450-1600*, Oxford University Press, 1975, p. 80, note 1.

[138] Ibid., p. 79, note 2; Barasch, *Theories of Art*, pp. 190 ff.; Panofsky, *Idea*, Chapter 7.

The Path Toward Beauty

Nature was the mistress of all artists, but Nature herself, just as for the Pythagoreans or for Aristotle, obeys certain laws of harmony. The artist who imitates Nature's way of operating thereby discovers her order:

> [Nature] is the greatest of all artists in the invention of forms, was always their model. Therefore, they collected the laws, according to which she works, … and introduced them into their method of building. (*On Architecture*, IX, 5).

> "It is very rarely even for Nature herself to produce anything absolutely perfect in every part." (Ibid., VI, 2).

> The artist "should be attentive not only to the likeness of things, but also, and especially, to beauty." (*On Painting*, III, 55).

> "We must always take what we paint from nature and always choose from it the most beautiful things." (*On Sculpture*).

Though art is once again related to *mimesis*, beauty is not attainable through imitation alone. Not everything in nature is beautiful; a selection is necessary. Naturalism and idealism merge once more. For Alberti, beauty (*concinnitas*) is based on harmony (figs. 39, 40 and 41):

> Beauty is a certain harmony of all the parts of a thing of such a kind that nothing could be added or taken away or altered, except for the worse (*On Architecture*, VI, 2).

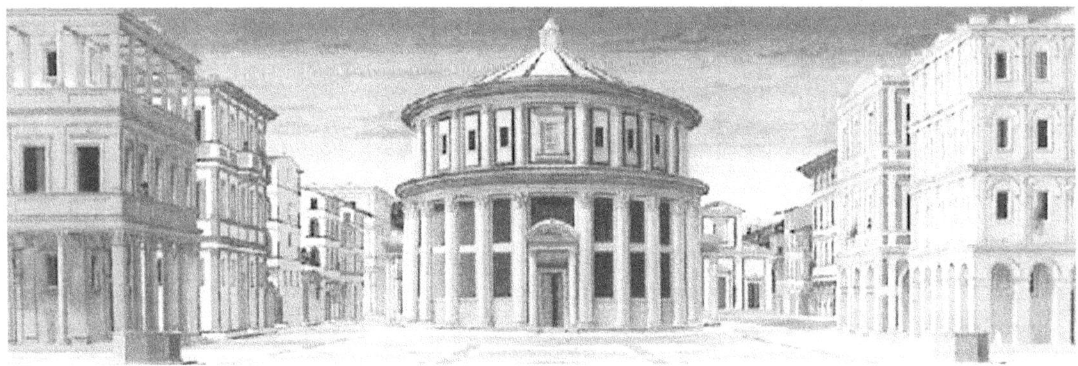

39　*Ideal City*, c. 1470, Urbino, Galleria Nazionale delle Marche (attributed to both Luciano Laurana and Piero dello Francesca)

> Beauty . . . is a kind of harmony and concord of all parts to form a whole which is constructed according to a fixed number, and a certain relation and order, as

symmetry, the highest and most perfect law of nature, demands (Ibid., V).[139]

While affirming that what is most beautiful is also pleasing, Alberti nevertheless insists that beauty is not related to taste, but on the contrary is based on the rules of art, imposed by a scientific, rational method, and hence related to knowledge (Ibid., VI, 2) and that:

The idea of beauty, which the most expert have difficulty in discerning, eludes the ignorant (*On Painting*, III, 56).

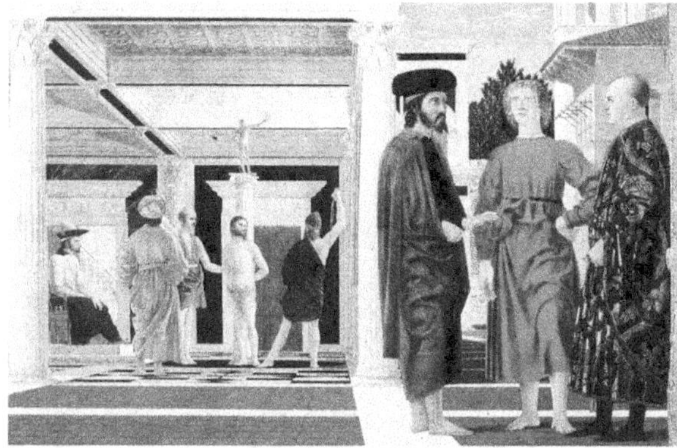

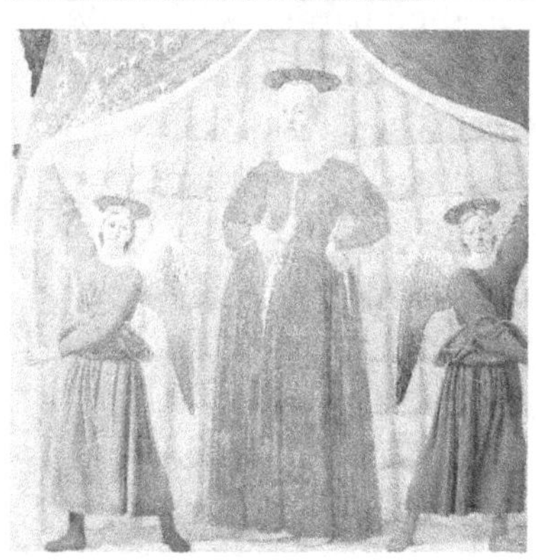

40   Piero della Francesca, *Flagellation of Christ,* c. 1460, Urbino, Galleria Nazionale delle Marche

41   Luciano Laurana, Courtyard, Ducal Palace, c. 1467-72, Urbino

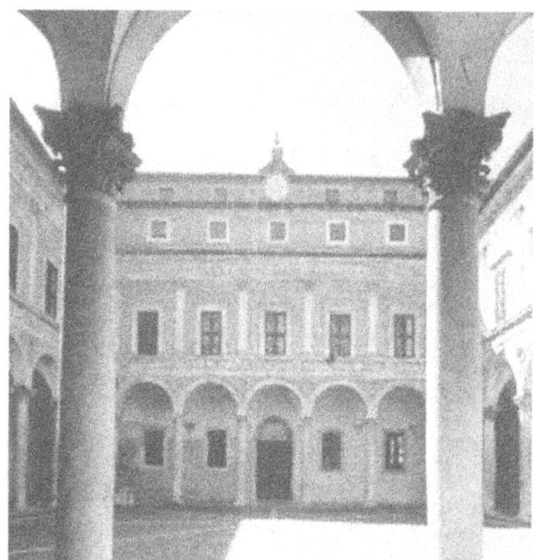

42   Piero della Francesca, *Madonna del Parto*, 1467, Chapel of the cemetery, Monterchi (detail)

Alberti's faith in nature as well as his rationalism originated in Greece, and were transmitted through Rome to all fifteenth-century humanists, without a trace of Neo-Platonic "mysticism."[140]

The paintings of Piero della Francesca (produced between 1452 and 1480), represent Nature perceived through truncated cylinders, spheres and ovoid shapes, all of them set in crystal clear perspective (figs. 40, 42-45). His pupil was the mathematician Luca Pacioli,

---

[139] Blunt, chapters I and V; Barasch, *Theories*, chapters III, ii and IV, iii; Panofsky, *Idea*.

[140] *Leon Battista Alberti on Painting and On Sculpture,* Edited with translation by Cecil Grayson, London, Phaidon, 1972; Blunt, op. cit, 1.

who became the friend of Leonardo da Vinci and wrote the *De divina proportione,* illustrated in part by Leonardo (fig. 68). Here geometry becomes metaphysics.[141]

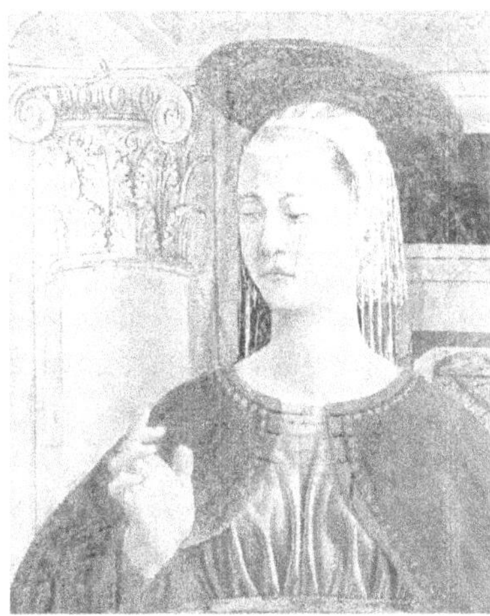

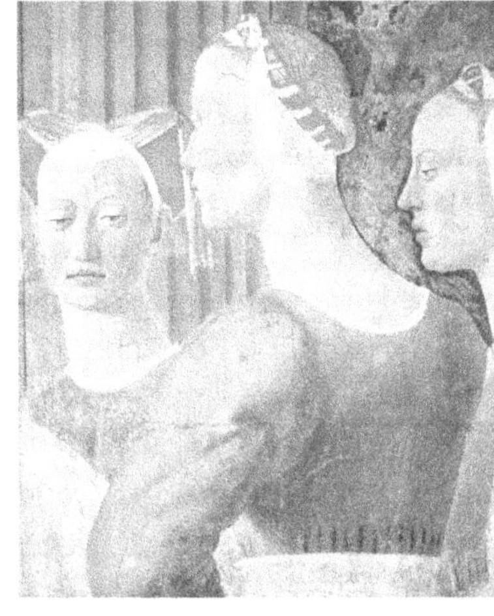

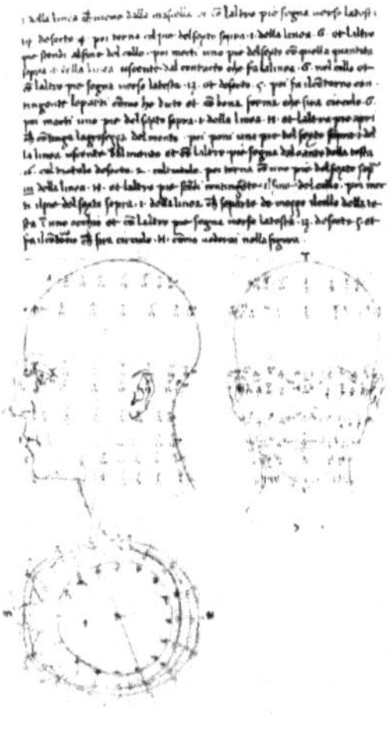

43

44

45

43   Piero della Francesca, *Annunciation,* detail from the Legend of the True Cross, c. 1455-60, San Francesco, Arezzo

44   Piero della Francesca, *Meeting of Solomon and Sheba,* detail from the Legend of the True Cross, c. 1455-60, San Francesco, Arezzo

45   Piero della Francesca, Manuscript drawings and notes, 1482, Rome, Vatican Library

46   *God as Architect of the World,* miniature from a moralized Bible made in Paris c. 1220, Vienna, Österreichische Nationalbibliothek

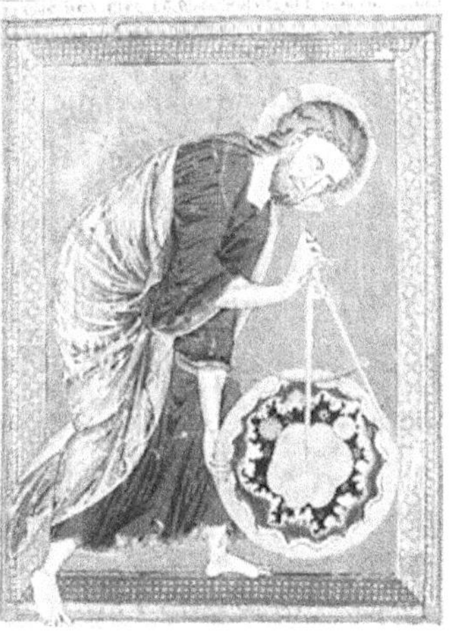

Throughout the Middle Ages and the Renaissance, God was imagined as a geometrician (fig. 46), creating the world with the compass. In the Renaissance, Nicolas of Cusa symbolized God by a circle, which, ever since Plato, had been considered the most beautiful of all geometrical shapes. The circle was thus to be at the origin of centrally planned churches, covered with the hemispherical heavenly vault, as defined or depicted in the *Ideal City* by Alberti or by Piero della Francesca (fig. 39).

---

[141] Luca Pacioli, *De divina proportione,* [First edition, Venice, 1509]; and ed. C. Winterberg, Vienna, 1899.

Although all these criteria and approaches to beauty are indeed of Greek origin, we find the same criteria in today's science. In 1991, in a dialogue between the Christian philosopher Jean Guitton and two physicists, the brothers Bogdanov, we encounter the same debate about order and disorder, chance and necessity, the nature of the real and the illusion of what only appears to be real:

> Beneath the visible disorder of phenomena lies a very profound order of an infinitely high degree, which might explain that which we still interpret as the result of pure chance.[142]

In the same dialogue, reference is made to Ilya Prigorine, who uses the example of snowflakes to underline the fact that "disorder is not a natural state of matter but, on the contrary, a state that precedes the emergence of a more elevated order." This tiny little object obeys, in fact, incredibly subtle mathematical and physical laws, and, although it is subject to all sorts of variables such as temperature, humidity and atmospheric pollution, it ultimately acquires a specific shape, which is unique in the world. Like works of art, no two snowflakes are ever identical. In the heart of each one we find an order, a subtle balance between the forces of stability and instability, each one obeying, once again, strict geometrical laws.

This constant reference to geometrical order, which we find universally among scientists as well as philosophers and artists, seems, of course, very reductive, even though it allows for the infinite variety of atoms, electrons, quarks or strings that modulate the universe, as well as the beauty and variety of forms in music and visual arts. Yet beauty cannot be reduced to the analysis or the awareness of order. Steven Weinberg, referring to the hope of finding a single unifying explanation for all the laws of the universe through the string theory, says:

> I will not attempt to give an answer to those who criticize modern science as being reductionist with a passionate debate on the beauties of contemporary science. Certainly, the reductionist point of view gives you the chill. But we have accepted it as it is, not because we like it, but because that is how the world functions.[143]

If one could not enter into Plato's Academy if one was not trained in geometry, neither, in his view, could there be any beauty without love and without a "vision" of beauty itself.

---

[142] Jean Guitton, Gricka and Igor Bogdanov, *Dieu et la science*, Paris, 1991.
[143] Steven Weinberg, *Le Rêve d'une théorie ultime*, Paris, 1997, quoted in Brian Green, *The Elegant Universe*, New York, 1999; p. 34 in the Fr. trans.

If the images of the gods belong to the realm of vision, how were they to be represented? And, if beauty is an attribute of most divinities, how was that beauty to be conveyed?

The term *visiones* is the Latin translation of the Greek term *phantasia*, and we will use it in the same way to mean a mental image, apparition or revelation, but not in the sense of eyesight.

Plato speaks of proportions that are based on *phantasia*, when an artist not only imitates nature, which is itself an illusion, and hence natural proportions, but also takes into account the optical illusion of the beholder (*Sophist*, 235 e, 236 a, 266 e, 268 c-d).

Aristotle uses the term of *phantasia* and analyzes it as the faculty of the soul to retain images that are derived from, but do not depend on, sense perception. In his view, imagination differed from sense experience (*aistesis)* but could not exist without it.[144]

Although the concept *phantasia* has its origin in Platonic and Aristotelian philosophy, where it refers to the imagination, it did not become an important concept until Late Hellenistic and Roman times, when it acquired the meaning of creative imagination, independent of any ordinary sense perception. Thus, we read in Quintilian the following definition of vision (*phantasia)*:

> There are things which the Greeks call phantasia and which we call visiones, through which images of things which are absent are so present to the mind that we seem to perceive them with our eyes and to have them present before us. Whoever perceives these vividly will best be able to generate emotions (*Institutes* 6.2.29).

When Plato writes about the Demiurge fashioning the world according to an ideal model, is he not, in fact, also talking about vision?

> The maker of any object, gazing at that which is always the same (the divine unchanging model), making use of a model of that sort, finishes to perfection its form and quality, that which results must be of necessity wholly beautiful, but if he gazes at what has relative existence, using a created model, it will not be beautiful (Plato, *Timaeus*, 28 a-b).

Plato imagines the Demiurge creating the universe which, as the most beautiful of all things, was in the image of something eternally beautiful, such as the sphere. The Demiurge uses all the geometrical forms that can fit into a circle for building materials and applies the Pythagorean harmonic ratios to the whole. Plato never refers to the supreme deity—the Good—in anthropomorphic terms.

---

[144] Aristotle, *De Anima*, 428 ff; Pollitt, *Ancient View of Greek Art*, p. 204.

The real question, whether a single cosmic deity was immanent and visible or transcendent and invisible, was raised since the second millennium B.C.E. in India, Egypt (fig. 47),[145] and Mesopotamia, but above all among the Hebrews.

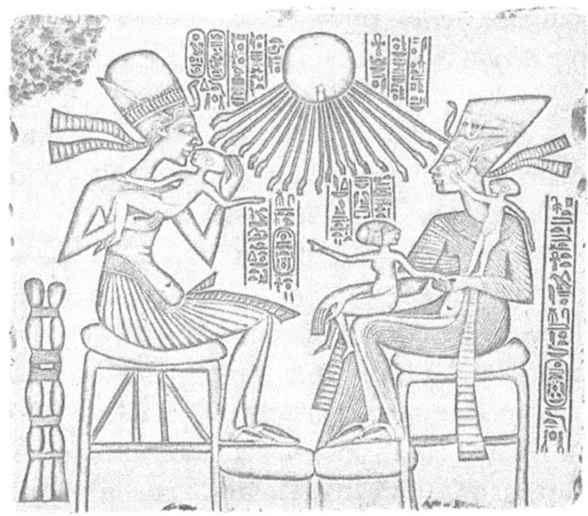

47 *Akhenaten, Nefertiti and their daughters under the protection of the rays of the Aten, the solar disk,* 18th Dynasty, Amarna Period, c. 1330 B.C.E. Berlin, Staatliche Museen zu Berlin – Preussischer Kulturbesitz, Agyptisches Museum

It was, in fact, Moses who first imposed the worship of a unique and utterly transcendent God: "But my face, He said, you cannot see, for no human being can see me and survive. . . . I will put you in the cleft of the rock and shield you with my hand until I have gone past" (Exodus 33:18 ff.). The Second Commandment prohibits making images not only of God, but of any living being created by God. Yahweh had appeared to Moses in a flood of light, or in the form of a devouring fire, first on top of Mount Horeb, and finally on Mount Sinai (Exodus 3:2; 19:16-20; 24:12-17). When Moses asked God who He was, He replied: "I am he who is" (Exodus 3:13-15). How could such divinity be represented? We have already seen what the Second Commandment implied. Let us simply add that, in *Exodus*, when God described how the Ark of the Covenant and the Sanctuary were to be made, he also singled out the artist, Bezalel, "and filled him with the spirit of God in wisdom, knowledge and skill in every kind of craft."(Exodus 31:2).

Throughout the Old Testament, God is described as light, although some prophets tried to portray their visions in slightly anthropomorphic terms. After all, God had created man in His own image. Thus, Ezechiel saw Yahweh enthroned, high above the four-winged, wheeled creatures with "the appearance of a human form" or "stretching out a hand with a scroll" (Ezechiel 1:26 and 2:9). Isaiah saw the Lord seated on a throne, surrounded by six-winged seraphs, or enthroned above the circle of the earth, while adding, nevertheless: "To whom can you compare God?" "What image can you contrive of him?" (Isaiah 2:19

---

[145] In the *Hymn to the Aten*, attributed to Akhenaton, we read: "O sole god, like whom there is no other, Thou dids't create the world according to thy desire. . . . " In the slightly later *Hymn to Amon—Re*, even the gods do not know what Amon looks like; "His image is not displayed in writings. No one bears witness to him, . . . He is too mysterious that his majesty should be disclosed, too powerful that he might be known. . . . " James Pritchard, *Ancient Near Eastern Texts*, Princeton, N.J., 1955, pp. 228-230 and pp. 365-367.

   The Path Toward Beauty

and 40:18). Habakkuk described Him as "His majesty covering the heavens and his glory filling the earth. His brightness being like the day and rays flashing from his hands where his power lies hidden" (Habakkuk 3:9).[146] All these and other Old Testament visions are, furthermore, accompanied by those of fantastic animals, angels with six wings, pavements of sapphire or platforms of crystal, huge clouds, and at the sound of thunder, earthquakes, stormy winds, trumpets or loud voices singing the glory of God. Enlightened prophets, who believed in the invisibility and transcendence of God, made these descriptions. At the same time, they warned their people against all forms of idolatry, the very sin for which Yahweh was punishing them. Nevertheless, they could only describe their visions in human, hence visual, if not representable, terms. These same visions were, in fact, to lead to the description of the apocalyptic Christ in Revelation 4, as well as to his representation on the portals of Romanesque churches.

The concept of the existence of a supreme principle underlying the diversity of things is also found, especially after 1000 B.C.E., in the Indian *brahman*, the concept of the unknowable Being or *atman*, the Self, beyond all speech and reference.

These same concepts were also expressed by the pre-Socratic philosophers of the sixth and fifth centuries B.C.E., e.g., the *apeiron*[147] (the indefinite, the infinite, the unlimited) of Anaximander, Pythagoras' mathematical principles underlying the harmony of the world, Xenophanes' "There is one God, who is greatest among gods and men, and who is not at all like men in either body or mind" (fr. 23), and, above all, Parmenides' Unchanging Being. That which is always changing was, for him, nothing but an illusion and the same held for any form of representation. We find exactly the same concept in Indian texts of the same period. How could such concepts be translated into visual terms?

For some pre-Socratic philosophers, the circle, or the sphere, as well as ratios such as 1:1, 1:2, 1:3 and so on, and the number one itself, symbolize the undefined, the eternal, the harmony of the universe, the Being or the One.[148]

In India, the *yantra*, a geometrical figure of interlocking triangles, circles, squares and polygons designated the supreme deity.[149] The square and the circle were also the elements of *mandalas*,[150] magic diagrams of the cosmos used for meditation, in the centre of which

---

[146] Wayne Meeks, "Vision of God and Scripture Interpretation in a Fifth-Century Mosaic, "*In Search of the Early Christians. Selected Essays*, ed. by A. Hilton and H. G. Snyder, New Haven, CT, 2002.

[147] Giovanni Semerano, *l'Infinito: un equivoco millenario. Le antiche civiltà del Vicino Oriente e le origini del pensiero greco,* Milano, 2001. According to Semerano, the *apeiron/epeiron* of Anaximander derives from the Semitic *apar,* from the Accadian *eperu* and the Biblical *afar,* which means *dust.*

[148] Thomas McEvilley, *The Shape of Ancient Thought, Comparative Studies in Greek and Indian Philosophies,* New York, 2002.

[149] K.C. Aryan, *Basis of Decorative Element in Indian Art*, New Delhi, 1981.

[150] M. Brauen, "Mandala extérieur, mandala intérieur," *Tibet, la Roue du Temps, pratique du mandala,* Paris, 1995; Idem, *Mandala: Sacred Circle in Tibetan Buddhism*, New York, 2009; J. Hopkins, *Kalachakra Tantra*, Rite of Initiation, London, 1985.

---

the Hindus could put Brahma and the Tibetans the Buddha, who were worshipped as the soul and creator of the universe (fig. 48).

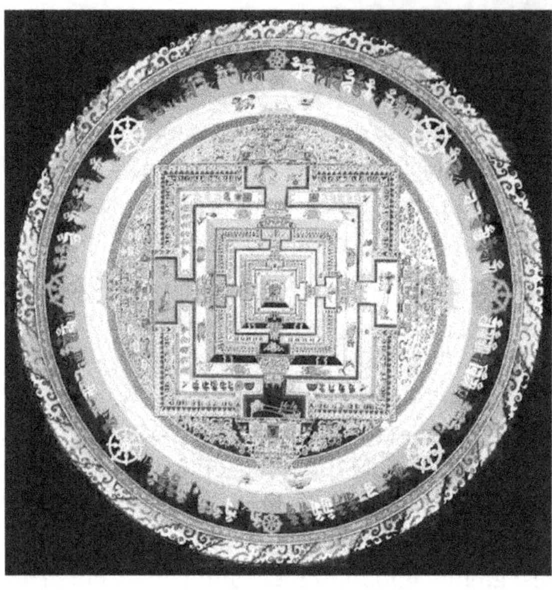

48 *Kalachakra (Wheel of Time) Sand Mandala.* Created over three weeks by monks from the Namgyal Monastery in Dharamsala, India

These geometrical forms, especially the square and the circle, were chosen as supports of contemplation. The Buddha (Gautama, Sakya-Muni) was, in fact, never represented in human form before the first century B.C.E., or five centuries after his death, and the fully developed type dates only from the Gupta period, i.e., of the fourth or fifth centuries. Buddhist art was, in fact, aniconic up to that period.[151]

The same geometrical concepts were also taken up by Byzantine, Islamic and Renaissance architects, who theorized about the square and the circle when building their places of worship, and used identical ratios while never creating identical buildings. In most sacred buildings, where man enters into communication with God, a link was established between the square as the symbol of earth, and the circle, or the cupola, as the symbol of heaven. For these builders, the deity was conceived as beautiful and so were these forms and ratios (figs. 49-50).

> The Byzantine church is an image of the Kosmos, symbolizing heaven, paradise, (or the Holy Land), and the terrestrial world in an orderly hierarchy, descending from the sphere of the cupolas, which represents heaven, to the earthly zone of the lower parts. The higher the picture is placed in the architectural framework, the more sacred it is held to be.[152]

---

[151] A.K. Coomaraswamy, *The Origin of the Buddha Image and Elements of Buddhist Iconography,* Louisville, KY, Fons Vitae, 2006.
[152] Otto Demus, *Byzantine, Mosaic Decoration,* Boston, 1955.

   The Path Toward Beauty

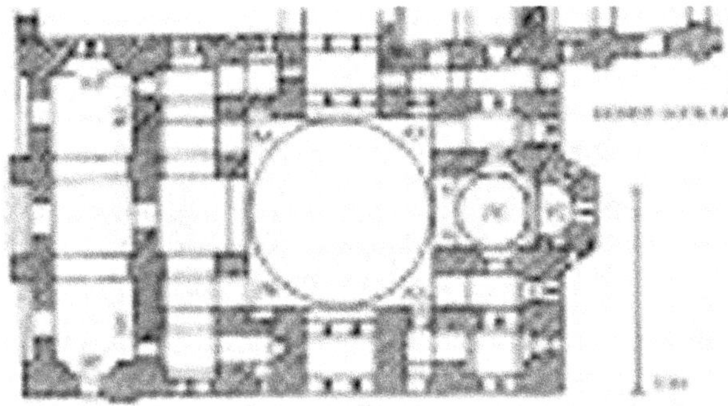

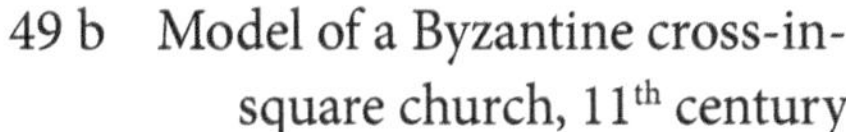

49 a   Floor plan, Daphni, Church of the Dormition, Daphni, Greece

49 b   Model of a Byzantine cross-in-square church, 11ᵗʰ century

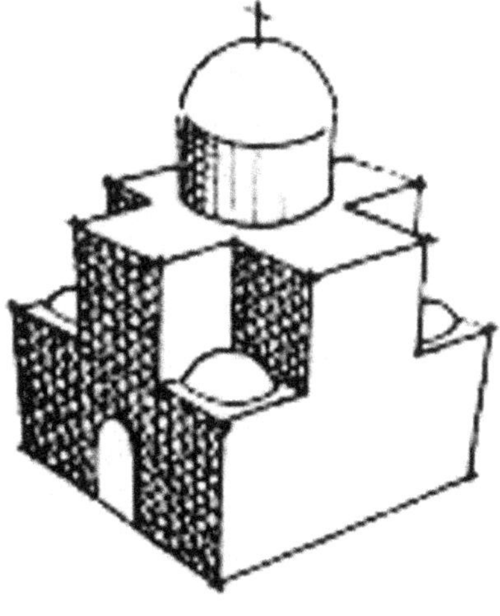

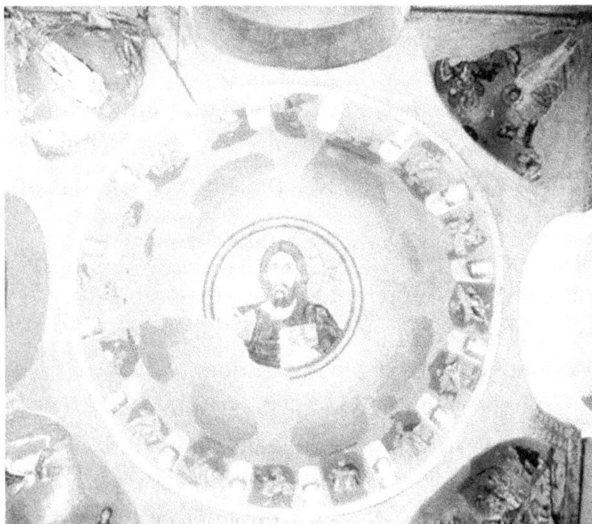

50   *Christ Pantokrator*, mosaic c. 1100, central dome, Church of the Dormition, Daphni, Greece

It is noteworthy that the abstract concept of the One emerged in Greece, despite a polytheistic and anthropomorphic religion which persisted even at the time when Chrysippus, the third century B.C.E. Stoic philosopher, thought that it was actually childish to represent the gods in human form. In both Greek and Roman civilizations the gods were, in fact, imagined as human beings, though immortal, and described as if they could appear at any time and at any moment to partake or intervene in the life of men.[153]

Although they were represented anthropomorphically, the statues were not consid-

---

[153] Gombrich, "Reflections on the Greek Revolution," *Art and Illusion*. Ernst Auerbach, *Mimesis. The Description of Reality in Western Literature*, Zurich, 1945, chapter 1.

ered divine equivalents. In Greece, in fact, the statues of the gods were not always called *omoiôma* (in the likeness of), *andrias* (from *aner*, man) or simply *eikones* (images), but rather *àgalma* or *agalmata* (from the verb *agallomai*, to pay honor to a god or to exult).[154] In Rome, statues of the divinities were not called *similitudines*, like statues of human beings, but *simulachra deorum* or *signa*. This distinction seems to indicate that these statues, while anthropomorphic, were either not to be considered in the same way as those of human beings or were not to be taken as likenesses of the gods, but merely simulacra. Nobody knew, in fact, what the gods looked like, in spite of the great familiarity that the Greeks had with their gods, especially through the detailed descriptions provided by Homer and Hesiod.[155]

Throughout time, and in most civilizations, anthropomorphic representations of gods have always indicated that human beings believed they were made in the image of a god, and hence could only imagine the deity through an idealized image of themselves. In most creation myths man does, in fact, partake of the divine.[156] The images of the gods belong, however, to the realm of vision.

By 100 B.C.E., Dio Chrysostomus was to stipulate that, in order to represent the gods, the artist had to have an image in his mind, or be "a divinely inspired creator." Thus, for Philostratus, in the early third century, Phidias and Praxiteles had represented the gods only thanks to *phantasia*, that is, vision and imagination:

> "Well, did artists like Phidias and Praxiteles," he said, "after going up to heaven and making copies of the forms of the gods, then represent them by their art, or was there something else which stood in attendance upon them in making their sculpture?" "There was something else," he said, "a thing full of wisdom." "What is that?" he asked. "Certainly you would not say that it was anything other than imitation (*mimesis*)?" "Imagination (*phantasia/visiones*)," Apollonius answered, "wrought these, an artificer much wiser than imitation. For imitation will represent that which can be seen with the eyes, but imagination will represent that which cannot." (*The Life of Apollonius of Tyana*).[157]

It was Plotinus (A.D. 205-270),[158] however, who put the greatest emphasis on the fact that an artist had to be expert in vision not only to represent the divinity, but also to reveal his beauty.

> The artist must have an inner vision, the image that he will create will be an emanation of God, hence an image of beauty. He creates a second cosmos and

---

[154] Liddell-Scott-Jones Greek lexicon.

[155] Gombrich, op. cit.

[156] For different creation myths see Mircea Eliade, *Histoire des croyances et des idées religieuses*, Paris, 3 vols. 1976-1983.

[157] Pollitt, *The Ancient View of Greek Art*, pp. 52 ff.

[158] For Plotinus, see above pp. 43 ff.

copies at every point the archetype, ... and has beauty as springing from the divine world. Beauty is of the divine and comes thence only (*Enneads*, VI 8, 12-13).

In Plotinus, the First Principle, the One, which is also the Good and the Beautiful, is inconceivable in itself, but when the Soul enters into union with the Beautiful, it perceives the Beautiful at the first glance, recognizes and welcomes it. (*Enneads*, I, 6, 2) For Plotinus, a work of art was beautiful only insofar as it was an emanation of the divine, and an artist could only have knowledge of it through an inner vision for which the Soul had to be trained:

> Such vision is for those only who see with the Soul's sight, and at the vision they will rejoice, and awe will fall upon them and a trouble deeper than all the rest could ever stir, now they are moving in the realm of Truth.
>
> This is the spirit that Beauty must ever induce, wonderment and a delicious trouble, longing and love and a trembling that is all delight. For the unseen all this may be felt as for the seen; and this the Souls feel for it, every Soul in some degree, but those the more deeply that are the more truly apt to this higher love (Ibid., I, 6,4).
>
> For the Soul, a divine thing, a fragment as it were of the Primal Beauty, makes beautiful to the fullness of their capacity all things whatsoever that it grasps and moulds (Ibid., I, 6,6).

It is Beauty then that awakens the Soul and makes man aware of the divinity, but what makes a work beautiful? It cannot be merely the use of particular ratios or the loveliness of any particular colour or the use of any particular material, such as gold, or the beauty of the individual stones of a house, not any part but only the unity and the harmony of the whole, which the artist can attain when entering into communion with the Ideal Form:

> For the Idea is a unity and what it moulds must come to unity. . . . Beauty enthrones itself, giving itself to the parts as to the sum: when it lights on some natural unity, a thing of like parts, then it gives itself to that whole. Thus, for an illustration, there is the beauty, conferred by craftsmanship, of all a house with all its parts, and the beauty, which some natural quality may give to a single stone.
>
> This, then is how the material thing becomes beautiful—by communicating in the thought that flows from the Divine (Ibid., I, 6, 2).

For Plotinus, even the beauty of colors is the outcome of a unification, achieved by the use of light overcoming the darkness of matter (Ibid., I, 6, 3). Plotinus draws an analogy between divine beauty and the splendor of light which would be stressed by all Neo-Platonic philosophers and would influence all medieval Western art. The analogy between the supreme deity and light, common to many civilizations, begins in the West, with the Semitic gods of Mesopotamia, such as Shamash and Yahweh, in the Old Testament.

The idea that an artist requires a vision to accomplish his work is also found in other civilizations. Thus, in an Indian treatise mentioned by Coomaraswamy, we read:

> The imager must be expert in vision (*dhyana*) and in no other way, certainly not in the presence of a model, can the work be accomplished.

> The mortal imager should resort to yoga visions, trance-visions, for thus, not otherwise, and surely not by direct perception, is the end attained.[159]

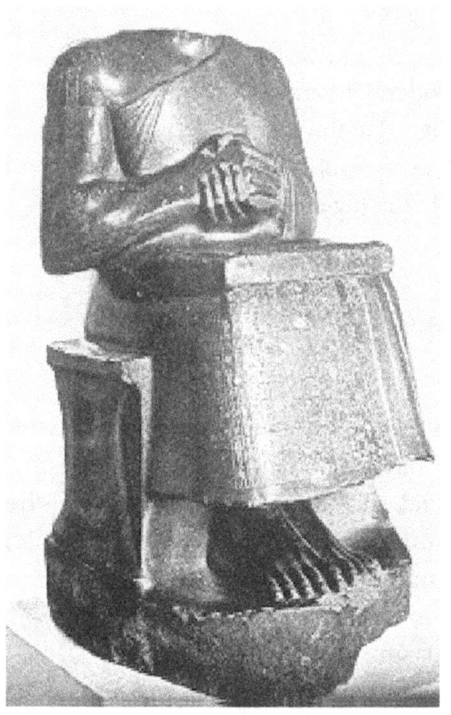

The Indian architect is also said to have visited heaven and to have sketched the prevailing forms of architecture, which he then imitates here below. The Indian artist is constantly represented as imitating heavenly forms, and it is the symbol that transmits knowledge of cosmic analogies.[160]

Dreams are considered to be equivalent to visions. Thus, on the knees of a seated Mesopotamian worshipper statue of Gudea (king of the city of Lagash/Telloh, c. 2130 B.C.E.),[161] a floor plan of a temple is engraved while, on his robe, a text explains that the god of his city appeared to the king in a dream, giving him that floor plan and asking him to build the temple in keeping with the heavenly model (fig 51).

51 *Gudea of Lagash, with a floor-plan of a temple engraved on his lap,* Paris, Louvre, c. 2130 B.C.E.

---

[159] Coomaraswamy, *Transformation*, p. 126 and pp. 165-166.

[160] A. Coomaraswamy, *Christian and Oriental Philosophy of Beauty*, New York, 1956, chapter 2, pp. 40 ff. and p. 79.

[161] The statue of Gudea is in the Louvre, next to that representing the king with the tools of an architect on his knees; it is reproduced in all books on Mesopotamian art, such as Henry Frankfort, *The Art and Architecture of the Ancient Orient*, Pelican History of Art, 4th edition, 1970, fig. 97.

Mesopotamian cities were planned in the shape of a constellation, which had two characteristics: the number of stars composing it and the geometrical figure they formed.[162] In the Ancient Orient, works were thought to be replicas of heavenly models, not for the sake of beauty, but to be ritually effective.

This correspondence between heaven and earth, between astronomy, numbers and music was most specifically emphasized in the Mesopotamian civilization but, centuries later, it was equally underlined by the Pythagoreans and by Plato, for whom music and astronomy were, in fact, sister sciences (*Republic*, 530 d). The seven-stringed lyre, whose invention is attributed to the Archaic Greek poet, Terpander, thus associated earthly music to the turning of the seven planets or to the music of heavens.[163]

In Egypt, the priests handed rules and formulae to builders, sculptors and painters, which they themselves had received from the gods. That explains the relative immobility of an art that reflects the eternal divine order and ensures thereby its ritual and funerary effectiveness. These numbers, these harmonic, visual or audible ratios, all reflect a concept of eternity as well.

> The only invariance that nature offers to the senses in the human life span are (1) the solar year and (2) the harmonic intervals.
>
> These invariances were joined in the concept of the Music of the Spheres—a doctrine attributed to Pythagoras, but quite possibly known in Mesopotamia a thousand years before his time.[164]

It would seem that beauty occurs when a correlation exists between earthly creation and heavenly models, in other words between the microcosm and macrocosm. This is a recurring concept.

We have already mentioned how contemporary science has gone much further into the exploration of this correlation, between the infinitely small and the infinitely large, and how it has confirmed it by other means and instruments, while continuing to search for the universal law that would encompass them both. Karl Popper points out how the artist, like the scientist, needs to sort out and schematize, how the artist also starts from a concept and

---

[162] Edward A. Maziarz and Thomas Greenwood, *Greek Mathematical Philosophy*, New York, 1968, p. 13; Ernest McClain, *Myth of Invariance: the Origins of the Gods, Mathematics and Music from the Rig Veda to Plato*, New York, 1976.
[163] Mc Evelley, op. cit., p. 46, referring to Walter Burkert, *Lore and Science in Ancient Pythagoreanism*, Cambridge (Mass.),1972, p. 349.
[164] Ibid., p. 81 ff. referring mostly to Mac Clain, op. cit.

not from a visual impression or experience. Abstraction precedes naturalism.[165] The mind seeks to dominate visual chaos, which explains the ingrained need for order and regularity we find in any human, scientific or artistic creation, as well as in any concept of formal beauty.[166]

The vision of the artist, whatever its content, originates in the human mind and, when beauty is one of the attributes of the divinity, as it was in India, ancient Greece, Islam and the medieval Christian East and West, then the vision of the divinity also has to be beautiful. Yet not all sacred images are beautiful, far from it. Why not?

> To any vision must be brought an eye that sees the mighty Beauty. If the eye that adventures the vision be dimmed by vice, impure, or weak, . . . then it sees nothing. . . . To any vision must be brought an eye adapted to what is to be seen, and having some likeness to it. Never did the eye see the sun unless it had first become sun like, and never can the Soul have a vision of the First Beauty unless itself be beautiful (Plotinus, *Enneads*, I, 6, 8).

> Therefore, first let each become godlike and each beautiful who cares to see God and Beauty (Ibid., I. 6, 9).

If the artist, who represented a deity, ever had such glimpse of Beauty, how did he represent it?

One day Malraux told Picasso about Bernadette of Lourdes to whom the Virgin Mother had appeared in a vision and of how none of the prints of any depicted Virgin, which she was shown by a delegate of the Church, resembled her. The illiterate young girl rejected them all angrily, except that of the icon of the cathedral of Cambrai[167] in which she recognized the beautiful Virgin of her vision. Picasso commented: "That the young girl recognized in that icon the Virgin that appeared to her is strange enough, but that a Byzantine painter invented her is even more amazing."[168] We do know that the painter of that particular icon

---

[165] Karl Popper, *Logic of Scientific Discovery*, London, 1959 and Popper, *Objective Knowledge*, Oxford 1972).

[166] Ernst Gombrich writes that: "there are different standards of life–likeness and the artist seeks to dominate a visual chaos" (*Art and Illusion*, p. 22). "The art originates in the human mind, in our reaction to the world, rather then in the visible world itself" (Ibid., p. 76). "This order is inherent in nature beyond any apparent chaos and indeed we seek it. If we cannot see it, we re-establish a visible order" (Gombrich, *Sense of Order*, London, 1979). How ingrained this need for order actually is becomes evident in the so-called new Science of Chaos, explained by non-Euclidian and fractal geometry, by other mathematical theorems and universal numbers, as if man could not cope with the unpredictable.

[167] Hans Belting, *Image et Culte*, French translation, 1998, pp. 592 ff., fig. X. (Translated into English by Edmund Jephcott as *Likeness and Presence*, Chicago, 1994.)

[168] André Malraux, *Tête d'Obsidienne*, 1974, pp. 121 ff.

  The Path Toward Beauty

certainly did not invent her, but used a prototype as a model. At one time, however, it was invented. This anecdote is actually at the heart of our concern.

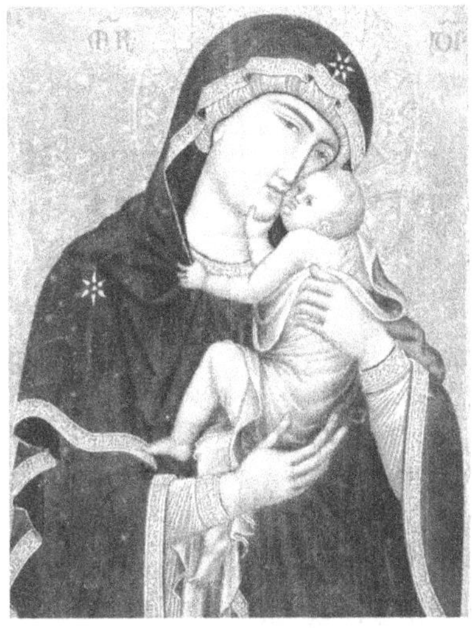

52   *The Cambrai Madonna*, c. 1340, New York, Metropolitan Museum of Art

This icon of Cambrai is probably a fourteenth-century Sienese copy of a Byzantine prototype of the Virgin of tenderness of the twentieth century,[169] itself a replica of an earlier icon (fig. 52). This miraculous icon was thought, along with so many others, to be the original authentic icon painted by Saint Luke, hence to be an actual portrait of Mary, inspired, however, by the Holy Spirit.[170] Through this portrait, as well as through all its replicas, Mary was believed to be still present on earth and, thus, to be able to intercede for mankind.

The representations of Christ and of Mary were justified and authorized by the Church, except during the iconoclastic period, only because they had assumed human form and had, thus, made themselves visible. Jesus could be represented only in his human form and certainly not in his divinity. But how were they to be represented? According to which archetype of ideal beauty?

It was believed that the prototype of Christ's portrait had not been painted by human hands (*a cheiro-poietos),* but had been miraculously imprinted on cloth, hence a portrait of divine origin. The most ancient sixth-century replica is the cloth with the portrait of Christ (the *Mandylion),* once among the holiest relics in the palace of the Emperor of Constantinople, now in the Vatican (fig. 53).[171] It was considered the archetype of all later images of Christ until it was replaced in about 1200, in Rome, by another portrait impressed on the cloth that Veronica (*vera icon)* handed to Jesus to dry his face when he was climbing up to Calvary. Each replica was then supposed to have the same power and the same beauty as the prototype or the archetype (*archetypia tou kallou),* but only insofar as it conformed to it, iconographically and stylistically. The icon of Mount Sinai is probably one of them (fig. 32), so are the *Mandylia* of Genoa, Church of San Bartolomeo degli Armeni, Novgorod (now in Moscow) and Laon Cathedral. As Belting notes, the prototype was considered an ideal of divine beauty, and all the replicas tried to come as close as possible to it.

---

[169] Belting, op. cit., pp. 385 ff., fig. 175.
[170] Ibid. op. cit., pp. 76 ff. and pp. 277 ff., 286, figs. 15, 128, 131 and plate III.
[171] Ibid.

In order to justify the use of images, John of Damascus (c. 750) wrote:

> Every image is declarative and indicative of something hidden. I mean the follow-
> ing: in as much as a man has no direct knowledge of the invisible. . . . The image
> has been invented for the sake of guiding knowledge and manifesting publicly
> that which is concealed.

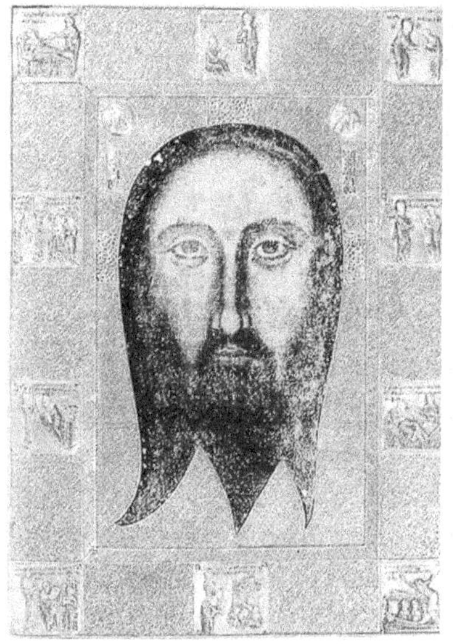

53 *Mandylion of Edessa (Portrait of Christ)* 6th century, Vatican, Rome

When the iconoclastic period came to end, the Byzantine Church was to impose the strictest iconographic and
stylistic rules on its painters.[172] Thus, the face of Christ
was always a replica of the earliest prototype. It always
had the same ratios, was drawn with a compass according to a three-circle scheme,[173] whereby the open radius
corresponded to the length of the nose, and the head
consisted of three of these units (figs. 50 and 54).

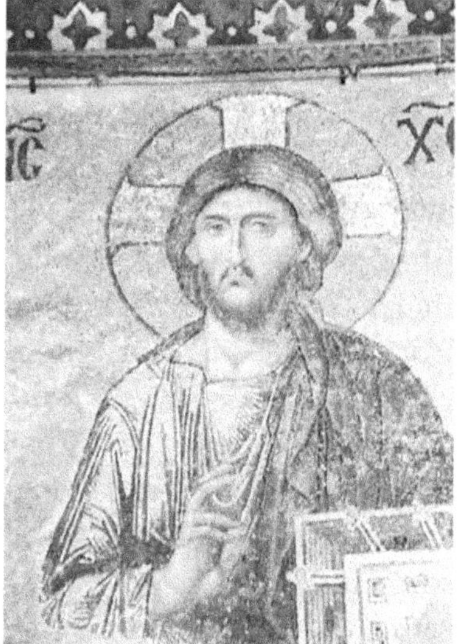

54 *Christ as Ruler*,
detail of the *Deesis*
mosaic, 13th century,
Istanbul, Hagia Sophia

We find the same conventions and very similar concepts in most other forms of religious arts. Thus, in the
making of an image of the Buddha, certain fixed canons
of proportion were imposed; the measures, having no reference to physical anatomy whatsoever, but to ideal and
canonical proportions (fig. 55). Some abstract spiritual
concepts had to be translated into physical form, such as
hand gestures (*mudras*), but every other detail was im-

---

[172] G. Mathew, *Byzantine Aesthetics*, London, 1963; Evdokimov, op.cit.; D. Menozzi, *Les Images. L'Église et les arts visuels*, Paris, 1991.

[173] Panofsky, "History of the Theory of Human Proportions," *Meaning in the Visual Arts,* pp. 102-112, p. 109 (fig. 2): the three-circle scheme.

  The Path Toward Beauty

posed (figs. 56, 91-93). The artist was not allowed to improvise on the established model, which alone reflected the ideal beauty of the sage.[174]

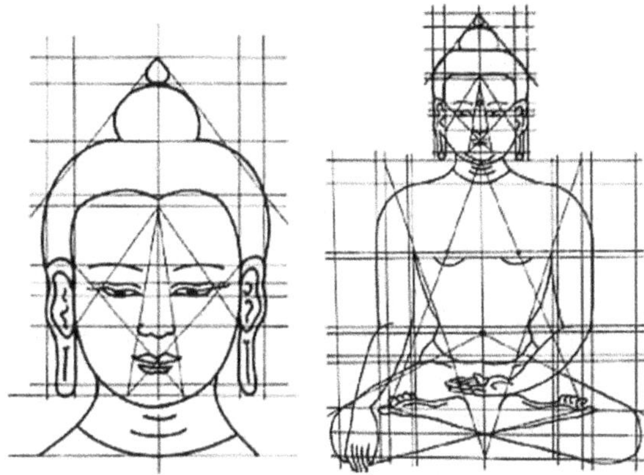

55   Canon of the ideal physical proportions of any representation of the Buddha

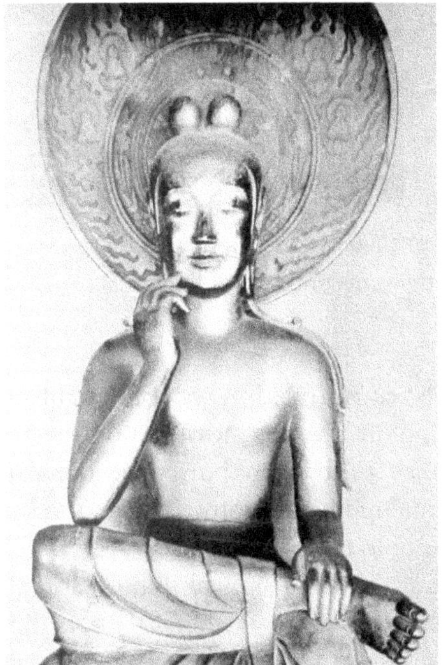

56   *Miroku Bosatsu*, 7th century, Nara, Chuguji Temple

The same sort of constraints applied in the making of statues of Shiva (fig. 15), which always had to be done according to a prototype, in order for the statue to be, if not beautiful, at least ritually effective and powerful, hence able to give access to the divine.[175]

> That image is said to be beautiful (ramie) which is neither more or less than the prescribed proportion (manna). . . . Is alone truly beautiful that which follows canonical proportions, none other. . . . Only an image made in accordance with the canon can be called beautiful; some may think that beautiful, which corresponds to their fancy, but that not in accordance with the canon is unlovely to the discerning eye.[176]

---

[174] Rowland, op. cit., pp. 153 -155.
[175] Ibid., 393 ff. and George Mitchell, *In the Images of Man,* Exhibition Catalogue, London, Hayward Gallery, 1982, p. 24.
[176] Coomaraswamy, *Transformation,* chapter 4, pp. 114, 115, 167.

In Japan, we find exactly the same approach used in making statues of gods or of sages, as in the case of Ganjin, the Chinese Buddhist priest, who had arrived in Japan in 753 (fig. 57). In this statue, the artist conveyed the beauty of peacefulness and interiority rather than representing the individual features of the blind man, but to do so the sculptor had also to conform to a very strict set of ratios and forms.[177]

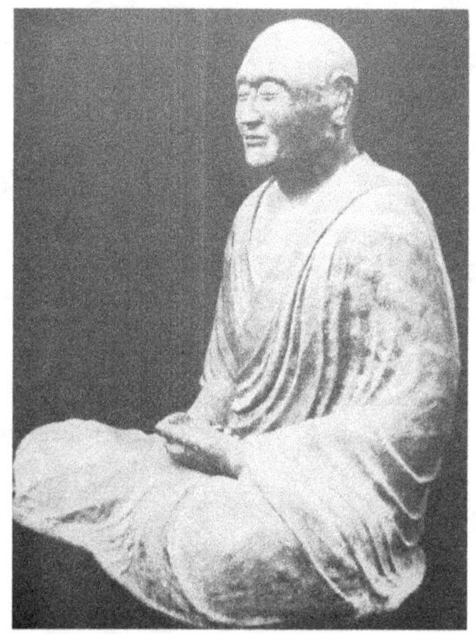

57   *Portrait sculpture of the Monk Ganjin,*
8th century, Nara, Toshodaiji

In all the above-mentioned civilizations, including ancient Greece, Byzantium and Renaissance Europe, the basic unit of the ideal proportions required to represent a deity was the face-length, from the hair on the fore-head, down to the chin. The various canons were, there-fore, designated as Five-face, Ten-face, Nine-face, and so on. This unit of measure could, as in classical Greece, be connected to smaller units, numbers or ratios.

These pre-established proportions, the precon-ceived ideals of divine beauty and the dependence on certain superhuman proportions and attributes, would properly transform the statue into an icon of divine perfection, and the result is an awe-inspiring and hieratic character of the representation of the Great Teacher.[178]

Many of these icons or statues had furthermore to be consecrated in order to establish the link between the worshiper and the deity, which did not necessarily mean that they were beautiful. On the contrary, some of them seem lifeless, as if they were purely mechanical reproductions, while others, although replicas of the same identical prototype, seem to be filled with a life of their own and, indeed, to "wake the soul to the consciousness of Beauty" (Plotinus, *Enneads*, I, 6,3). It is as if some artists have had "the soul's sight and the vision of the First Beauty, because their soul was beautiful as well" (Ibid., I, 6,9), whereas others did not, to put it in Plotinus' words.

Some of these works were done with love, love for the divinity through the love for his work, without which, however precise the replica, there can be no beauty, but that com-

---

[177] R.T. Paine and A. Soper, *Art and Architecture of Japan*, Pelican History of Art, 3rd edition 1981, p. 59, fig. 26.
[178] Rowland, op.cit., note 136.

          The Path Toward Beauty

ponent of beauty, that creative spark, remains forever indefinable by words or measures, totally elusive and yet undeniable.

The images of the gods also reflect the human need for tangibility as proof of their existence, and the sight of an artist, like that of the patron or beholder, can indeed be *"dimmed by vice, impure and weak, seeing nothing"* (Plotinus, *Enneads*, I, 6, 6), hence incapable of grasping beauty as well. How many, in fact, can say:

> We ourselves possess beauty when we are true to our own being; . . . our self-knowledge is our beauty; in self-ignorance we are ugly (Ibid., V, 8, 13).

When Western theologians of the eleventh century, such as the abbots of Cluny in Burgundy, insisted on the mystery of the Incarnation, through which God had made Himself visible, they once again justified His representation. That led to the revival of monumental sculpture on the great portals of Romanesque churches, all representing theophanies, or visions of God (figs. 58 and 59).

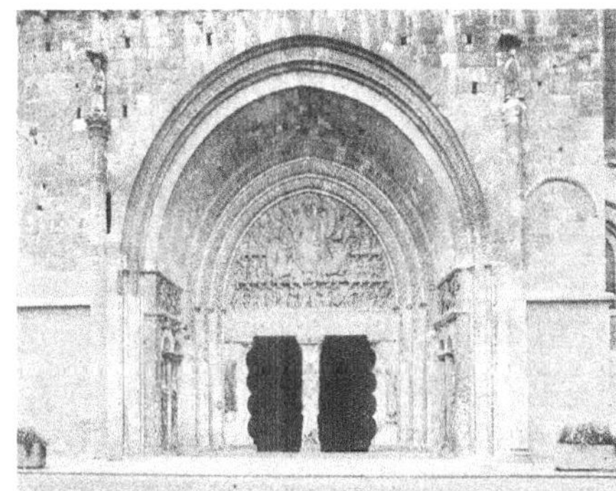

58 a

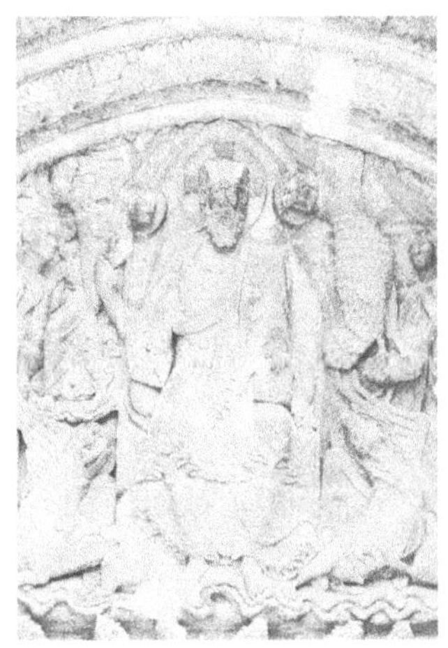

58 b

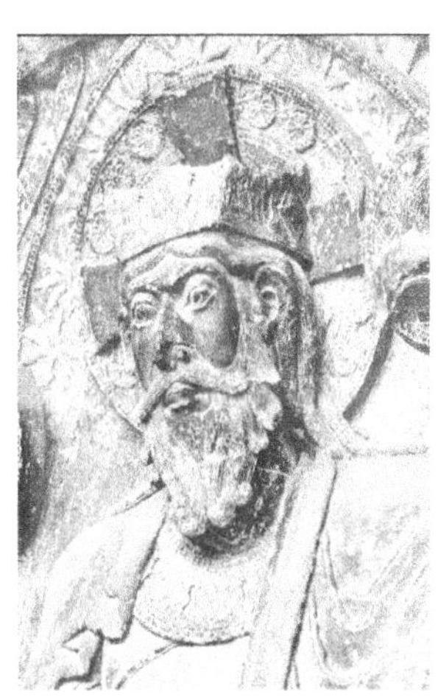

58 c

58 a   South Portal and Porch, priory church of Saint-Pierre, c. 1120, Moissac
58 b   *Second Coming of Christ* (Revelation 4-5), c. 1120, detail of the tympanum showing *Christ in Majesty*
58 c   Detail of 58 b

Besides the biblical texts mentioned at the beginning of this chapter, John Scotus Erigena, the ninth-century neo-Platonic philosopher, imagined the vision as follows:

> All the lines are issued from one unique point, in which they all converge in order to find again their unity. . . . That which every creature searches for is incom-

prehensible, and is endlessly searched for; in an endless motion, . . . the object of their search escapes reason. I call theophanies those visible forms by which beauty makes us know that God exists, and not what he is, but only that he does exist, because the nature, the essence of God cannot be spoken nor thought of. That inaccessible light is beyond all comprehension.

God himself tells us that he is rest, . . . that the term of our agitation is to reach the immobility of God. It is he who moves us and moves us towards him. . . . The movement of the spirit consists in knowing him. . . . In knowing God, man starts to love him. Pulled outside himself by the object of his love, man enters into ecstasy: he precipitates himself, in always more vehement motion, and will not stop until he is totally within the beloved being, as if wrapped up by him from all parts. With what joy does he allow himself to be enclosed, circumscribed by he whom he loves![179]

In the Romanesque portals, such as those of Moissac (fig. 58), Autun, Charlieu or Vézelay (fig. 59), the figures seem, in fact, to stretch, to bend over, in a totally non-naturalistic way, endowed with a motion of their own. The closer they are to the central vision of Christ the more vehement their movement and the larger they become, a hierarchy of sizes is used: at the bottom is man, at the top is God, followed by angels and apostles. The bodies were considered as accessories of the soul and were not represented according to any anatomic observations (fig. 62 b). The place of a theophany is eternity, hence unrelated to perspective. These portals appear as the visual equivalent of the visions described by the Prophets of the Hebrew Bible and Revelation, as well as by some Neo-Platonic texts.

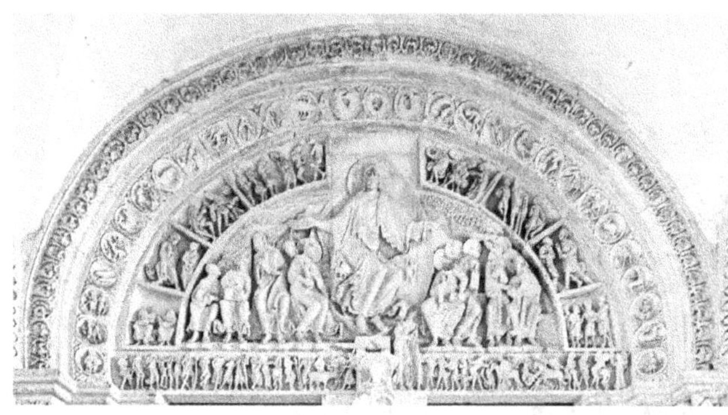

59 a *Christ Giving the Gift of the Spirit to the Apostles*, c. 1130, tympanum, central portal inside the narthex, Vézelay, Benedictine abbey church, Sainte-Marie Madeleine

[179] *De Divisione Naturae*, V, cited by Yves Christe, "Esthétique", *Les Grands Portails Romans*, Geneva, 1969, chapter 1 and translated into English by Hearn, *Romanesque Sculpture*, New York, 1981.

The Path Toward Beauty

An extremely rigorous geometrical order underlies Romanesque sculptures (fig. 60), which display at the same time the most extraordinary freedom of invention.[180]

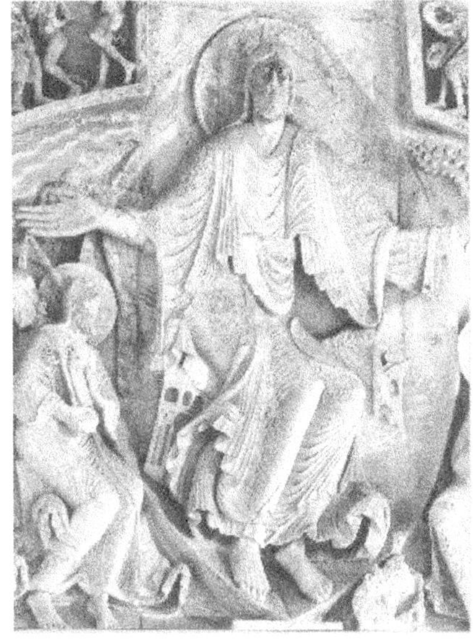

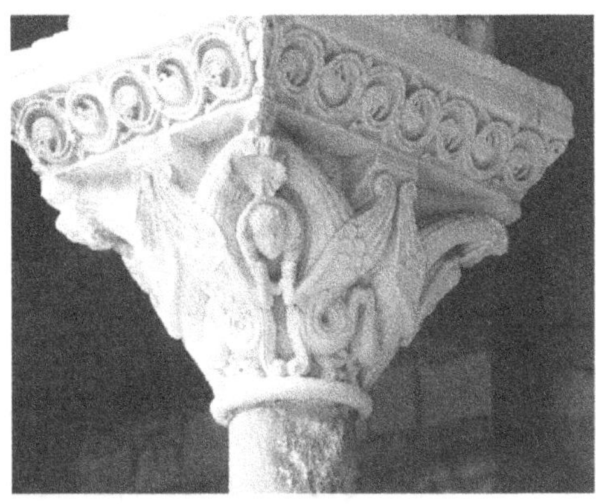

59 b   Detail of the figure of Christ.

60   Ornamental capital, c. 1100, cloister, Moissac, priory church, Saint-Pierre

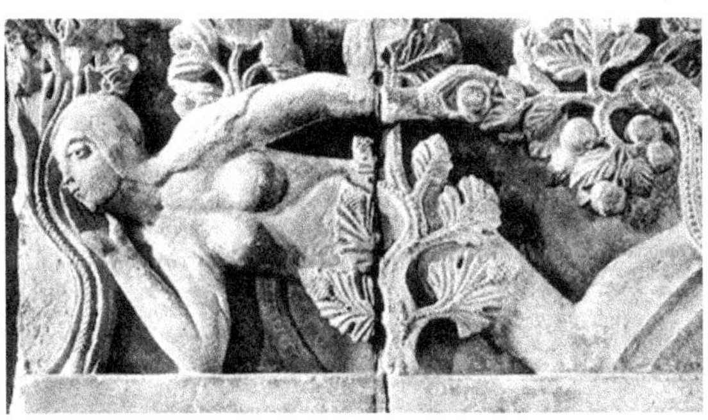

The geometrical order may even have allowed artists to convey their vision in an intelligible way without entering into competition with God's creation (fig. 61). Gombrich shows that the more a child desires to ride, the less important it is that the horse resemble a real horse[181] and, as Kitzinger points out, the more urgent man's need to pray or communicate with God is, the less he needs naturalism, which can actually become a hindrance to communication.[182]

61   Gislebertus, *Eve*, c. 1130, fragment of a lintel from the church of Saint-Lazare, Autun. Now in the Musée Rolin, Autun

---

[180] Henry Focillon, *L'Art des sculpteurs romans*, 1931, new edition 1983. J. Baltrusaitis, *Formation, déormation. La stylistique ornementale dans la sculpture romane*, Paris, revised edition 1986; Yves Christe, op. cit.
[181] Gombrich, *Meditation on a Hobby Horse*, New York, 1963, p. 8.
[182] Kitzinger, op. cit., pp. 106-107.

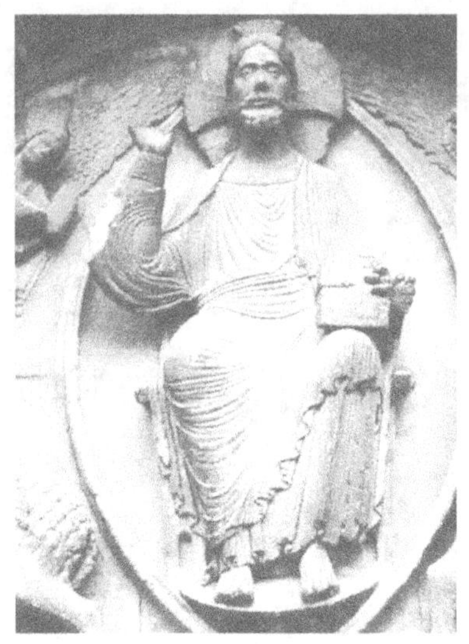

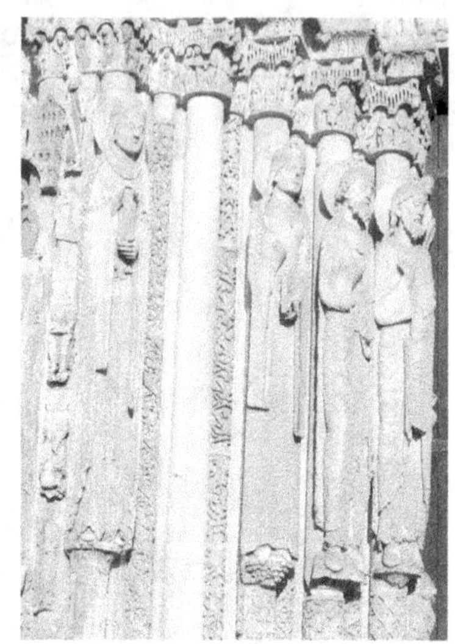

62 a *Apocalyptic Christ*, c. 1155, detail from the central tympanum, west façade, Chartres Cathedral.
62 b *Kings and Queens*, c. 1155, jamb statues, central portal, west façade, Chartres Cathedral

Let us recall that an African mask (fig. 64) was also considered a theophany, a visible manifestation of a divinity, and that it could only act as such if it was beautiful.[183] We mentioned earlier a few of the criteria of beauty concerning Yoruba art.

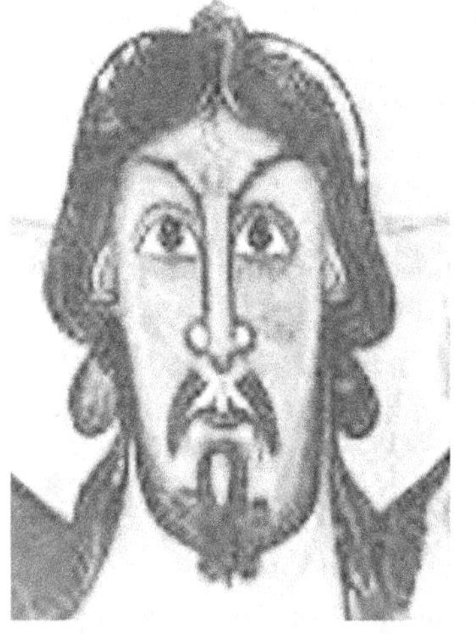

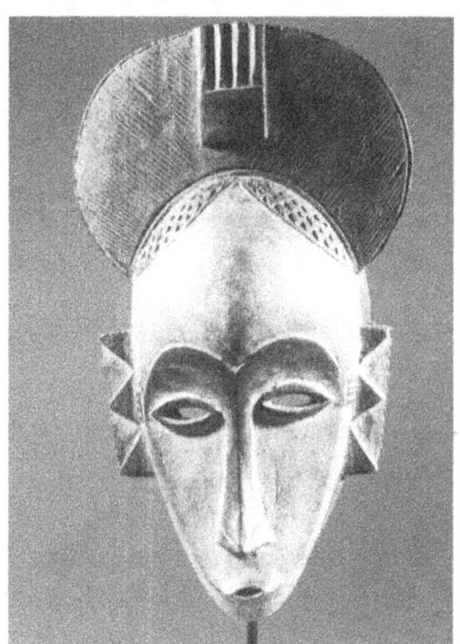

---

[183] Michel Leiris, *Afrique Noire. La création plastique*, Paris, Univers des Formes, 1967, p. 45.

 The Path Toward Beauty

63 *Christ in Majesty*, detail, apse painting, from Lerida, Church of Tahull, c.1123. Now in the National Museum of Catalonia, Barcelona, Spain

64 *Guro Mask*, Ivory Coast, Private Collection

When Plotinus asked himself what we should do in order to have a vision of the inaccessible beauty of god, he suggested that we put aside all material references and visible support.

> He that has the strength let him arise and withdraw into himself. His eyes, turning away forever from the material beauty that once made his joy. . . . Close the eyes and call instead upon another vision, which is to be waked within you, a vision, and the birth-right of all, which few turn to use. . . . Withdraw into yourself and look . . . (*Enneads*, VI, 8, 9).

> By these steps we are led to know that the primary nature of Beauty must be formless (Plotinus, Ibid. VI, 7, 33).

When twentieth-century artists turned away from the world of natural forms, of things and objects, their vision of the inaccessible became abstract or unnameable.

Thus, Malevich's abstract painting, *Black Square*, 1915 (fig. 65), took the place of a Christian icon:[184]
The form becomes an allusion to space and the painting, an allusion to painting, revealing the essential, the supreme or essential being, a world without objects.

65 Kazimir Malevich, *Black Square*, 1915, St. Petersburg, Russian Museum

Beauty in Creativity

Throughout the centuries, beauty has been either the means or the aim of art conceived as a "receptacle of the sacred,"[185] and all those arts therefore followed a set of traditions, as we saw in the previous chapter. Their shape, their visual and emotional power was determined by sacred and canonical texts. The artists had to observe pre-established rules and imitate

---

[184] Lipsey, op. cit., p. 136.

[185] Belting, *Image et Culte,* 1998 (translation of German edition of 1990), p. 618.

models that were more or less fixed. Beauty was a metaphysical concept, and the beauty of the deity was conveyed through forms that were based on iconographical schemes and mathematical principles. In the various texts and civilizations, the artist was usually considered the instrument of a deity or an institution, rather than a creator in his own right. Little or no importance was given to his inventions, if they were accepted at all, or to his individual identity.

To create, as we said earlier, means, etymologically, to make (from the Sanskrit *Kri*) and it corresponds to the Greek *poïein*. Every created thing is literally *poësis*, even though it can take various forms.

> By its original meaning, poetry (*poësis*) means simply creation, and creation, as you know, can take very various forms. Any action which is the cause of a thing emerging from non-existence into existence might be called poetry and all the processes in all crafts are kind of poetry, and all those engaged in it are poets . . . (Plato, *Symposium*, 205 b).[186]

To create means to bring into being.

When Plato referred more specifically to the creation of works of art such as the epic poems of Homer, he used another term, procreation, *tòkos*, from the verb to beget, to engender (*tekéein*). He considered artists spiritual procreators. In the *Symposium* (line 206 b ff.), the aim of love, as we saw earlier, was to procreate, physically or spiritually, in view of immortality, and Beauty (*Kalloné*) presided over everything divine, and hence is immortal. Procreation was the only way in which human beings could approach the immortality of the gods, and it was only through love and beauty that this was possible. According to these definitions, every artwork is a creation, but not every one has earned immortality for its author or survived the judgment of time. Inventiveness or novelties are never mentioned.

From the sixteenth century onward, creativity, in the sense of inventiveness,[187] was, on the contrary, praised in the Western world. It was also in the Cinquecento that greater interest began to be shown for the life and the character of the individual artist. The artist was glorified as a genius, and compared to God, imagined as being captured by the *"furore*

---

[186] For the different definitions of "creation" see: George Steiner, *Grammars of Creation*, 2001, p. 21 ff.

[187] George Steiner underlines how "the intricate play of differentiation and overlap between 'creation' and 'invention' has been little explored," how one would never say, for example, that God invented the universe. He analyzes how the stories of the inception of the cosmos relate to those of the birth of a work of art: *Grammars of Creation*, 2002, p. 16 ff.

                    The Path Toward Beauty

dell'arte,"[188] an artistic ecstasy. The "heroization of the artist" had begun.[189]

Before the Cinquecento, creation had first and foremost been associated with God (Genesis 1 and 2), who created the world out of nothing and made it alive, lastly creating man "in the image of God, male and female he created them." He "shaped man from the soil of the ground and blew the breath of life into his nostrils and man became a living being."

This concept of creation is not only that of the Western world and of the Bible, but it is found, with some variants, in nearly all creation myths, as if the myths not only reflected human dreams, but also human experience. In some cases, these myths cannot date back further than the invention of pottery, since God is often imagined as a Potter, creating man out of clay, even if not on a pottery wheel, as in the Egyptian myth of Chnum.[190]

During the Middle Ages, God was often compared to an artist, but in the High Renaissance, the artist was equated to God.[191] Even if artists give form to the formless, their forms do not come out of nothing. No art form comes out of nothing . Every artist is a member of a very old lineage; every work of art is a bead on a long necklace of other beads. "My new 'I' comes from something very old" (Brancusi).[192] Every form of art is the outcome of a given culture, at a given moment in time.

It either continues a tradition or breaks with it, it innovates or does not innovate, protests against the rules or follows them, but it is never a creation *ex nihilo* like the Biblical creation of God. And yet, even God's creation did not come out of nothing! According to rabbinic exegesis, twenty-six aborted creations are said to precede the one recorded by Genesis. Twenty-six drafts, *maquettes*, or rough sketches.[193] Originality itself is antithetical to novelty; originality refers in fact to origins.

> Meaningful art, music, literature, are not new, as is, as must strive to be, the news brought by journalism. Originality is antithetical to novelty. The etymology of the word alerts us. It tells of "inception" and "instauration," of a return, in substance and in form, to beginnings. In exact relation to their originality, to their spiritual-

---

[188] *PietroAretino, Il primo libro delle lettere, 1531* and Giorgio Vasari, *Vite de' più eccellenti pittori, scultori ed architettori*, 9 vols., 1568. Ed. G. Milanesi, Florence, 1878.

[189] Ernst Kris and Otto Kurz, "The Heroïzation of the Artist in Biography," in *Legend, Myth, and Magic in the Image of the Artist. A Historical Experiment*, chapter 2, New Haven, 1979 and E. Zilsel, *Die Entstehung des Geniebegriffes*, Tübingen, 1926; R. Wittkower, "Genius: Individualism in Art and Artists", *Dictionary of the History of Ideas*, vol. 2, New York, 1973, pp. 297-312, esp. section IV.

[190] Mircea Eliade, *A History of Religious Ideas*, 3 vols., Chicago, 1978-1985.

[191] Aretino called Michelangelo a divine person (*persona divina*) and characterized Titian's brush stroke as divine.

[192] Quoted in Lipsey, *An Art of Our Own*, p. 242.

[193] George Steiner, *Grammars of Creation*, 2001, p. 31.

formal force of innovation, aesthetic inventions are "archaic." They try in them the pulse of the distant source.[194]

Notwithstanding all these observations, it was not until the Cinquecento that the artist's creation was to be paralleled to that of God and his imagination and inventions exalted. One of the earliest and most significant examples of this shift was Leonardo da Vinci (1452-1519),[195] the earliest artist to stress the creative role of the artist in his own writings.[196] He considered painting as a science, based first on the experience of Nature, which was then controlled by the mind.

> All our knowledge has its origin in our perceptions (Richter, 1147).

> All sciences are vain and full of errors which are not born from experience (Ibid., 33).

> My intention is first to record the experience and then by means of reason to show why it must be so (Ibid., 1148 A).

Leonardo's vision was based on eyesight, and not on any mystical vision. For him, the painter competed with Nature (Richter, 662), the mistress of all things and the master of all masters (Richter, 660). Painting, however, had an advantage over Nature, which was to

> preserve the likeness of a divine beauty of which Nature's example has been destroyed by time and death (Ibid., 33).

---

[194] George Steiner, *Real Presence*, London, Faber, 1989, pp. 27-28. For Giordano Bruno, around 1585, originality is the non-adherence to tradition. For William Duff, in 1767, originality is associated with genius: "By original, we mean that native and radical power which the mind possesses, of discovering something new and uncommon in every subject on which it employs its faculties." By the end of the eigthteenth century, originality is associated to genius and to imagination. The twentieth-century artist claims to have overthrown all authority and tradition, "to have destroyed anything which hampers his access to origins. He sets in motion a twofold movement: re-creating the origin and creating the original (creation *ex nihilo*)." (C. Grenier, *Big Bang*, Exhibition Catalogue, Pompidou Centre, 2005, p. 16).

[195] On Leonardo and his writings: J.P. Richter, *The Literary Works of Leonardo da Vinci*, 2nd. ed., London, Oxford University Press, 1939, 2 vols. (Richter's numbers refer to *items*, not pages.) See also C. Pedretti, *The Literary Works of Leonardo da Vinci Compiled and Edited by John Paul Richter. Commentary*, 2 vols. Oxford, Phaidon, 1977; A Blunt, *Artistic Theory in Italy, 1450-1600*, Oxford University Press, 1975, chapter 2, pp. 36-37; K. Clark, *Leonardo da Vinci*, rev. ed., Penguin Books, 1967; Barasch, *Theories*, pp. 132 ff. [Unavailable to the editors is the third edition of Richter (London, Phaidon, 1970).]

[196] As Panofsky has shown, Leonardo avoided, however, the term *creare* when speaking of the artist, even though he designated the painter as "master and god" of the world of images which he shapes in his work (E. Panofsky, *Renaissance and Renascences in Western Art*, 2nd. edition, Stockholm, 1965, note 3, p. 188).

The Path Toward Beauty

The painter did not only represent what he perceived in Nature; he could also invent what Nature had not yet created and, consequently, be like God. It was Leonardo da Vinci who marked the transition towards this new concept of the artist when he wrote

> about that divine power, which lies in the knowledge of the painter, transforms the mind of the painter into the likeness of the divine mind, for, with a free hand, he can produce different beings, animals, plants, fruits, landscapes, open fields, abysses, terrifying and fearful places.[197]

> For Leonardo, the painter was, in fact, a creator:
> If the painter wishes to see beauties which will make him fall in love with them, he is a lord capable of creating them (*generarle*), and if he wishes to see monstrous things that arouse real compassion, he is their lord and creator (*n'è signor e dio*) (Richter, 19). [198]

The parallel between the creativity of the artist and that of God would have been considered utterly blasphemous not only in Judaism and Islam, but also among Christians, at least up to the sixteenth century. As Barasch summarizes it: "The creative nature of the artist is underscored by comparing him to the principal creator, God."[199] In Judaism, the prohibition against representation was prompted primarily by the fear of idolatry. The same was true for Islam, where the artist who attempted to represent a living being in any life-like form was condemned to hell according to the *hadith*, not only due to fear of idolatry, but because the artist had competed with God without being able to bring his creation to life.

This parallel between the artist and the Creator was also unthinkable among the Yoruba in Africa or in the various periods of Indian and Chinese art as well as in most other civilizations. The Yoruba sculptor, as we saw earlier, had to incorporate into his work the vital energy of the divinity while respecting established traditions. At the same time, he had some freedom, but certainly could never consider himself equivalent to a deity. That same sculptor, could, however, be possessed by a deity, just as the Aztec sculptor who was said to have "god in the heart"(*yolteotl*), or to have, "put the deified heart into the objects" (*tlayol-*

---

[197] Blunt, *Artistic Theory*, p. 37; Heinrich Ludwig, ed. *Leonardo da Vinci, Das Buch von der Malerei*, Quellenschriftentrür Kunstgeschichte, 18. Wien, Braumüller, 1882, §68, p. 139.

[198] The entire passage reads: "Sel pittore vol vedere bellezze che lo innamorino, lui è signore di generarle, e se vol vedere cose mostruose che spaventino, o che sieno buffonesche e risibili, o veramente compassionevole, lui nè signore e dio. E se vol generare siti e deserti, lochi ombrosi o foschi ne' tempi caldi, lui li figura, e così lochi caldi ne' tempi freddi. Se vol valli, se vole delle alte cime de' monti scoprire gran campagne, e se vole dopo quelle vedere l'orizzonte del mare, egli nè signore, e se delle basse valli vol vedere li alti monti, o delli alti mondi le basse valli e spiaggie. Et in effetto cio chè ne l'universo per essenzia, presenzia o immaginazione, esso l'ha prima nella mente, e po nelle mani, e quelle sono de tanta eccellenzia, che in pari tempo generano una proporzionata armonia in un solo sguardo qual fanno le cose."

[199] Barasch, *Theories*, pp.186 ff.

teuhuiani), which describes the action of introducing divine breath into the material, or to "confer with his heart" (*moyolnonotzani*) which describes those who feel the divine touch and shape it into a work of art.[200] These concepts are found, *mutatis mutandis*, in very many civilizations.

In China, artists were considered divine (by the critics and never by themselves), not because they had invented or created new forms, "striving and competing with Nature," but because they had, on the contrary, succeeded in capturing, with an effortless brush stroke, the vital breath of Nature itself. In so doing, they succeeded in attaining harmony with that universal breath of life, which is the Tao. The Chinese, it must be said, had no concept of a creator God, to whom the artist could be compared; they had no myth of creation *ex nihilo*. For them, the world had begun with the breath of life itself, and the constant interaction of the *yang* and the *yin* within a Totality, the Tao, as order triumphed over chaos. This order was not conceived or translated into mathematical terms, but into the Taoist balance and interaction of *yang* and *yin*.[201] A painter was considered divine when he was in harmony with the Tao of the universe. This implied that the artwork had to reflect a correlation between microcosm and macrocosm, and that the brush of the painter helped things to come out of chaos.

While some of Leonardo's drawings of water, clouds and plants also seem to have captured the breath of Nature, they were the result of a very different creative process, even though he, too, observed the correlation between micro- and macrocosm, between man and the universe.

> By the ancients, man has been called the world in miniature; and certainly this name is well bestowed, because, inasmuch as man is composed of earth, water, air and fire, his body resembles that of earth; and as man has in him bones, the support and framework of his flesh, the world has its rocks, the support of the earth; as man has in him a pool of blood in which the lungs rise and fall in breathing, so the body of the earth has its ocean tide which likewise rises and falls every six hours, as if the world breathed; as in that pool of blood veins have their origin, which ramify all over the human body, so likewise the ocean sea fills the body of the earth with infinite springs of water. The body of the earth lacks sinews, and this is because the sinews are made expressively for movements and, the world being perpetually stable, no movement takes place, and no movement taking place, muscles are not necessary. But in all other points they are much alike (Richter, 929).

---

[200] Barasch, *Theories*, pp. 186 ff.

[201] Anne Cheng, *Histoire de la penséee chinoise*, Paris, 1997, pp. 37 ff., 49, 139; Mircea Eliade, *A History of Religious Ideas*; Marcel Granet, *La Pensée chinoise*, Paris, Albin Michel, 1964.

　　　The Path Toward Beauty

So that we might say that the earth has a spirit of growth; that its flesh is the soil,
its bones the arrangement and connection of the rocks of which the mountains
are composed, its cartilage the tufa, and its blood the springs of water. The pool
of blood which lies round the heart is the ocean, and its breathing, and the increase and decrease of the blood in the pulses, is represented in the earth by the
flow and ebb of the sea; and the heat of the spirit of the world is the fire, which
pervades the earth (Richter, 1000).

Man was in the image of the world, but by his physiognomy, his gestures and the movements of his limbs, man's body was also an outward and visible expression of the mind
(Richter, 350-389). Painters had to learn how to represent one through the other. Other Renaissance artists also stressed this relation between the microcosm and the macrocosm as it
is reflected in the human body. They speculated on the harmony between the two through
the theory of human proportions, which was also the secret of its beauty.

Leonardo wanted to penetrate into the mind of Nature itself and understand its laws.

The painter's mind must of necessity enter into Nature's mind in order to act as
an interpreter between Nature and art, it must be able to expound the causes of
the manifestations of her laws (Richter, 41).

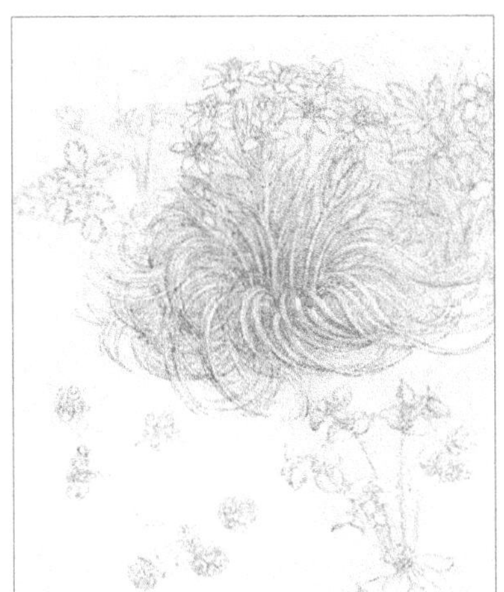

66 Leonardo da Vinci, *Star of Bethlehem*, c. 1506, Windsor
Castle, Royal Library

This is why Leonardo studied the growth of plants (fig.
66), the movement and reflection of water, the clouds, and the geology of the rocks. He also studied all kinds of physiognomies, human anatomy and proportions and was also among the first to have dissected corpses to better understand the human body (fig. 67).

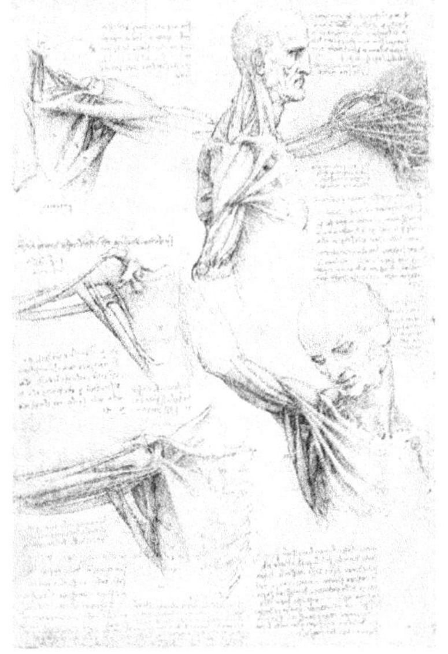

67 Leonardo da Vinci, *Anatomical studies of
an old man*, 1510, Windsor, Royal Library

He studied the folds of draperies (fig. 73), various landscapes (Richter, 393-478) and so on not in order to catch the living breath of life, as the Chinese painters would have done, but to penetrate beneath the surface of things and understand what caused their outer appearances.

In Leonardo's competition with Nature, painting was based on his experience, but sight had to be controlled by mathematical demonstrations to be understood by the mind (Richter, 1145, 1148A, 1158).[202] "Let no man who is not a mathematician read the elements of my work" (Richter ed. by Pedretti, 1, 112).

Nevertheless, Leonardo's affirmation that all certainty and truth could be determined only by mathematics and his interest in the beauty of human proportions,[203] are in keeping with an entire Western tradition, first and foremost Plato's *Timaeus* and Vitruvius' *Book on Architecture*, but also the Florentine artists of the fifteenth century, such as Alberti, Piero della Francesca, and his pupil, the mathematician Luca Pacioli, Leonardo's friend (fig. 68).

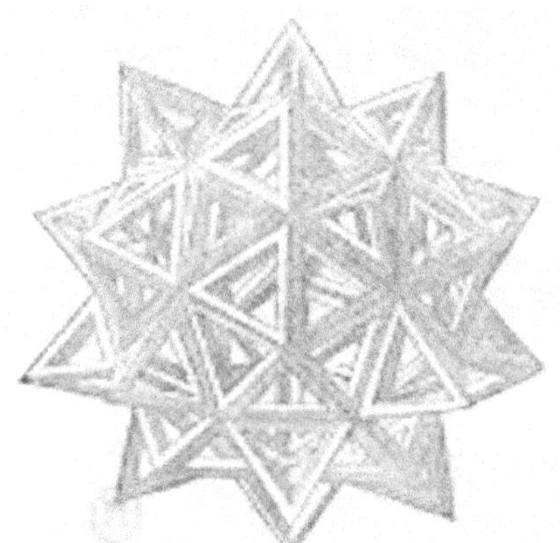

68 *Dodecahedron* (after a drawing by Leonardo da Vinci), Woodcut, in Luca Pacioli's *De divina proportione*, 1509, Paris, BnF.

Leonardo's insistence on the primary importance of sense experience, however, was far removed from Plato's theory of knowledge and from any Neo-Platonic concept of art and beauty. For him, painting was a science, and all sciences begin with experience, outside which there could simply be no truth:

No human investigation can be called true science without passing through mathematical tests (*dimostrazioni*), and if you say that the sciences which begin and end in the mind contain truth this cannot be conceded and must be denied for many reasons. First and foremost, because in such mental discourses experience does not come in, without which nothing reveals itself with certainty (Richter/ Pedrettti, 1, 32).

Experience does not feed investigators on dreams, but always proceeds from accurately determined first principles, step by step, in true sequences, to the end, as

---

[202] For the drawings, A. E. Popham, *The Drawings of Leonardo da Vinci*, New York, 1945 and the two *Exhibition Catalogues of Leonardo's Drawings*, New York Metropolitan Museum and Paris, 2003.
[203] "Human beauty composed of proportional, beautiful parts." (Richter, 651-652).

     The Path Toward Beauty

can be seen in the elements of mathematics founded on numbers and measures
called arithmetic and geometry, which deals with discontinuous and continuous
quantities with absolute truth (Richter/Pedretti, 1, 34).

Experience never errs, only your judgements err by expecting from her what is
not in her power (Ibid., p. 240).

Contrary to the far younger Michelangelo (1475-1564), Leonardo da Vinci was not really influenced by Ficino's Neo-Platonic philosophy, for whom "Beauty is the splendor of God, whose rays come down to earth, . . . a kind of force or light shining from Him through everything,"[204] hence, also through works of art. Michelangelo, too, conceived of art as a gift from heaven and beauty as an emanation of God.

The greatest artist has no conception which a single block of marble does not
potentially contain within its mass, but only the hand obedient to the mind can
penetrate to this image.

The Divine Hammer who dwells and abides in Heaven, not only shapes beauty
in others but, by so doing, makes His own beauty greater still," (Michelangelo,
Sonnet, ed. by A. Blunt, *Theories*. p. 72).

Unlike Michelangelo, Leonardo rarely wrote about God, leaving such discourse "to the imagination of the friars" (Richter, 837).

For if we are doubtful about the certainty of things that pass through the senses,
how much more should we question the many things against which the senses
rebel, such as the nature of God and the soul and the like, about which there are
endless disputes and controversies (Richter, 6).

Contrary to all Florentine neo-Platonists, Leonardo was interested only in the truth that experience and science could demonstrate and not

in the sophisticated reasons and frauds of wits in great and uncertain things (Richter, 1168).

When Leonardo wrote about beauty, it was either in contrast to the ugly (Richter),[205] or about the beautiful proportions of an angelic face (Richter, 25), or the beautiful effects of perspective at the spot where the sun's rays fall (Richter, 313). He compared the proportions of painting to the harmonious concord "which reaches the eye just as a chord in music af-

---

[204] Hofstadter and Kuhns, pp. 203-238.
[205] Barasch, *Theories*, p 139.

fects the ear" (Richter, 25), music being the sister of painting even though painting ranks higher than music because it does not fade away as soon as it is born (Richter, 32).

His anatomical drawings in the Windsor castle manuscripts as well as his drawing of the human head (fig. 69) and of the Vitruvian man in the Academy of Venice (fig. 70), not only illustrate a theory of ideal human proportions, defined once and for all by Greek principle of *symmetria*, but also Leonardo's own accurate study of the human body (fig. 67).

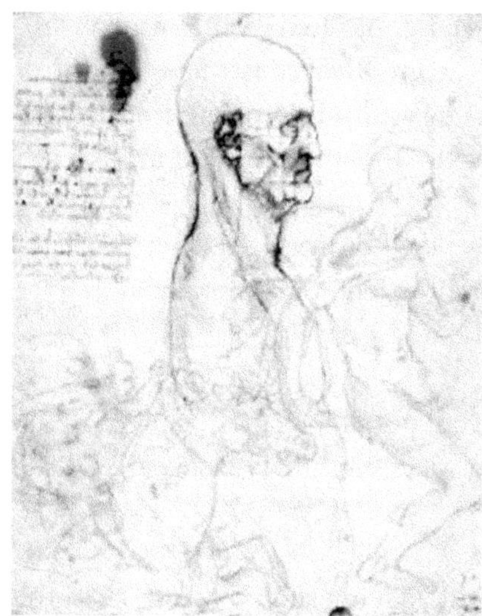

69 Leonardo da Vinci, *Facial Proportions of a Man in Profile; Study of Soldiers and Horses*, c. 1490-95, Venice, Gallerie dell'Accademia

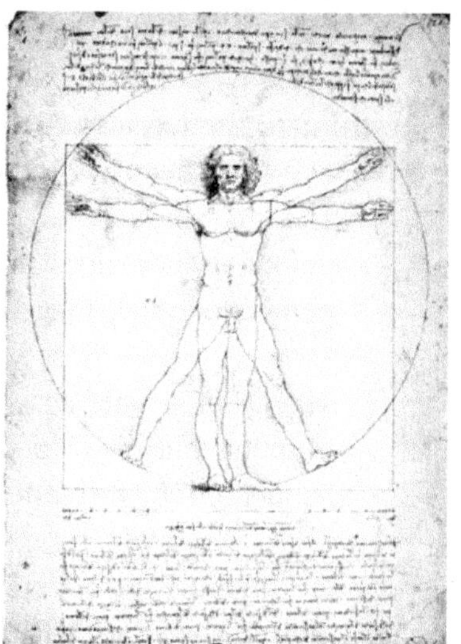

70 Leonardo da Vinci, *The Vitruvian Man (The Proportions of the Human Body According to Vitruvius)*, 1492, Venice, Gallerie dell'Accademia

Leonardo drawing interprets the following text in Vitruvius' *De Architectura* 3.1.3.
The navel is naturally placed in the centre of the human body, and, if in a man lying with his face upward, and his hands and feet extended, from his navel as the centre, a circle be described, it will touch his fingers and toes. It is not alone by a circle, that the human body is thus circumscribed, as may be seen by placing it within a square. For measuring from the feet to the crown of the head, and then across the arms fully extended, we find the latter measure equal to the former; so that lines at right angles to each other, enclosing the figure, will form a square.

Leonardo observes that the man's navel marks the centre of the circle, but not that of the square, marked by the top of the genital organs (Richter, 343).

Leonardo was nevertheless not indifferent to ideally beautiful features, especially when drawing or painting those of Christ, and some of the apostles for the *Last Supper* of Milan, or the *Virgin and Saint John the Baptist* in the Louvre. Contrary to the Greeks, however, and to L. B. Alberti or to Renaissance speculation about beauty based on a theory of ideal

The Path Toward Beauty

human proportions,[206] Leonardo always advised the painter not to improve on Nature, not to select or idealize. Thus, he refused any fixed, measurable, ideal set of proportions when painting "ordinary" faces or bodies, because in Nature there is a great variety of human features and proportions, none of which was more beautiful than the other:

> But if you wish to make your figures on the basis of one and the same measurement, know that they cannot then be distinguished from one another, which is something never seen in nature.[207]

Any fixed ideal of beauty would necessarily have been in conflict with the observation and correct representation of nature; hence, there could not be only one type of beauty within Nature, which was beautiful in all its aspects.

> Though human ingenuity may make various inventions . . . it will never devise any invention more beautiful, nor more simple, nor more to the purpose than Nature does; because in her inventions nothing is wanting and nothing is superfluous . . . but she puts into them the soul of the body which forms them (Richter, 837).

Is there any more concise definition of beauty?

Though Leonardo repeats, over and over, that painting is a science, he also admits that it is a gift and that the anatomical study of human and animal bodies and of their proportions was only a means of investigation towards an end which transcends it (Richter, 1155). The actual painting was far superior to the science which preceded it and which could be taught, whereas painting "cannot be taught to those not endowed by Nature, like mathematics" (Richter/Pedretti, 1, 35).

> The scientific and true principles of paintings first determine what is a shaded object, what is direct shadow, what is cast shadow, and what is light, that is to say, darkness, light, colour, body, figure, position, distance, nearness, motion and rest. These are understood by the mind alone and entail no manual operation; and they constitute the science of painting which remains in the mind of the contemplators; and from it is then born the actual creation, which is far superior to the science that preceded it (Richter/Pedretti, 1, 34).

It was Dürer who was to formulate the duality between the objective artistic rules, the binding laws of correctness and beauty. He also observed that one artist can produce something more valuable in an unpretentious drawing than another in a major painting that had occupied him for months and years, that one man can prove himself to be a greater artist by the representation of an ugly figure than another by the representation of a beautiful one

---

[206] E. Panofsky, "History of the Theory of Human Proportions," *Meaning in the Visual Arts* (1955).
[207] Leonardo da Vinci, *On Painting*, ed. and trans. A. P. McMahon, Princeton, 1956, n. 291.

and that "this gift is wondrous. For often God gives to one man the intellectual power, the understanding, to make something good."[208]

The concept of the inspired artist goes back to Plato's concept of the god-sent madness (*maniké* and *manìa mousòn*) which inspires the poet in the *Phaedrus* and the *Ion*. Technique alone was not sufficient to make a good poet; inspiration was necessary and that was a gift of the gods. This idea was picked up again during the sixteenth century, especially in Vasari's *Lives*, where the artist is imagined as creating his work in a state of artistic ecstasy. This state was conceived as a wondrous gift, as if driven by God, which leads to the worship of genius.[209] The praise of creativity, inventiveness and imagination, and the parallel between the artist and God, seem to have been interrelated in all sixteenth century art theory, but were first expressed in Leonardo da Vinci's own work and writings at the very beginning of the century.

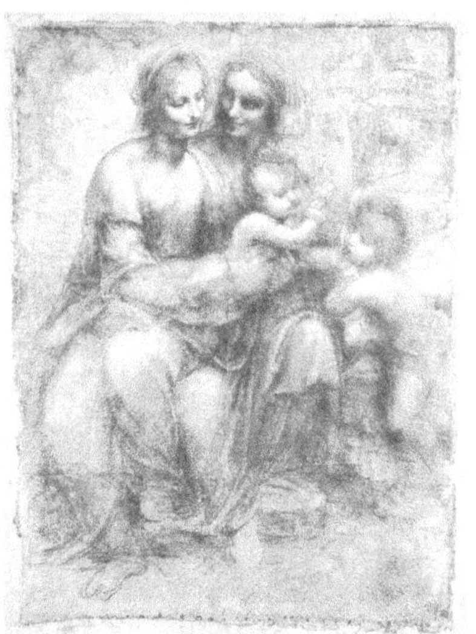

When standing in front of Leonardo's charcoal drawing of the *Virgin and Child with St. Anne* and the young *St. John* of the National Gallery of London (fig. 71) or in front of the early *Adoration of the Magi* (left unfinished in 1481), in the Uffizi (fig. 72), one has the overwhelming feeling of witnessing the creative process itself. It is as if this painting was, to quote Kenneth Clark, an overture to all of Leonardo's work,[210] but even more, to Leonardo's own "competition" with Nature's own creative process.

71 Leonardo da Vinci, *Madonna and Child with St Anne and the Young St John*, Charcoal with white chalk heightening on paper, 1500-01, London, National Gallery

---

[208] E. Panofsky, *Idea. A Concept in Art History*, Harper and Row, Engl. Trans, 1968 (German edition, 1924), pp. 121 ff.

[209] E. Kris and O. Kurtz, op. cit., pp. 48 ff. refers to E. Panofsky, *Idea*, in which he refers to Dürer's "dualism between law and reality, rule and genius," "object" and "subject."

[210] K. Clark, *Leonardo da Vinci*, 1967, p. 40. Maurizio Seracini revealed, through infrared reflectography, a great number of original drawings covered up by a brownish paint, which was actually applied a century after Leonardo had left Florence for Milan and abandoned the drawing of the *Adoration of the Magi*, commissioned for the Church of San Donato a Scopeto, in Florence. This discovery only enhances this overwhelming feeling of witnessing Leonardo's creative process. Cf. F. Camerota, A. Natali, M. Seracini, *Leonardo da Vinci. Studio per l'Adorazione dei Magi*, 2006.

 The Path Toward Beauty

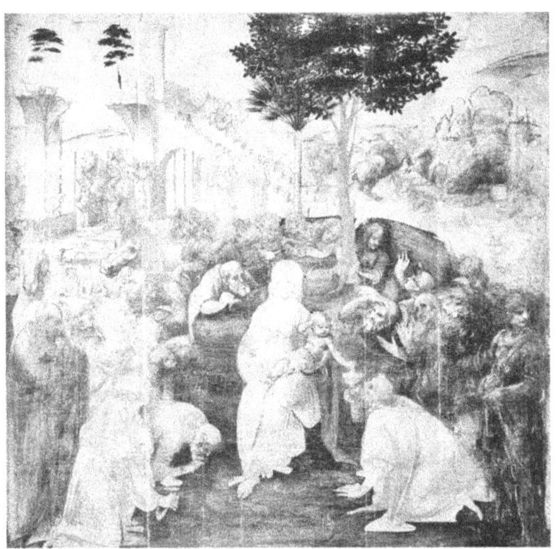

72   Leonardo da Vinci, *Adoration of the Magi*, c.1481, Florence, Uffizi Gallery

The same thing happens when one looks at certain of Leonardo's drawings and at paintings by Titian, Rembrandt or Velasquez or even at fragments of some of these artworks (fig. 73). One begins to wonder if beauty does not, in fact, lie in the process and power of creation itself, when these are at work.

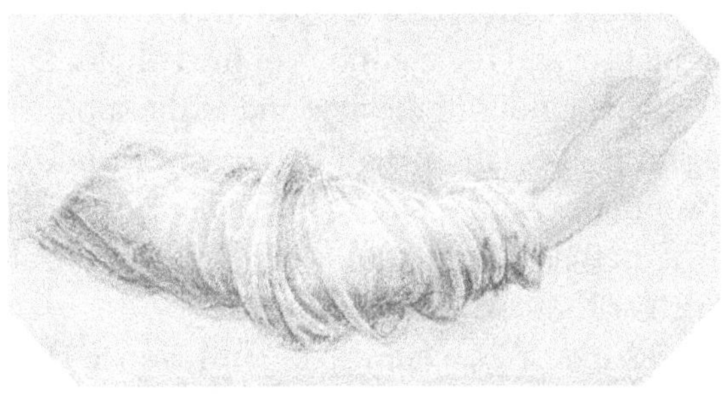

73   Leonardo da Vinci, *Detail of arm, hand and sleeve drapery*, study for the painting of *The Virgin and Child, St. Anne and St. John the Baptist*, 1508-12, Windsor, Royal Library

Through the painting in the Uffizi, and the charcoal cartoon of the National Gallery, one not only enters into Leonardo's investigations and experiences, but into an image of a world recreated by

> and that divine power, which lies in the knowledge of the painter, transforms the mind of the painter into the likeness of the divine mind (Richter/Pedretti, p. 24).

Nature's beauty is, nevertheless, ephemeral, while that of Leonardo's painting is not. The aim is always immortality.

> How many paintings have preserved the likeness of a divine beauty of which Nature's example has been destroyed by time or death, and the work of the painter has thus become of greater value than that of Nature, his teacher (Richter, 33).

This divine beauty may well be that of life itself, conveyed by every stroke of Leonardo's own hand, however trained and corrected by his sense of sight and by his mind.

After reading thousands of Leonardo's notes and seeing hundreds of his drawings, we still do not know anything about his personal life and feelings, while each drawing seems to reveal his exceptionally inquisitive mind. The "heroization of the artist in biography" was to be done by others.

Michelangelo's own Neo-Platonic approach to art and beauty remained exceptional in the sixteenth century. The admiration or worship of Michelangelo during the late eighteenth and early nineteenth centuries was, however, to become admiration for his subjective art, creative power, expressive genius, depth of feeling and stormy passions that fascinated Reynolds in the 1780s, and "a disruptive force at the very foundation of the defence of tradition in art" that led to the Romantic exaltation of the emotional.[211]

The concept of the artist as genius and the praise of imagination and creativity have been emphasized ever since the sixteenth century. They were literally exalted in the second half of the eighteenth century, especially by the Romantics, who were fascinated by the mystery of artistic creation, the individual character and psychology of the artist and his intuitive side. Furthermore, they emphasized the importance of the artist's inner life and emotions, conveyed or evoked by the work of art, which also aimed at stimulating the imagination and the emotions of the beholder.[212]

The notions of the new and of the subjective were praised first in the Hellenistic period, again in the Italian High Renaissance, and then throughout Western civilization up to the twentieth century. During these periods, Western art was related to the imitation of Nature, whether idealized or not, when it was not related to the imitation of ideally beautiful models such as those of Antiquity.

Works of art were also commissioned by an ever more varied and individualized public. Art patronage began to change during the sixteenth century, and so did the concept of the artist and of the role of art and of beauty, as we shall see in the following chapter. The skill of the artist and his compliance with workshop traditions and guild commissions were no longer judged by other artists, but by merchants or critics, who were rarely artists themselves. The social status of the painter, sculptor and architect was slowly changing, too; from a skilled manual labourer he came to be gradually respected as a liberal artist, knowledgeable in the sciences and therefore treated as a gentleman.[213] He was expected to interpret religious, historical, allegorical and mythological themes with ever greater freedom, hence independently of any established canon.

The great art patrons were no longer the city guilds, religious orders or the Church. Works of art were no longer made solely in honour of the gods of the city, as in ancient Greece, or commissioned by a major city guild, as in Florence during the fourteenth and the fifteenth centuries, nor were they made only to celebrate the glory of God or to commemorate the deeds of a saint. More and more often, they were commissioned to glorify

---

[211] Barasch, "The Late Renaissance", *Theories*, chapter 5 and idem, *Modern Theories of Art* 1, pp. 138-141.
[212] Barasch, *Modern Theories*, 1, pp. 284 ff.
[213] Blunt, "The Social Position of the Artist," op. cit., chapter IV; Barasch, "The Artist and the Medium; Some Facets of the High Renaissance," *Theories,* chapter 4.

the ambitions of an art patron, eager to enhance his own personal prestige or that of his household. They were made to please his curiosity and his taste. It is in this general context that artworks became elements of decoration, exalting the individual, rather than a means of worship. Beauty was no longer defined by measurable means and metaphysical references only but, far more frequently, by the pleasure it gave the beholder or the prestige it conferred.

The belief that there was an ideal beauty, which the artist could attain through correct representation, the art of perspective, and a set of ideal geometrical forms and mathematical ratios, once shared by Alberti or Piero della Francesca, Raphael, and so many others was threatened by the late sixteenth century and by the classicizing academism of the seventeenth and eighteenth centuries.

When reading the texts of artists, critics and philosophers written during the three centuries following the Italian Renaissance, we always run up against the same criteria developed in the previous chapters, to which we must, however, add the increasing importance given to imagination, to pleasure and to subjectivity, leading to Kant's *Critique of Judgment* (1790). Greater weight was also put on symbols as mediators between the visible and the invisible, and to the inner spiritual life of the artist and of the beholder, starting with Hegel (1835-38).[214] Throughout these centuries Western art continued, however, to be conceived as an imitation of nature.

It is only in the early twentieth century, that Western artists rejected the legacy of Antiquity and the Renaissance, because it had become nothing but an academic heritage, devoid of life and meaning, dead. Artists could no longer find the source of their creativity in the imitation of the appearances of nature, or in the creation of works of art considered beautiful according to academic criteria and canonical models or, for that matter, the taste of the *Salons* of the period.

Four centuries after Leonardo da Vinci, Paul Klee (1879-1940), among others, was to write about art and creativity: "Art is a simile to the Creation. Each work of art is an example, just as the terrestrial is an example of the cosmic."[215]

In his *Lectures on Modern Art*, of 1924, he wrote:

> [The artist] surveys with penetrating eye the finished forms which nature places before him. The deeper he looks, the more readily he can extend his view from the present to the past, the more deeply he is impressed by the one essential image of creation itself, as Genesis, rather than by the image of nature, the finished product. Then he permits himself the thought that the process of creation can today hardly be complete and he sees the act of world creation stretching from the

---

[214] Hegel, *Vorlesungen über Aesthetik, 1835-1838*, trans. by T. M. Knox, *Aesthetics: Philosophy of Fine Art*; Oxford, 1975; Barasch, *Modern Theories*, 1, pp. 178 ff. and chapter 4: "The Symbol," pp. 224 ff.; Tzvetan Todorov, *Théorie du symbole*, Paris, Seuil, 1977, especially pp. 179 ff.

[215] Paul Klee, 1920, in Chipp, *Theories of Modern Art*, p. 186.

past to the future, Genesis eternal! . . . Presumptuous is the artist who does not follow his road through to the end. But chosen are those artists who penetrate to the region of that secret place where the primeval power nurtures all evolution. There, where the powerhouse of all time and space—call it the brain or heart of creation—activates every function; who is the artist who would not dwell there? In the womb of nature, at the source of creation, where the secret key to all lies guarded. . . . What springs from this source—whatever it may be called, dream, idea or fantasy—must be taken seriously only if it unites with the proper creative means to form a work of art. Then those curiosities become realities—realities of art, which help to lift life out of its mediocrity. For not only do they more or less revitalize the visible, but they also make secret visions visible.[216]

In his Notebooks of 1922 (edited by J. Spieller, 1961), Klee also wrote:

The power of creativity cannot be named. It remains ultimately mysterious. What does not shake us to our foundations is no mystery. Down to our finest particles we ourselves are charged with this power. We cannot formulate its essence, but we can, in some measure, move towards its source. In any case, we must reveal its power in its functions, just as it is revealed to us. . . . Merged with matter, it must enter into a form that is alive and real. And it is thus that matter takes on life and order, from its smallest particles to its subsidiary rhythms and its higher structures.

Creation lives as genesis invisibly under the surface of the work.[217]

The new is not acknowledged in its own right by Leonardo or by Klee, but neither is the deceptive power of a work of art that takes Nature as its point of reference. Klee, like most artists of his time, had moved away from the imitation of Nature, which had dominated Western art from the Renaissance onward. He placed more value "on the powers which do the forming than on the final forms themselves."[218]

The growing importance given to novelty, the craving for so-called originality, seems especially associated with twentieth-century art, art theory and art criticism. Thus, Apollinaire was to describe Cubism as New Painting and emphatically praise its innovations, but Picasso, one of the creators of Cubism and one of the best examples of "modern" creativity, wrote:

---

[216] Roger Lipsey, "Paul Klee," *An Art of Our Own, The Spiritual in Twentieth-Century Art*, Boston, 1988, pp. 178-179.

[217] Ibid., p. 192.

[218] Paul Klee, *On Modern Art*, 1925, *Modern Artists on Art*, ed . Robert Herbert, 1964, p. 87.

　　　　　　　　The Path Toward Beauty

To me there is no past or future in art. If a work of art cannot live always in the present it must not be considered at all. The art of the Greeks, of the Egyptians,

of the great painters who lived in other times, is not an art of the past; perhaps it is more alive than it ever was.[219]

74 a Pablo Picasso, *Guernica*, 1937, Madrid, Museo Nacional Centro, de Arte Reina Sofia

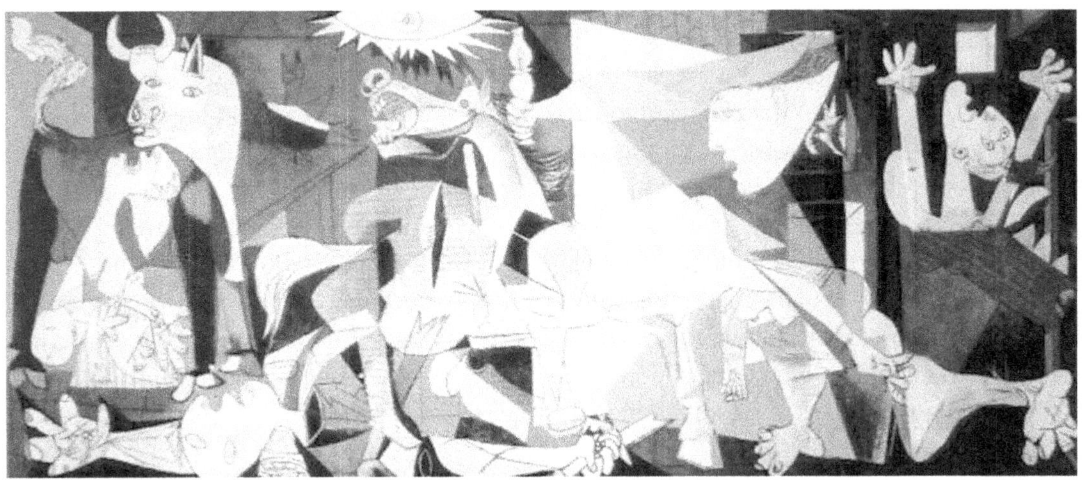

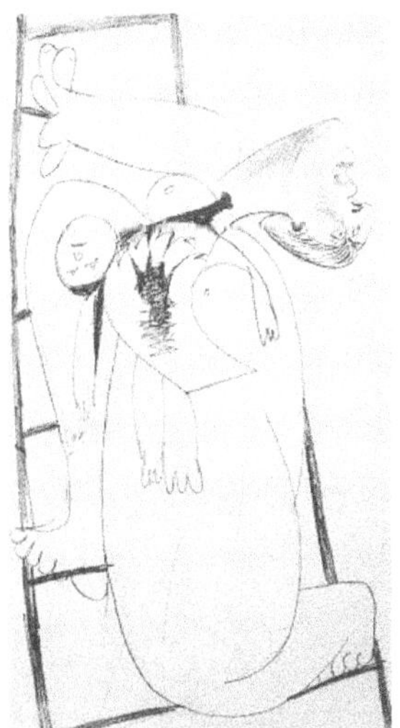

74 b Pablo Picasso, study for *Guernica*

The artist is a receptacle of emotions that come from all over the place: from the sky, from the earth, from a scrap of paper, from a passing shape, from a spider's web. When we invented Cubism we had no intention whatever of inventing Cubism. We wanted only to express what was in us.

Academic training in beauty is a sham. We have been deceived, but so well deceived that we can scarcely get back even a shadow of the truth. . . . Art is not the application of a canon of beauty, but of what the instinct and the brain can conceive beyond that canon. . . . It is not what the artist does that counts, but what he is. . . .

---

[219] Pablo Picasso, *Statement,* 1923, in Chipp, *Theories of Modern Art*, p. 264.

We have turned pictures into petty and ridiculous things. We have been tied up
to a fiction, instead of trying to sense what inner life there was in the men who
painted them.[220]

When we look at *Guernica* (fig. 74 a) or at so many of his other works, we do not ask ourselves whether or not it is beautiful.

In front of Picasso's work as well as in front of the works of others, past and present,
signed or anonymous, we would like to conclude this section with Henry Moore, writing
about his own sculpture:

> For me, a work must have a vitality of its own. . . . When a work has this power-
> ful vitality, we do not connect the word Beauty with it . . . Beauty, in the Greek
> and Renaissance sense, is not the aim of my sculpture. . . . Beauty comes by the
> way and can never be an end in itself. . . . Between beauty of expression and
> power of expression, there is a difference of function. The first aims at pleasing
> the senses, the second has a spiritual vitality, which for me is more moving and
> goes deeper than the senses. Because a work does not aim at reproducing natural
> appearances it is not, therefore, an escape from life, but may be a penetration
> into reality. . . . Not a decoration to life, but an expression of the significance of
> life, a stimulation to greater effort in living.[221]

Twentieth century art did not only reject the mimetic heritage of the Renaissance, but
also the eighteenth-century notion that a work of art "demanded to be experienced aesthetically," that its aim was to be beautiful and that beauty was that which pleased the taste
of the beholder. But how did these notions emerge in the first place?

---

[220] Pablo Picasso, *Conversation*, 1935, in Chipp, *Theories of Modern Art*, pp. 271-72.
[221] Henry Moore, in Herbert, *Modern Artists on Art*, pp. 138-144.

It is generally assumed that beauty is that which pleases, and that the faculty of judging whether something is beautiful or not is related to taste and based solely on subjective grounds. Although rooted in the art theories of the Late Italian Renaissance and of the European academies of the seventeenth and eighteenth centuries, this assumption is essentially an eighteenth-century hypothesis and mainly Western.

Aesthetics[222] (the term itself was invented by A. Baumgarten in 1750) had become increasingly important by the second half of the eighteenth century and referred to sense knowledge as opposed to intellectual knowledge. This new philosophy is also based on the premise that intuition and imagination must also have determinate rules in human representations. It became, more generally, the philosophy of art and of its beauty. Thus, many philosophers in England, France and Germany were to analyze the link between art, beauty and the feeling of pleasure, most importantly David Hume (in 1757), and especially Immanuel Kant (in 1764 and in 1790). Because this link has become a commonplace, we will try to understand its origin and development in both art theories and philosophy.[223]

Art Theories
The general art theories of the late sixteenth and seventeenth centuries are also at the origin of the earliest art criticism, which deals more specifically with individual works of art or exhibitions, e.g., the *Salons* of D. Diderot (1713-1784).[224] The term *beaux–arts* was coined around 1750, establishing a decisive, though very ambiguous, semantic link between beauty and art. The aim of art has not always been, and is becoming less and less, to be beautiful or to please. Academic teaching, art theories and art criticism also established some terms, if

---

[222] Recall Plato's "Theory of Knowledge" (*Republic*, 505 ff. and 514 ff.), how he divides reality into sensible reality (*to aistheton*), and intelligible reality (*to noeton*). The knowledge of the former leads only to changeable opinions (*doxa*), that of the latter to the knowledge of truth *(episteme)*. In *Hippias Major* (297 e-298 a), Plato rejects the idea that beauty is that which pleases the senses of sight and of hearing. In *Philebus* (63 a-66 b), Plato shows how intelligence partakes far more of beauty than pleasure.

[223] D. Summers, *The Judgment of Sense, Renaissance Naturalism and the Rise of Aesthetics*, Cambridge, University Press, 1987. (This book was brought to my attention only at the very end of my own research, enough to make me aware of the extent to which the eighteenth-century approach to beauty was rooted, not only in late Renaissance thought, but also in ancient and medieval thought. Summers goes into greater depth on each one of the important points than the scope of this book would have allowed. I have been able, however, to insert a few of his definitions and observations here, especially in footnotes and strongly recommend the book to the reader.)

[224] D. Diderot, *Oeuvres esthétiques*, ed. P. Vernière, Paris 1968. Excerpts in Diderot's *Selected Writings*, trans. D. Coltman, New York and London, 1966; Y. Belaval, *L'esthétique sans paradoxe de Diderot*, Paris, 1950. Diderot wrote more about it in the *Encyclopédie* in the chapters concerning: "Beauté," "Peine," "Plaisir," "Sensation" (1751-1772). See also Diderot, *Traité du Beau et autres esssais*, ed. R. Ganzo, Paris, 1973.

---

not standards, of good taste, which became synonymous with beauty.

Within a very short time, "ideas emerged and forms of reflection and study were shaped that decisively determined thinking on the visual arts for the next two centuries."[225] At the same time, the philosophers, who were primarily concerned with epistemology rather than with art, stipulated that one could not reason about beauty, because there was no innate idea of beauty and that no logical argument or scientific demonstration could prove its truth or establish its criteria. Thus, for Hume in 1757, "Beauty is no quality in things themselves: It exists merely in the mind which contemplates them; and each mind perceives a different beauty. . . . There is no standard of taste."[226] For Kant (in 1790), who pursued the reflection and the critique of Hume but carried it much further: "That which pleases is beautiful. . . . Everybody has his own taste as regards to the pleasant. . . . Beauty without a reference to the feeling of the subject is nothing in itself, . . . and there can be no objective rule of taste to determine by means of concepts what is beautiful."[227]

How did this link between beauty and taste, whereby the beholder became, in fact, the main focus of interest rather than the work of art itself come to impose itself?

First of all, this connection, or this notion of beauty as that which pleases and is relative to taste, exists only in the West, where it arose in periods during which art was conceived as an "imitation" of Nature, "mistress of all things" (Alberti). Ancient Greece, as we saw earlier, based its art on *mimesis* and Aristotle emphasized how all arts were based on man's instinct and desire for imitation, but also on how much we enjoy looking at the most accurate representations of things, recognizing them and learning from them (*Poetics*, 4, 1448 b).[228] For him, pleasure is "the consciousness through the senses of a certain kind of emotion" (*Rhetoric*, 1370a 25 ff.).

At the time of the revival of "mimetic" art in Florence, Alberti wrote that "the painter's work is intended to please the public. So he will not despise the public's criticism and judgment" (*Della Pittura*, 1435, III, 62). He knew that the artist's fame depended on his pleasing

---

[225] Barasch, *Modern Theories, 1.* p. 89. This chapter is greatly indebted to this author.

[226] David Hume, "Of the Standards of Taste," *Four Dissertations*, London, 1757, ed. by J. Stolnitz, *Aesthetics,* London, 1965.

[227] Immanuel Kant, *Beobachtungen über das Gefühl des Schönen und Erhabenen*, Königsberg, 1764, ed. and trans. into French by R. Kempf, *Observations sur le sentiment du beau et du sublime*, Paris, 1969; "Critique of the Aesthetical Judgment," *Critique of Judgment*, originally published in Berlin in 1790 and in 1793, ed. and trans. J.H. Bernard (Dublin, 1892), New York, Hafner Library of Classics, 1968. We used this old translation, but more recent translations are available, such as that by Paul Guyer and Eric Matthews, *Critique of the Power of Judgment*, Cambridge University Press, 2000.

[228] *Poetics* was rediscovered, translated and edited in Italy at the end of the fifteenth century and re-edited many times throughout the sixteenth. See the Introduction of J. Hardy, ed., Aristotle, *Poétique*, Paris, Belles Lettres, 1969.

   The Path Toward Beauty

the public, thanks to the accuracy of his representation of Nature[229] for which there were objective standards of evaluation, mostly based on mathematical rules such as the principles of human proportion and perspective. He also knew that the same standards were used by those who had to judge the work of art, i.e., the guild patronage of Florence, the learned humanists, as well as the artists themselves. The latter led to what Gombrich called the "Renaissance conception of artistic progress, whereby each artist wanted "to demonstrate certain problem-solutions . . . for the admiration of all, but principally with the eye on his fellow artists and the connoisseur who can appreciate the ingenuity of the solution put forward."[230] This spirit of demonstration, to show "the unusual and ingenious way in which the great master solves the artistic problem" is also found in the work of Leonardo da Vinci and was never to disappear entirely from Western thought. It goes back, in fact, to ancient Greece and to competitions, such as that between Pheidias, Polikleitos, Kresilas and two other sculptors around 440 B.C.E. for a statue of a *Wounded Amazon* to be erected in the temple of Artemis in Ephesus (Pliny, XXXIV, 53). These ideas of "progression," "contribution," and "demonstration," as well as praise of what was to be called "modernity" (from the Latin *modo*, meaning "now") also were characteristic of Impressionists and Cubists.

The idea of progress emerges in the history of ancient Greek and Hellenistic Art and, *mutatis mutandis*, again in the Florentine Renaissance.[231] It certainly implied an ideal of perfection as well, which the Western artist hoped to attain when the "imitation" of nature and his own idea of beauty converged: Lysippus' sculpture and Zeuxis painting were considered the ideal of perfection by Pliny the Elder; Raphael's paintings and Michelangelo's art, as a whole, by Vasari.[232] This idea of progress through competition brought an entirely new dimension into how art was viewed by artists, by client-patrons and by any educated beholder; all of them shared, in fact, the same visual experience. Baxandall shows how "the customer's participation" and "agreement" functioned in fifteenth-century Florence.[233] At the same time, one still thought that art was a means to discover and understand nature, which began with the quest of scientific rules and principles that guided the artist in his

---

[229] Let us remember, however, that likeness was by no means the equivalent of beauty. For Alberti (*Della Pittura* of 1435 or *De Statua* of roughly 1460), beauty was conceived as an ideal, hence the result of a mental reconstruction. In Lorenzo Valla's *Elegantiae*, written at about the same time, beauty (*pulchritudo*) derived from the suitability of things and persons to both place and time, it applied to virtues, when it is called "decorum" and does not refer so much to virtue itself, but to what common opinion considers to be virtuous, beautiful and fitting (Baxandall, *Giotto and the Orators,* 1971, pp. 10 and 37-38).

[230] Ernst Gombrich, "Renaissance concept of artistic progression," *Norm and Form*, 1971, p. 7.

[231] Pliny the Elder, *Natural History*, Books 34 and 35, London, 1968 (The Loeb Classical Library, n. 394). In Florence, this concept is also found in Dante (*Purgatory,* XII, 94-6) and in Boccaccio (*Decameron*, VI, 5), when the concept of art as an imitation of Nature-emerged with Giotto, around 1320-30. See also: Barasch, *Theories,* pp. 114 ff. and Baxandall, *Giotto.*

[232] Vasari, *The Lives.* See also E. Panofsky, *Idea, A Concept in Art Theory,* New York, Icon,1968.

[233] M. Baxandall, *Painting and Experience in Fifteenth-Century Italy*, Oxford, 1972, and idem, *Giotto.*

work and led him to scientific knowledge of the world. These rules were thought to reflect the unchanging laws that underlie the beauty of the cosmos, still conceived as mathematically ordered. Early Renaissance art theory refused to recognize various forms of beauty. Beauty and truth were synonyms and the judgment was an intellectual one, not a matter of taste or of sense experience.

The aim of most all other art forms in the world was not to please the beholder's taste. Why not? Because none of them had the Greek, Roman and Renaissance concept of *mimesis*, whereby the quality of the work was supposedly compared to the forms of Nature, however ambiguous that comparison may have been, and however much it changed according to the place and period. In all other civilizations, however, artists also had a model of reference in their minds, but it was not in competition with the visible world or with other models.

In China, for example, the landscape painter is not trying to "imitate" Nature in its outer appearance, but to capture, with brush and ink, its breath of life, the *ch'i* which animates the *yin*, the *yang* and the omnipresent Void in between, forming together the Tao. Every individual painter, as well as beholder, is thought to participate thereby in the process of creation and its constant transformation. There was, in fact, no model other than the paintings of the great masters of the past. Though traditional rules are certainly followed, nothing prevents the calligrapher painter from capturing the *ch'i* with his brush and ink. A Chinese painting is, furthermore, never envisaged as the equivalent of a window frame, but, on the contrary, as a space of freedom where all the vital elements or components (water and mountain, *yin* and *yang*, the empty space of the canvas, or the Void) are constantly interrelated.

In other civilisations, when there was an ideal of perfection, it was linked to the idea of the divinity and to the act of worship, of which art was one of the elements. Indian *Sastras* codified the rules that the artists had to follow; works of art were made to be offered to the deity, had to imitate older canonical models rather than nature, and had to please the gods.

Let us come back to Western mimetic art, and to the emergence of the notion that the aim of art was to please. In the second part of the sixteenth century, treatises were no longer written in Italy only by artists and for artists, as it had been the case in the fourteenth and fifteenth centuries, but also by learned humanists for spectators and art collectors. Thus, when Ludovico Dolce wrote that "painting was invented primarily to give pleasure" (*Dialogo della Pittura, intitolato l'Aretino*, Venice, 1557), this pleasure was independent of any knowledge of the accuracy of representation. It was an intuitive judgment made by a cultivated public, discussing the grace and delicacy of Raphael, which pleased them far more than the awesomeness (*terribilità*) of Michelangelo, thus introducing a comparison, which was to become a commonplace thereafter. One conversed among enlightened people, not among artists, wondering whose work was more attractive, which work one liked more or less, slowly rejecting the dictatorship of rules or of any other objective criteria.

When Vasari published his *Lives* (1550 and 1568), although he was an artist and wrote

 The Path Toward Beauty

about artists, his text seems to be addressed to art collectors and friends of art, whom he had met in the palace of an enlightened art patron (i. e. the Cardinal Farnese) rather than to artists .

With Vasari, grace (*grazia*) and facility (*facilità*), became important aesthetic values. Grace, however elusive its meaning, was related to softness and sweetness and could only be judged, once more, by an intuitive reaction of the spectator, by a judgment of the eye (*giudizio dell'occhio*), which was not subject to any scientific demonstration. For Vasari, judgment (*giudizio*),[234] or the spectator's eye, is the final arbiter of the quality of a work, and Vasari explicitly asserted its superiority over objective measurements. Facility is a synonym for virtuosity, for the ease or the lack of any apparent effort in making a painting or a sculpture, which can also be a source of its grace. We have thus shifted from the concepts of beauty and truth through accurate representation, which had been those of Alberti or of Piero della Francesca, to those of grace and facility, both of which aimed at pleasing the spectator. Thus, we have also shifted from objective to subjective standards of judgment.[235]

The notion that the aim of art is to please, with all its variations, has continued up to today, along with the judgment of the eye, neither of which is related to reason or to any objective criterion.

But to which type of pleasure did the theoreticians or the public refer? To sensual as well as intellectual pleasure. Pietro Aretino, for example, was attracted by the sensual qualities of the colors of Titian,[236] by the feeling of texture that certain painters can convey, or by the beauty of a woman's body.[237] Others were delighted by invention (*invenzione*), or the subject matter chosen by the artist, and found pleasure in deciphering the riddles and iconography of a painting, criticising errors of interpretation, and "translating the encoded meaning of figures and objects into comprehensible terms,"[238] through their own knowledge of numismatics, epigraphy, emblem books (Alciati, 1531), mythology (Giraldi, 1558 and 1596; Conti

---

[234] Baldassar Castiglione refers to the *giudicio naturale* of each artist, each one having a different style. *The Book of the Courtier*, ed. by D. Javitch and C. Singleton, New York, Norton, 2002. Raphael made the beautiful portrait of Baldassar Castiglione, which is in the Louvre. Already in the fifteenth century, Luca Pacioli, pupil of Piero della Francesca, teacher and friend of Leonardo da Vinci and author of the *Divina Proporzione* (ed. by C. Winterberg, Vienna, 1899), wrote about irrational proportions or those that one could not prescribe to the artist, which were left to the discretion of his eye.

[235] Barasch, *Theories*, pp. 209 ff.

[236] Titian made three portraits of Aretino, one of which is in the Pitti Palace of Florence, and another in the Frick Collection in New York.

[237] Ibid., pp. 251-2.

[238] Ibid., p. 263.

1551; Cartari, 1556), astrology (Lomazzo, *Trattato*, II 1591)[239] and iconography (Cesare Ripa's *Iconologia*, 1593 and 1603, which is a dictionary of personifications of ideas and abstract notions).[240] Thus, by the end of the sixteenth century, "historical" and "mythological truth" became another central criterion for judging the value of a work of art.[241]

Furthermore, by 1600, still life, genre painting (whose subject matter was taken from daily life), landscape painting, and portraiture had become independent pictorial art forms, first in the Netherlands and then in all of Europe, each kind with its own secular subject matter. In Protestant countries, such as Holland, the altarpiece with its religious subjects had by then almost disappeared. In short, by the late sixteenth and early seventeenth centuries, pleasure was no longer that which one experienced in front of an accurate representation. It had become sensual pleasure and liking; the subjective judgment of the eye; the beholder's pleasure at recognizing the obscure meaning of the subject matter; its decorative function; and, more importantly and with more reaching consequences, the emotional impact of a work of art.

At the same time, as already mentioned in the previous chapter, there was also greater interest in the creative process itself, and in the psychology and personality of the individual artist, hence, his genius. A work of art became, therefore, a more subjective matter of appreciation. While one of the declared aims of art was indeed to please the beholder, the other was to touch his emotions. On the one hand, we see allegories, mythological subjects, portraiture, independent still–life painting and landscape, subjects taken from daily life, hence an ever greater variety of subject-matter, pleasing an ever wider body of art collectors and laymen from an ever wider social spectrum,[242] and, on the other, religious subjects selected and censored by the clergy: paintings decorating the walls of private homes and paintings above altars.

Let us not forget that we are in the aftermath of the Counter-Reformation, which imposed strict dogmatic rules on religious painting and sculpture, whereby the artists had to make literal representations of Biblical or hagiographic texts, conform to the dogmas of the Church, follow imposed schemes for church architecture and decoration, and accept the censorship of the clergy. What mattered to the censors was not the "uplifting" beauty of a

---

[239] G. P. Lomazzo, a Milanese painter trained in Leonardo's tradition, became an art theoretician after he turned blind, c. 1570. He developed the notion of *moto*, not as motion of the body, but of the soul. He stressed the importance of the subject matter in relation to an entire cultural background, to what we would classify today as iconography and emphasized the variety of personal styles within the same period, hence of various forms of beauty. Barasch, *Theories*, pp. 271-291.

[240] Ibid., pp. 262 ff.

[241] Ibid, pp. 269.

[242] This phenomenon was especially apparent in seventeenth-century Holland, in the decoration of the houses of Dutch burghers. See Simon Schama, *The Embarrassment of Riches,* London, 1987, chapter 5 and Appendix II, pp 619-20, which is an inventory of the estate of an Amsterdam burgher with the list of paintings that decorated the various parts of his house.

     The Path Toward Beauty

work of art, as in the Middle Ages, but total respect for what they considered to be a spiritual truth. For them, the aim of art was not to please, but to be a didactic instrument and awaken deep religious feeling. The Church was reacting not only to the Protestant Reform and its rejection of images within the church, but also to the rational and critical approach of the earlier humanists, their freedom of interpretation, and especially their fascination with pagan Antiquity. The censorship of Michelangelo's *Last Judgment* (1536-1541) and Veronese's *Feast in the House of Levi,* 1573) illustrate these points,[243] but so does Michelangelo's last *Pietà* (known as the *Rondanini Pietà,* 1555-1564: fig. 38), in which he himself, having reached the eve of his own death, under the impact of the Counter Reformation as well, recognizes the vanity of all arts and, in fact, of all physical beauty.[244]

Nevertheless, while the theoreticians discussed the aim of art (primarily that of painting), and seem to have agreed that it was either to give pleasure or to touch the emotions, they did not discuss beauty, nor establish any correlation between the pleasure that a work of art could provide and its beauty. For Lomazzo (*Treatise on Painting,* 1584) or Zuccari (*L'Idea de' pittori, scultori et architetti,* 1607), beauty had, in fact, remained a reflection "of God's supreme light," or "a splendour that comes from the light of God's face," of which the harmony of the work of art was only a visible expression. Beauty, therefore, remained a metaphysical concept, "a spark of divinity."[245]

By the early seventeenth century, we are very far removed from the beliefs of the Early Renaissance artists, for whom only perfect beauty could serve as the model for all creation, through which the artist discovered the truth by piercing the secrets of Nature's way of operating as well as the unchanging mathematical rules reflected in the unchanging harmony and beauty of the universe. For art theoreticians of the late sixteenth century, on the contrary, mathematical rules were thought to imprison the imagination and the creative power of the artist, and were, therefore, rejected (F. Zuccari, 1593-1607, Patrizi, 1586, Giordano Bruno, 1585).[246] These theories were nevertheless even farther removed from the most forceful painter among their own contemporaries, namely Caravaggio (1573-1610),

---

[243] Blunt, op. cit., p. 80, note 1 and see following note.

[244] Michelangelo's *Sonnets,* trans. by Frey: "Thus I know now how fraught with error was the fond imagination which made Art my idol and my king. . . . No brush, no chisel will quiet the soul, once it is turned to the divine love of Him who, upon the cross, outstretched his arms to take us to Himself"(c. 1554). "I have let the vanities of the world rob me of the time I had for the contemplation of God" (c. 1555).

[245] Panofsky, *Idea.* chapter 5; Summers, op. cit., pp 283-310.

[246] Giordano Bruno (1548-1600) recognized that "beauty is of many kinds," differing one from the other. He was aware that the essence of beauty, like the essence of pleasure and of the good, is indefinable and indescribable. He seems to have been one of the very earliest thinkers to have believed that the task of the artist was to create something that had never been created before, that was original and not in compliance with tradition. Bruno set the artist's personality and creativity in place of traditional rules. His *Degli eroici furori* (1585) was published in England, which is not without interest. For Giordano Bruno, who was ahead of his time, see Barasch, *Theories,* pp. 294-295; Panofsky, *Idea,* p. 219, note 76.

---

who was to revolutionize Western art.

The art theories of the time, even those of Federico Zuccari, himself a renowned painter then and president of the newly founded Academy of San Luca in Rome, appear totally anachronistic in relation to Caravaggio's work.[247] It is as if none of these theoreticians was capable either of recognizing or accepting the genius of the younger artist and the overwhelming emotional power of his work. At the same time, they had given greater importance to the personality of the individual artist, the rejection of normative rules, and the importance of the emotional impact of art. As Barasch underlines, in relation to Lomazzo: "the contradiction between the artist's individual psychology and the aesthetician's idea of a normative style came into the open, becoming a focal problem of any thought on art."[248] While the theories and the art of Zuccari and Lomazzo marked the end of a period, it was Caravaggio's paintings (fig. 75) that announced a new one, and it was Rubens (1577-1640), the other contemporary giant of Western painting (fig. 78), who was to recognize his exceptional quality.[249]

Caravaggio, on the other hand, as so many artists thereafter, did not seem to have been interested in these speculations about art, and even less in making beautiful works of art. His work lacked, in fact, all "grace," "facility" or "decorum," because Caravaggio's aim was not to please, but to stir the deepest and most sincere religious emotions. It thus becomes a very good example of a work that went against the established criteria of beauty, as well as all the theories of art of its own time, yet nevertheless defied the judgment of time (fig. 75).

75 Caravaggio, *Entombment*, 1602-03, Rome, Pinacoteca Vaticana

Giovanni Bellori wrote his text (*Vite*, 1672, prefaced by an essay of 1664, entitled *Idea del Pittore,*

---

[247] Such as the *Calling and Martyrdom of Saint Matthew* (c. 1598-1602) in San Luigi de' Francesi in Rome, or the *Entombment* (c. 1603), now in the Vatican Museum and, above all, his very last paintings: *Late Caravaggio*, Exhibition Catalogues, Naples and London, 2005.
[248] Barasch, *Theories*, p. 291.
[249] Walter Friedländer, *Caravaggio Studies*, Princeton, 1974, p. 195.

   The Path Toward Beauty

dello scultore e dell'architetto scelta delle bellezze naturali superiori alla Natura),[250] according "to the counsel of Nicolas Poussin," in which he bitterly criticised Caravaggio's crude
"naturalism" and even wondered how a man like Caravaggio could seriously "aspire to art
without understanding what art really is." For Bellori, art was the expression of an ideal of
beauty; hence, he could criticize Caravaggio because he did not "carry any idea in his mind"
and "accustomed himself to ugliness and error." He accused Caravaggio of appealing to the
lower classes who "refer everything they see to the visual sense, they praise things painted
naturally, being used to such things; they appreciate beautiful colours," whereas the noble
and the learned refer what they perceive to ideas rather than to ordinary objects of daily experience, they are in love with beauty and prefer beautiful forms and line to colour (Hume
and Kant were still to share that preference).

Bellori was, therefore, to re-establish the link between art and beauty by reasserting that
the aim of a work of art was to embody and manifest beauty. For him, a work of art had to
surpass Nature, creating ideally beautiful forms, though not in accord with a canon of beautiful proportions, as for Alberti, but because it was made by an artist who turned inward to
rediscover in himself the ideal, divine models. While this is reminiscent of Plato's *Timaeus*
and the demiurge creating the world according to ideal, unchanging, divine forms, Bellori
also acknowledged the existence of different types of beauty, one drawing on the beauty
of ancient statues, another on the natural beauty of the models or on grace, and revealing
still another beauty through line (*disegno*) and relief (*rilievo*). As much as he rejected the
"naturalism" of Caravaggio, he venerated Raphael's painting and was fascinated by Roman
antiquities.

For the French painter, Nicolas Poussin (1594-1665), Bellori's friend, "we must not
judge by our senses alone but by reason."[251] For him, painting had two aims: to move and
to please the beholder. It moved the beholder by representing human actions and emotions
and by conveying the mood of the scene convincingly. Depending on the emotion to be
conveyed, various movements of the body had to be chosen, focusing on the essentials of
the story, avoiding excessive details, and aiming at "simplicity." The painter had to please the
spectator, by making sure that he also understood and could read the story he was looking
at. In 1665, Poussin wrote: "painting is an imitation made on a surface with lines and colors
of everything one sees under the sun; its aim is delight (*sa fin est la delectation*)" (1665).[252]
Was he referring to sensual and intellectual pleasure, or to some sort of mystical state of
grace?[253]

---

[250] Panofsky, *Idea,* chapter 6 and Appendix II; Barasch, *Theories,* pp. 315 ff.

[251] Letter of Poussin to Chantelou, November, 1647, *Nicolas Poussin: lettres et propos sur l'art*, ed. A. Blunt,
Paris, 1964, p. 123.

[252] Ibid., pp. 163-165 and Barasch, *Theories,* pp. 324 ff.

[253] Barasch, ibid., p. 325: "Traditionally, *delectatio* carried mainly the connotation of sensual pleasure, but
in the mystical trend of the Baroque, it was frequently connected with the experience of divine grace."

Bellori's theories and Poussin's principles were to become those of the classical trend in the Parisian Academy of Painting and Sculpture, founded in 1645, where Bellori's concept of the *beau ideal* was pursued and became an essential part of any art education (fig. 76).

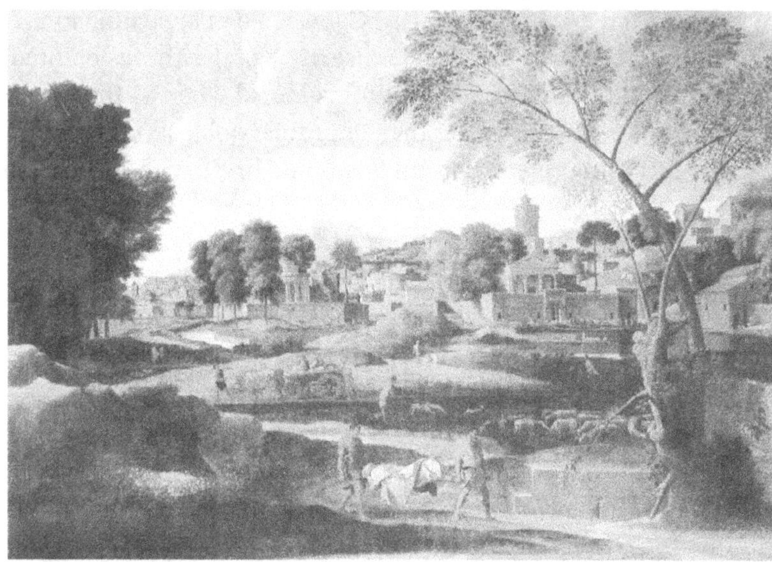

76 Nicholas Poussin, *Landscape with the Funeral of Phocion*, 1648, Paris, Musée du Louvre

For Charles Le Brun (1619-1690), the court painter of Louis XIV, and head of the Parisian Academy from 1663 to 1683 (date of Colbert's death),[254] ideal beauty could be obtained by copying exemplary works of art, such as ancient Roman statues and relief, or Raphael and Poussin, "in order to learn from them how one should draw from nature, and how to employ antiquity, in what manner the masters knew to correct nature itself, and to grant beauty and grace to those parts (of the body) that are in need of them."[255]

Recall how Leonardo da Vinci, on the contrary, had warned young artists not to learn from the masters, but from Nature herself, not to be a grandchild of Nature, but to be her son. As Barasch summarises: "Inherited forms and tradition are the essence of academism . . . to replace direct observation by ready models. . . . Culture was replacing experience." For Le Brun, the aim of art was not only to lead to perfection, but also to convey human emotions, not through the postures, movements and gestures of the body, as had been done so

---

[254] A. Blunt, *Art and Architecture in France, 1500 to 1700*, Pelican History of Art, 7, 1957, pp. 183 ff.

[255] Lectures of Charles Le Brun (1619-1690) in A. Fontaine, *Les doctrines de l'art en France*, chapters 3 and 4 and p. 64; N. Pevsner, *Academies of Art*, pp. 83-87; Barasch, *Theories*, pp. 331 ff. We will see how, on the contrary, Kant (1790), thought that beautiful art was produced only by a genius and could not be copied, below, pp. 131-133.

The Path Toward Beauty

far, but through facial expressions as well, since every single emotion was reflected on the human face and could be codified (fig. 77 a-b).

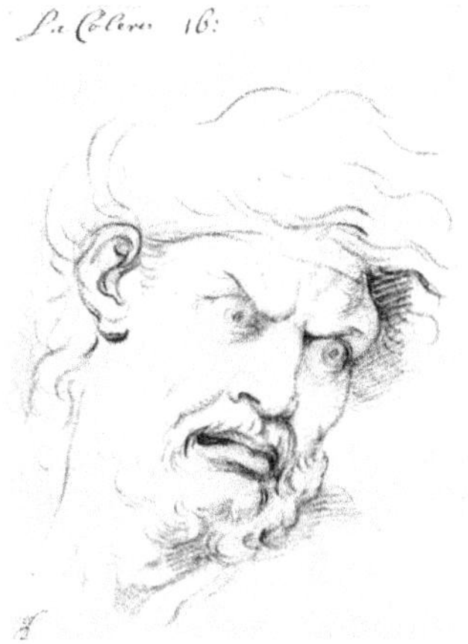

77 a   Charles Le Brun, *Anger* from *Expressions of the Passions of the Soul* c. 1670, Paris, Musée du Louvre

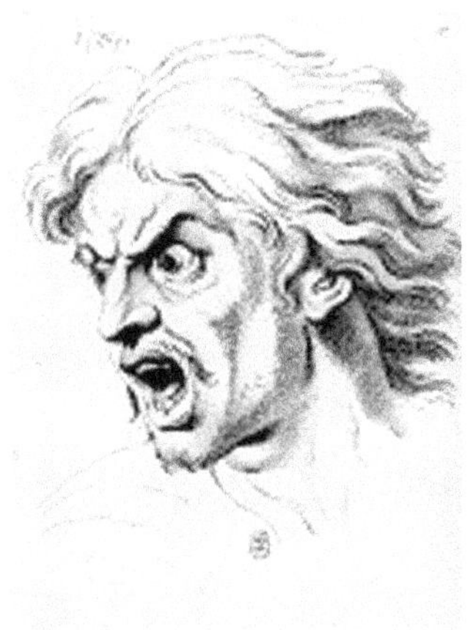

77 b   *Terror*, 18th century, engraved by Gérard Audran, Paris, Bibliothèque nationale (ms. BnF, Est, Kc 21, pl. 17)

His *Method to Learn to Draw the Passions* was illustrated by his own drawings as models (Descartes' *Passions of the Soul* was printed in 1649 and influenced Le Brun).[256] The portrayal of "passions," or of expression, was to become an important part of painting, along with composition, line and color, and was one of the contributions to art theory of the Parisian Academy. Under the leadership of Le Brun, a painting had to appeal essentially to the mind, and it was drawing that embodied reason, whereas colors appealed only to the eye and to the senses.[257] The Parisian Academy was also to propose criteria of judgment, which clearly revealed its own preferences. Thus, in 1667, Felibien established for the students of the Academy a hierarchy of pictorial genres according to subject matter. At the bottom of the ladder were still-life and landscape paintings, at the top the historical and allegorical paintings depicting the actions of man, God's most perfect creation.[258] Academic theory was furthermore to classify these figures, according to their social status, and to the scene in which they appeared. Hence, Le Nain's genre paintings belonged to the lowest level. Spectators were expected to share the same rigid judgment, even though the validity of many of

---

[256] What did Le Brun know about Hellenistic Pergamene sculpture, hence about their representation of *pathos* (see figs. 30 and 96-97)? Had he seen the *Laocoön*, excavated in Rome in 1506?

[257] This preference for drawing was to remain that of Hume as well as Kant, and for the same reasons.

[258] The same hierarchy was to be proposed by William Duff, *Essay on Original Genius,* 1767, and was to survive into the nineteenth century.

these rules was soon to be questioned, especially by the followers of Le Brun, among them Roger de Piles (president of the Parisian Academy in 1699).

The latter was to support the first passionate debate within the Academy about the role and significance of color in painting. Slowly, color rose to the top of the hierarchical ladder, taking the place of drawing and becoming the major component of painting. Rubens' paintings (fig. 78) became the models to be imitated instead of Raphael's or Poussin's. (fig. 76)

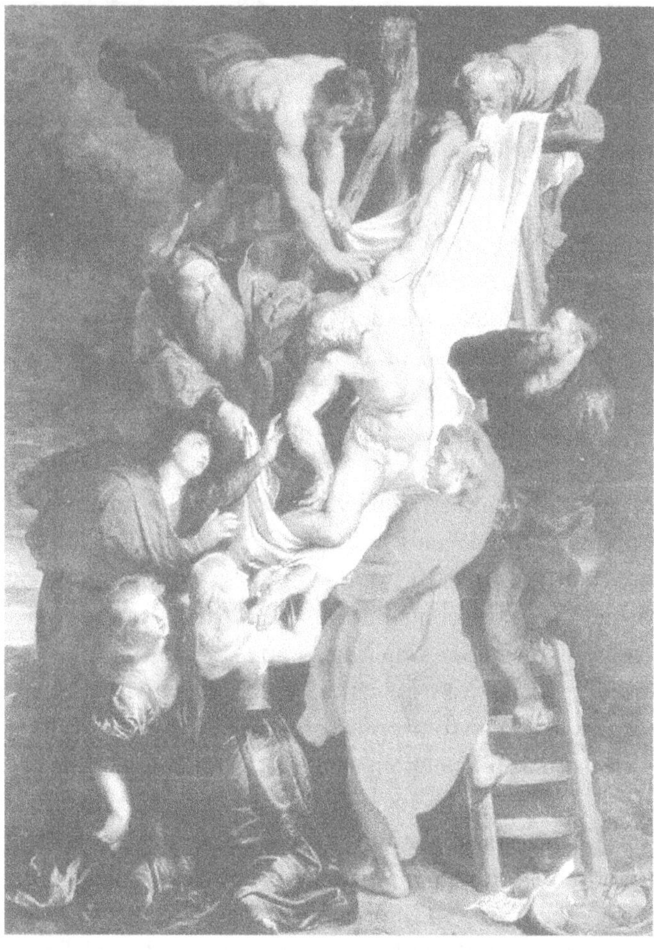

78 Peter Paul Rubens, *Descent from the Cross*, 1612, Antwerp, Cathedral

The recognized aim of painting remained, however, that of deceiving the eye, but color achieved that deception more convincingly than drawing.

Another dispute had reached its climax by the beginning of the eighteenth century, known as the *"Quarrel between the Ancients and the Moderns,"* which led to a new awareness of the value of the art of the present, no longer as an imitation of the ancients, but, on the contrary, superior to them. Thus, the reign of Louis XIV was considered superior to that of Augustus, and the art of all the artists who were at his service, superior to that of Antiquity and the Renaissance. As a result, royal patronage necessarily became the model for other art patrons.

In 1708, Roger de Piles even proposed a rating system of a certain number of selected artists of different "nations," according to a scale in which 20 stood for perfection. The artists were graded in composition, line, color and expression. Raphael still received the highest grades throughout, followed by Rubens. Even for expression, Raphael was rated 18, while Caravaggio was given 0, and Velázquez was not even mentioned. We are obviously confronted with a sample of personal preferences, reflecting those of the Parisian Academy, whereas de Piles believed that he was judging according to objective rules. Beauty, in the sense of the outstanding quality that defies the judgment of time, was not, or could not, be an academic criterion, nor could it be recognized by the taste of most "aestheticians," bound as they were to the taste of their own time.

What about taste? Just as the notion that the aim of art is to please and to move the emotions actually goes back to ancient Roman rhetoric, so, too, the notion of taste, which is either personal and subjective, or is "supra personal." These models, scales and hierarchies of genres were all meant to become standards of normative taste, which the Academy of the time of Le Brun called *grand goût* or "Grand Manner," and which also became the embodiment of social conventions as well as a synonym for good taste and beauty. At the beginning of the eighteenth century, de Piles still insisted: "There must be something great and extraordinary to surprise, please and instruct, which is what we call the *gran gusto,*" and "in painting the *gran gusto,* the sublime, the marvellous are one and the same thing."[259] He also distanced himself from the dogmatism of Le Brun, for whom only Antiquity, Raphael and Poussin could serve as models, and recognized different types of "good" art: "I love everything that is good in the work of great masters. . . . I love the diversity of schools: I like Raphael, I like Titian, I like Rubens." While acknowledging different types of beauty, de Piles also correlated each one to a different type of truth, either ideal truth based on the idea of the artist, simple truth consisting in the faithful representation of nature, or composite truth, which was the combination of both. Truth had ceased, by that time, to be one and absolute; it was composite and relative, and so was beauty related to the changing taste of the public.

Very gradually, this concept of the relativity of taste as well as of truth, appeared not only in the teaching of the Academy, but also in the judgment of an ever larger and more diversified audience that visited the exhibitions of academic artists (*Salons* of 1699 and 1725), admiring, criticizing and judging the works of art on display.[260] While the public became the judge, the appreciation of what appealed the most to the largest number of people, to "the public eye," was also to impose itself.

One example of this public judgment was J. B. Du Bos (*Critical Reflections on Poetry and Painting,* 1719) for whom art had to appeal to feelings (*sentiments*) and not to reason: it had to please and move.[261] Du Bos was read and discussed in England by David Hume and in Germany, translated by Lessing himself, the author of the *Laocoön* (in which Lessing, like Du Bos, compares poetry and painting) and was most probably also known to Kant. For Du Bos, the function of art was neither to instruct nor to move, but merely to give pleasure

---

[259] *Cours de peinture,* 1702, translated into English in 1707.
[260] Barasch, *Theories,* pp. 349 ff.
[261] Barasch, *Modern Theories,* 1, p. 11, n. 29, pp. 16 ff.; A. Lombard, *L'Abbé Du Bos: un initiateur de la pensée moderne,* Geneva, 1969.

to the beholder. What interested him was the spectator and not the artist. In his view, human beings experience pleasure when they cease to be bored and: "The pleasure one feels in looking at the imitations that the painters and the poets know how to make of objects that are apt to evoke passions in us, had they been presented to us in reality, is a pure pleasure, . . . capable of occupying us for a moment but not involving real suffering or emotion." The emotion was simply pure pleasure, which could not be provided by any painting in which the beholder would have confused art with reality because, in such a case, he would not have been removed from real passions. This concept of "pure pleasure" announced what Shaftesbury and Kant were to call "disinterested pleasure." Du Bos was also to reject all allegorical paintings because they depicted actions or figures that had never existed, and hence did not speak the language of the passions and could not move the spectator, but only stimulate his imagination. In any event, the spectator was the ultimate judge of the work of art; it is he who had to understand its meaning.

In very broad lines, the aim of art was thought to be that of pleasing the taste of the beholder, whose judgment was formed by social conventions and art theories promoted by the teachers of the Academy and critics, as well as by the exemplary patronage of the king and his followers. What was pleasing was also considered to be of good taste, and hence to be beautiful.

Eighteenth Century Philosophy and the Triumph of Subjectivism

Though artists, theoreticians of art, philosophers, and scientists of seventeenth and eighteenth-century Europe approached the world from different points of view, they all grew out of the same context and influenced each other. The historical and cultural developments of this period are too complex to discuss at length here, but we should keep in mind some scientific discoveries that profoundly affected Western thought. The discoveries of Copernicus (1473-1543), Kepler (1572-1630), Galileo (1564-1642), and Newton(1642-1727), the invention of new instruments of observation such as the telescope and the microscope, and the rise of the empirical approach to nature forced most intellectuals to interact differently with the world and to adopt a more sceptical view of their own beliefs and of theoretical knowledge. Not only was the earth no longer at the centre of the solar system,

> but one revolutionary conclusion of Galileo's new system was that power need not continually flow from God once nature became endowed with, uniform intrinsic necessity of its own. The communication of motion, which had played such an important role in the ancient world view and on which major arguments for the existence of God had rested, lost its significance in a mechanistic order where bodies, once they moved, would continue to do so until stopped by an external cause. . . . The new science of mechanics did not dispense with a Cre-

The Path Toward Beauty

ator who would initiate motion, but it appeared to withdraw God from nature after his creative act.[262]

Nature had become self-supporting, self-moving.

The laws of causality and traditional cosmology were called into question by various scientific discoveries. Increasingly, science was to define the story of the world and the last word no longer belonged to theology or Scripture as interpreted by the Church. The various religious reforms of the sixteenth century also encouraged a more critical approach to religion itself.

The philosophers of the seventeenth and eighteenth centuries were no longer theologians, and they no longer based their theories of knowledge strictly on logical arguments, but rather on sense experience and on scientific observation. They were no longer certain that the world was made according to the ideal geometric forms of Plato's *Timaeus*. As Dupré points out:

> Newton . . . questioned Copernicus and Kepler . . . and Galileo, . . . who still believed or rather presupposed nature's inclination towards a perfect geometrical order.[263]

The meaning of objectivity and subjectivity, of certitude and of doubt also changed. The subject became increasingly important as "he who thinks" and thus as a subject who conceives of the world, not as it is, but as he perceives and thinks it. The ontological proofs of God's existence were also undermined, and Kant, although he believed in God's existence, was to write in 1790: "I cannot know what God is."[264]

The status of the artist had also drastically changed during the Late Renaissance, when he was recognized as being "blessed with the creative gifts since his cradle" (L. Dolce, 1557; P. Aretino, 1550s; G.P. Lomazzo,1590) or was called a "mortal god" (Michelangelo, Raphael and Titian). In the second half of the eighteenth century, the artist also became a psychological type and his relation to his work and issues such as talent, genius and imagination, became matters of great concern.[265]

From this starting point, then, how were philosophers to deal with the concept of beauty?

Descartes, when asked by a musical theoretician to define beauty, answered doubtfully: "What pleases most people can be called simply the most beautiful, but this is not anything well defined." In *The Passions of the Soul* (1645-1656), he mentions emotions such as joy, sadness, love, and hatred that we may experience in reading stories or in watching theatre

---

[262] Louis Dupré, *Passage to Modernity,* New Haven, 1993, pp. 68 ff.

[263] Ibid., p. 78.

[264] Kant, *Analytic of the Teleological Judgment,* § 91. See below, p. 121.

[265] Barasch, *Theories,* p. 182 and pp 188 ff.; and idem, *Modern Theories,* 1, pp. 284 ff.

performances, but also wonders how these same passions can give us pleasure, "an intellectual pleasure which can arise from sadness in the same way as from the others." He also insisted on how the response of the spectator was influenced by his own recollections.

In the second half of the seventeenth century, Pierre Nicole, a teacher of philosophy at Port Royal (the center of the Jansenist movement), wrote a treatise about beauty in itself (*The Treatise on True and False Beauty*, 1659), demonstrating how true beauty does not, in fact, change; rather it is our point of view about beauty that is subjective and changing:

> If a thing is to be, it is not that it should be in accord merely with its own nature;
> it must also have the right relationship to ours. . . . Our taste is nearly always determined by custom and the attitude of others.

Pascal was also to declare that: "The broader one's mind, the greater the number of diverse beauties one sees."[266] Elsewhere, he calls that definable quality that appeals to people, and which we call beauty, the *je ne sais quoi*, the "I do not know what."[267]

While philosophers had doubts about the validity of a universal beauty recognized as such by all, they also observed that beauty was related to the pleasure of sense experience, hence to the changing taste of human beings. The existence of beauty in itself, like the existence of God, could no longer be demonstrated by reason or by science. Kant wrote:

> If we expressed this proposition dogmatically as objectively valid, it would be:
> There is a God. But for us men, there is only permissible the limited formula: We
> cannot otherwise think and make comprehensible the purposiveness which must
> lie at the bottom of our cognition (Kant, "Critique of the Teleological Judgment",
> *Critique of Judgment*, § 75).

This shift from a concept of absolute beauty (tantamount to the concept of God) to that of relative beauty determined by human taste took place at the same time as the Parisian Academy of Painting and Sculpture was striving, on the contrary, to impose a norm of taste through academic rules. At the same time, art teachers and theoreticians, critics and philosophers became increasingly interested in the spectator and his judgment, hence, in how to please him. A work of art was no longer made as an offering to God, but as an object to be enjoyed by a beholder.

Thus, for Hume[268] (1757) and for Kant (1790), beauty was also related to sense experience, providing a feeling of satisfaction and of "disinterested" pleasure (with no desire for possession, no utility and no moral implication) in the spectator. Both philosophers were not only deeply rooted in classical philosophy, but profoundly marked by the changes that

---

[266] *Discourse on the Passion of Love*, no. 31.
[267] Barasch, *Theories*, pp. 350-52.
[268] All references to David Hume, "Of the Standards of Taste," *Four Dissertations*, London, 1757, are taken from *Aesthetics*, ed. by J. Stolnitz, London, 1965.

occurred in Western thought during the seventeenth and early eighteenth centuries.

Hume declares that beauty exists only in the mind that perceives it, and that each mind perceives a different beauty, hence:

> To seek the real beauty or real deformity is as fruitless an enquiry as to pretend to ascertain the real sweet and the real bitter. . . . Though it be certain that beauty and deformity, more than sweet and bitter, are not qualities in objects, but belong entirely to sentiments.
>
> Beauty had to give pleasure, which differed from one person to another. There was, in fact, no innate idea of beauty; beauty was perceived and experienced subjectively and was always related to taste for which there was, in fact, no standard. [269]

While Hume used what he called "good sense,"[270] he also recognized that:

> The same Homer who pleased in Athens and Rome, is still admired in Paris and in London. All the changes of climate, government, religion and language have not been able to obscure his glory. . . . It appears then that, amidst all the variety and caprice of taste, there are certain general principles of approbation and blame, whose influence a careful eye may trace in all operations of the mind.

He also observed that in all nobler productions of genius one could find "a mutual relation and correspondence of parts" (the good, old principle of *symmetria*), and that "every work of art had also a certain end and purpose for which it was calculated, deemed more or less perfect as it was more or less fitted to attain this end." This concept of purpose was at the heart of the philosophy of the time. It was related to the question of causality and predetermination, i.e., did God will everything, did He endow nature with purposiveness, or, on the contrary, are human beings the ones who give meaning and purpose to the world?

Hume also states that certain authors "gain public applause, which they maintain forever" that there are general uniform principles of taste in human nature.

> Where men vary in their judgments, some defects or perversions in the faculties may be commonly remarked, proceeding either from prejudices, from want of practice, or want of delicacy; and there is just reason for approving one taste and

---

[269] D. Summers, defines judgment as taking place between *means* and *standards*. A mean is "a point in a continuum between two extremes, a standard is something above any actual thing, relative to which the truth or validity of an actual thing may be determined. The relation between *means* and *standards* being, of course, a difficult thing". (*The Judgment of Sense*, pp. 23 ff.) Plato was interested in *standards*, as were most other civilizations. Aristotle, whose writings had more influence on Kant, was interested in *means*.

[270] For the meaning, not of *good*, but of *common sense*, from Aristotle to Kant, see D. Summers, op. cit., pp. 78-109.

condemning another. . . . In that case a certain degree of diversity in judgment is unavoidable, and we seek in vain for a standard, by which we can reconcile the contrary sentiments. . . . At twenty, Ovid may be the favourite author; Horace, at forty and perhaps Tacitus, at fifty. . . . We choose our favorite author as we do our friend, from a conformity of humour and disposition. . . . A certain degree of diversity in judgment is unavoidable, and we seek in vain for a standard, by which we can reconcile the contrary sentiments.

For him, the spectator, as judge, must necessarily have the same knowledge as the artist and therefore have "the same address and dexterity, which practice gives to the execution of any work." The spectator had to be able to judge "how far the means employed are adapted to their respective purposes" and to have:

The same clearness of conception, the same exactness of distinction, the same vivacity of apprehension, essential to the operation of true taste. A man who has a just taste has also a sound understanding. . . . Thus, though the principles of taste be universal, and, nearly, if not entirely the same for all men, yet few are qualified to give judgment on any work of art, or establish their own sentiment as the standard of taste.

This link between the "appreciation" of beauty and adequate knowledge and understanding was common to many philosophers: beauty has to do with knowledge, wrote Saint Thomas Aquinas.[271]

While Hume mentions specific authors, such as Homer, Virgil, Aristotle, Plato, Epicurus, Descartes, Cervantes and Milton, but no visual works of art, he also recognizes that there must be some universal principles of taste since there is universal agreement on their work, which defied the judgment of time. Nevertheless, he insists that there is no standard of taste, hence no universal criteria by which to judge beauty.

Kant was to pick up where Hume left off, while going much farther. His *Critique of Judgment* (1790) became the most important, or rather, the best known, contribution to the Western concept of beauty in the modern age, just as Plato's dialogues and certain Neo-Platonic texts had been the most important for Antiquity, the Middle Ages and the Renaissance.[272]

Towards the end of the eighteenth century, a work of art was generally envisaged as an

---

[271] Petrarca and Boccaccio declared that the ignorant could not understand the beauty of Giotto's paintings, which could only be grasped by those who knew (Baxandall, *Giotto and the Orators*, 1971, p. 60). Alberti wrote that "the idea of beauty, which the most expert have difficulty in discerning, eludes the ignorant" (*Della Pittura*, III, 56).

[272] Platonic and Neo-Platonic philosophy of beauty was to be revalidated all the way up to the abstract painters of the twentieth century.

object to be enjoyed aesthetically by an increasingly large number of people, and its beauty was meant, as we saw before, to elicit a feeling of pleasure in the beholder. The work of art was seldom considered in relation to its specific function, its *raison d'être*, which constituted its iconographical meaning. All of those would have referred to the purpose of the work, and not only to its form. As we mentioned above, the issue of purpose was an important philosophical issue, linked to that of causality, and not to iconography: did God will a thing to be as it is, or is it the human being who endows it with purpose? This question was raised by Francis Bacon in the early seventeenth century and was to remain one of the main issues for Kant as well.

Furthermore, the mathematical idealism of Pythagoras and of Plato, according to which the cosmos was conceived as mathematically ordered, which had dominated the Italian Renaissance up to the late sixteenth century, had lost its hold. Similarly, as we saw earlier, the idea that artistic forms had to reflect that order through ideal proportions or conformity to the circle or to the square, was abandoned. Nowhere, in fact, does Kant refer to a mathematical order, even when he writes about beautiful art, although he still seems to perceive nature as a well-ordered totality.

In his *Critique of Judgment*,[273] Kant deals with the beauty of nature as well that of art, but this *Critique* is the third and last volume of a trilogy.[274]

Philosophically, the term *Critique* itself assumes a precise meaning in the eighteenth century. A critical attitude of the mind consists in observing how that very same mind functions, what it means to think and to comprehend, which mental operations ensure or enable our knowledge, and what are the validity and limits of knowledge.

---

[273] "Judging" derives from the Latin *iudicare,* which translates the Greek *krinein,* meaning to distinguish, to discriminate or separate, which also gives the substantive of *kritikon,* the faculty of judging. In Latin, we also have the verb *cernere,* to discern.

[274] The *Critique of Judgment* consists of two parts, the *Critique of the Aesthetical Judgment* and that of the *Teleological Judgment.* We are essentially concerned with the first part, the *Analytic* and the *Dialectic of the Aesthetical Judgment.* The *Analytic* itself is furthermore divided into two books: the *Analytic of the Beautiful* and the *Analytic of the Sublime.* This *Critique of Judgment* is, however, also the last part of a trilogy, and is preceded by *The Critique of Pure Reason* (1781 and 1787) and by *The Critique of Practical Reason* (1788); hence, it cannot be understood independently. *The Critique of the Teleological Judgment* must thus be considered as the conclusion to all three *Critiques* and not only to the *Critique of Judgment.* In the same way the *Analytic of the Sublime* must also be understood as the continuation of the *Analytic of the Beautiful* or as the second step in one and the same analysis. Immanuel Kant, *Critique of Judgment*, originally published in Berlin in 1790 and in 1793, translated in English by J. H. Bernard, (Dublin, 1892), New York, The Hafner Library of Classics, 1968. Bernard's translation is archaic, and readers may prefer to consult more recent ones, such as that by Paul Guyer, published by Cambridge University Press, 2000.

"What can I know?" is the question raised by the The *Critique of Pure Reason* (1781).[275] For Kant, knowledge has two different but totally intertwined origins: our mental apparatus, prior to any experience, hence a priori, and the subsequent a posteriori experience. We experience and understand natural phenomena through principles (*Verstandesbegriffe*) that are determined by our own mind, and not by the outer world, hence by the subject and not by the object. Kant maintains, for example, the necessity of a causal law as an a priori category of our faculty of knowledge, which therefore precedes our experience, and which is necessary and universal. Hence, it is not a posteriori and it is not based on habit or imagination, as Hume had asserted. It is our mind which structures nature through its own a priori laws and not the other way round, but we can only assert that which we can also experience and nothing else. We cannot experience nature outside a priori notions of time and space. We cannot understand the world outside a number of a priori categories or concepts (*Kategorien oder Verstandesbegriffe*) such as that of the relation of cause to effect. We cannot think or know the objective world of phenomena outside any of these subjective and a priori principles and other forms of consciousness (*Erkenntnissbegriffe*), but we can only apply these principles to the world of appearances (*phenomena),* which is the only one which is real, and not to that of things in themselves (*noumena*) ideas such as that of the world in itself, or for that matter of anything in itself, or of the soul as such, or of the existence of God. Knowledge can only exist and be proven to be exact when a priori concepts are applied to *phenomena*, not to *noumena* of which we cannot know anything. These are related to a priori ideas that Kant defines as "concepts of reason" (*Vernunftbegriffe),* outside the notions of time and space and of the a priori concepts or categories of understanding. Reason cannot demonstrate what it knows, hence all the so-called proofs of God's existence are not genuine demonstrations.

In the second *Critique of Practical Reason* (1788), Kant is no longer concerned with pure theory, but with practice, not with man's thinking, but with his actions, i.e., with morality, whose subject is the good. Here, he is focused on the human necessity to respect moral law, to assume it as a guiding principle for human conduct and to act according to duty. He thinks that moral law determines human nature, although it can only be put into practice through the free will of the individual according to his individual conscience. Thus, there is a moral law, which belongs to the sphere of reason, and there is moral feeling, linked to the human desire for happiness and hence for pleasure, though the one does not determine the other. Nevertheless, this pleasure belongs to the world of subjective experience and not of objective knowledge. In the third and last work, the *Critique of Judgment,* Kant does not deal with reason or with morals, but only with feelings, and more specifically, with the feel-

---

[275] See also D. Summers, op. cit. for the definition and the historical background of most of the terms that were to be used by Kant, such as pleasure of sense, imagination, free will, common sense, taste, spirit, genius, and so on.

   The Path Toward Beauty

ings of pleasure and pain. In the *Critique of the Aesthetical Judgment,* Kant deals with the beauty of nature and art as if they were analogous, insofar as art is an imitation of nature, but produced by man. To view nature in its overall beauty or, on the contrary, as chaos, gives us either pleasure or pain, while it also makes us wonder if there is any finality, or purpose in this beauty. If nature is purposeful, i.e; if there is a purpose (*Zweck*) in what we find beautiful, then this aim towards a purpose is the secret of its beauty; or, is man alone purposeful, and hence, is there a purpose only in *his* products, i.e., in beautiful art?

The Analytic of the Beautiful (§ 1 - § 22)

Aesthetic judgment rests on no rational concepts and does not tell us anything about the object. It refers only to pleasure. For Kant: "The object of such satisfaction is called beautiful"(§ 6).

> Everyone has his own taste as regards to the pleasant" [276] and "there can be no rule according to which anyone is to be forced to recognize anything as beautiful" even though, "if we call the object beautiful we believe that we speak with a universal voice and we claim the assent of everybody. . . . The judgment of taste itself does not postulate the agreement of everyone (for that can only be done by a logically universal judgment because it can adduce reasons). . . . The universal voice is only an idea" (§ 8).

The pleasure in the object precedes the judgment of taste, and this pleasure is subjective, hence independent of any concept of the object; it is nothing but a state of the mind.

> Beauty without a reference to the feeling of the subject is nothing in itself (§ 9).

> The faculty for judging the beautiful is not related to reason, but is a feeling resting on subjective grounds (§ 15).

> There can be no objective rule of taste to determine by means of concepts what is beautiful. . . . To seek for a principle of taste that might furnish, by means of definite concepts, a universal criterion of the beautiful is fruitless trouble, because what is sought is impossible and self-contradictory (§ 17).

---

[276] See § 29 and § 44 where Kant differentiates between "the pleasant, . . . which has no reference to culture, but belongs to mere enjoyment," and "the beautiful, which requires the representation of a certain *quality* of the object, that can be made intelligible and reduced to concepts; . . . and it cultivates us in that it teaches us to attend to the purposiveness in the feeling of pleasure." This distinction will become clearer as we proceed.

The beautiful is that which, without any concept, is known as the object of a necessary satisfaction (§ 22).

Beauty, as a thing in itself, is for Kant an indemonstrable idea, along with the beauty of nature and of art.

Aside from his native Koeningsberg, what natural beauty, and which visual works of art, besides the few that he seems to have known only through secondary sources, did Kant ever see?[277] It would appear, in fact, that Kant was only interested in epistemological problems, and not in art. He seems never to have left his native town, nor ever to have experienced a "sublime" alpine landscape. He also refers only exceptionally to the beauty of any specific object, but speaks generically of the beauty of the tree, the garden, the building, the painting, the piece of music, etc.

When he refers to the "formative arts" (*bildende Form*: painting, sculpture, architecture, horticulture), he considers *delineation* or drawing in general as "the proper object of the pure judgment of taste and of what pleases," and not the colors that belong to charm (§ 14 and § 53). Delineation and composition "constitute the proper object of the pure judgment of taste, whereas colors awaken and fix our attention on the object itself" (§13); and "ornaments," used "merely to recommend the painting by its charm" thus are "finery" and detract from "genuine beauty" (§ 13). In spite of Kant's apparent lack of exposure to any major work of art, his own artistic taste, if he had any, was in keeping with that of his contemporaries. Thus, he shared Hume's preference for drawing. He also preferred the imagination found in English gardens to the stiff regularity of French formal gardens, or "what is not subject to the constraint of artificial rules" (§ 22), while he considers "that taste barbaric which needs a mixture of charm and emotions in order that there may be satisfaction" (§ 13). Within the overall context of the history of art, Kant wrote his trilogy between the

---

[277] In the "formative arts," he mentions only two classical Greek statues: Polycleitus' *Spear Holder* and the *Cow* of Myron (§ 17), neither of which he had ever seen, but which he might have known through Winckelmann's *History of Ancient Art* (1757). For Winckelmann and his enormous impact on the history of the visual arts, cf. Barasch, *Modern Theories,* 1, pp. 97-121. Kant, however, does not consider the two statues beautiful in relation to any ideal of beauty, or because of any principle of *symmetria*, but simply because they are correct representations of men. He also mentions the pyramids of Egypt and Saint Peter's in Rome (§ 26), because of their well known size. In literature, he mentions Homer, only once (§ 47), and another time a play by Voltaire (§ 54). For music, he mentions no work at all. More literary works were mentioned in his earlier *Observations on the Feeling of the Beautiful and the Sublime* (1764). On the other hand, he makes frequent references to contemporary philosophers.

　　　　　The Path Toward Beauty

triumph of Neo-Classicism and the approaching "upheavals" of Romanticism.[278]

At this stage of his analysis of the judgment of taste, Kant seems to refer only to the beauty of formal elements, as if the beautiful had no other purpose beyond its formal characteristics. If the object had any objective purpose, such as utility, it could not give us any immediate satisfaction, "which is the essential condition of a judgment about beauty." If, on the other hand, its purpose is perfection, which is the concept closest to that of beauty, this perfection could only be formal and therefore in accordance only "with the subject's internal feeling," it could not give any cognition (*Erkenntniss*) of the object itself. Beauty is not ideal for Kant either, because "there can be no objective rule of taste to determine by means of concepts (*Begriffe*) what is beautiful (§ 17).

Therefore:

> The satisfaction in beauty is such as presupposes no concept. . . . If now the judgment of taste in respect of the beauty of a thing is made dependent on the purpose in its manifold aspects (*das Mannigfaltige*), like a judgment of reason, and thus limited, it is no longer a free and pure judgment of taste (§ 16).

He then refers to two types of pleasure, and hence to two different judgments of taste, according to whether or not one knows the purpose of the object. In the first case, the pleasure is sensuous, and it is only related to the object one has in front of one's eyes; in the second case, it is an intellectual pleasure that refers to what one has in one's mind.

> By means of this distinction, we can settle many disputes about beauty between judges of taste by showing that one is speaking of free, the other of dependent

---

[278] Winkelmann's writings, as representative of Neo-Classicism, were published between 1755 and 1768: *Thought on the Imitation of the Greek Works of Painting and Sculpture,* 1755, and *History of Ancient Art,* 1768. For him, ideal beauty was devoid of any emotional expression and was not supposed to arouse passions. He was against the art of Bernini, but also against that of his own time. Beauty consisted in shape and not in color. For him, the beautiful was never detached from the morally good. Diderot's *Essays and Criticism* (1750s and 1760s), his "Essay on Beauty," in the *Encyclopédie* were published in 1772. In the latter, he defends beauty especially in relation to the person experiencing it. Elsewhere, he defends the spontaneity of the sketch against the finished quality of the Academy's paintings, denying the importance of rules that "injured the man of genius," while also insisting on the morality of the subject matter, which often resulted in poor judgment. In Joshua Reynolds's *Discourses* (1769 and 1790), especially in his thirteenth discourse, he is concerned with imagination which becomes "the residence of truth," against imitation. He worships Michelangelo, especially in his last discourse of 1790, as the prototype of "subjective" art, of the creative power of genius (independent of tradition), and of the sublime. Raphael remained the representative of the academic tradition. Special attention should also be paid to William Duff's *Essay on Original Genius* (1767). Works of other German authors and artists, not to mention English or French philosophers, as well as Italian art theoreticians, might also be mentioned, all of them belonging to Kant's Zeitgeist: Lessing's *Laocoön* (1766), Herder's *Plastik* (1778), etc. Kant's own first *Observations on the Beautiful and the Sublime,* dates from 1764. All precede Kant's *Critique of Judgment* (1790).

---

beauty, that the first is making a pure, and the second, an applied judgment of taste (§ 16).

In today's terms, we would relate intellectual pleasure to what we now call an iconographic analysis, through which we attempt to understand the overall meaning of the work of art in the context of its own time and its particular function or purpose. Kant could only envisage art as an imitation of nature, thus "beautiful art must look like nature although we are conscious of it as art," (§ 45) and natural beauty is *a beautiful thing*, whereas artificial beauty is *a beautiful representation* of a thing (§ 48). In the *Analytic of the Beautiful*, Kant deals, in fact, only with the pleasure of the beholder and with the pure judgment of taste, showing how beauty is not related to the object at all, and hence to its purpose, but solely to the spectator's feeling of disinterested pleasure. Beauty is thus a state of mind, which cannot be explained by rational or moral means, nor be understood through the critique of pure or practical reason. The judgment of taste, however, like any judgment, claims, or indeed demands, universal assent (§ 19); when we call an object beautiful, we believe we are speaking for everybody, which is nevertheless an illusion, because: "There can be no rule according to which anyone is to be forced to recognize anything as beautiful," and hence, there cannot be any claim to universality. But in that case, how can we share this judgment of taste with everyone? If "the beautiful is that which, without any concept, is known as the object of a necessary satisfaction," we can only communicate "some subjective principle which determines what pleases or displeases only by feeling, and not by concepts, but yet with universal validity"(§ 20). Thus, we can only communicate our subjective feeling of pleasure universally, even though it is not based on any concept, but rather on what we call "common sense."

Kant is not very clear about this alleged "common sense" (§ 22). For Aristotle, common sense was related to knowledge linked to the sensations of the five senses, but also to intuition or what he called a "common sensation," a kind of middle term between sense and reason, or between what we know through the senses, which is particular, and that which we know through the intellect, which has universal validity. Kant may already be thinking of another faculty, that of imagination.[279] He ends, in fact, the *Analytic of the Beautiful*, with another definition of taste, as "a faculty of judging an object in reference to the imagination's free conformity to laws," which he illustrates with the image of "the sight of the changing shapes of a fire on the hearth or of a rippling brook; neither of these has beauty, but they bring with them charm for the imagination because they entertain it in a free play" (§ 22). Kant uses this image to provide a transition between the *Analytic of the Beautiful* and the *Analytic of the Sublime.*

Whereas, in the former, Kant deals only with a finite world and with the sense experi-

---

[279] For the overall concept of "Common Sense," see Summers, op. cit, Chapter 5, pp. 71 ff.

ence of the beholder, in the latter, he deals with the beholder's imagination as an instrument of reason, used to think or imagine the infinite and the non-definable, as well as with the imagination of the artist or the genius who produces beautiful art. Beautiful art is thus an integral part of the *Analytic of the Sublime*! Kant is gradually moving from the world of the beholder to that of the maker, from the world of sense experience to that of imagination, and from the first to the second step of the *Critique of Aesthetical Judgment*.

In the *Analytic of the Sublime* (§ 23-54),[280] Kant is concerned at first with the infinite,[281] the boundless, the indefinable, the immeasurable, with the sheer vastness of Nature:

> We call that sublime (*das Erhabene*) which is absolutely great, . . . great beyond all comparison (§ 25).

> Nature is therefore sublime in those of its phenomena whose intuition brings with it the idea of its infinity . . . The bare capability of thinking this infinite requires in the human mind a faculty itself suprasensible (*übersinnlich*), . . . because it is great beyond all standards of sense (§ 26).

Kant first relates the Sublime to magnitude and might in nature, as well as to anything that excites a feeling of fear and pain or a feeling of awe. Hence, he refers to the "Sublimity" of God, and to the awe—not the fear—of God, whose divine greatness one admires; to the "Sublimity" of that "Being" which induces respect in us, but which, like beauty, resides in no outer object, but only in the mind (§ 28).

> That the mind be attuned to feel the sublime postulates a susceptibility of the mind to ideas. . . . In fact, without development of moral ideas, that which we, prepared by culture, call sublime presents itself to the uneducated terrifying as terrible (because fearful) (§ 29).

Kant thus establishes a link between the feeling of the sublime and moral feeling, which he believes to be common to all human beings who have had a moral education (Kant calls it "moral culture"), and which prepares them to be attuned to the feeling of the sublime. For Kant, "the bare capability of thinking this infinite requires in the human mind a faculty itself suprasensible," and the aesthetic judgment of the sublime in nature requires far more cultivation than a judgment of the beautiful (§ 29) because it has to use a "mental dispo-

---

[280] The sublime is a concept that dates back to Longinus, a Greek rhetorician of the third century B.C.E. It resurfaced as a conceptual category in the eighteenth century when it was related to the visual arts, e.g., Burke. Barasch, *Modern Theories*, 1, pp. 73 ff. and bibliography.

[281] In his *De l'infinito*, Giordano Bruno (1548-1600) describes the infinite universe without a fixed center and without bounds, "stretching out beyond any calculation of space and time": see L. Dupré, *Passage to Modernity*, New Haven, 1993, p. 61. See also: A. Koyré, *From the Closed World to the Infinite Universe*, New York, 1958.

sition," imagination. Through the imagination, Kant leads us into a region beyond sense experience and beyond what we can conceive through the intellect, as if imagination was neither perception nor thought, although still related to perception. It is as if imagination[282] was, as Aristotle wrote, "the point where sense and reason meet."[283]

Kant considers imagination as an instrument of reason, as the faculty or ability of the mind to form images or ideas, even though it does not refer to concepts. It is only related to reason through "a subjective presupposition," which is common to all men, along with moral ideas. Kant "ascribes necessity" to the aesthetical judgment of the sublime, just as he "ascribed necessity" to the law of causality in the *Critique of Pure Reason* and to moral law or duty, in the *Critique of Practical Reason*. What is important is that Kant does not consider this "subjective presupposition" any less valid than any "objective supposition." This observation seems particularly significant in the context of our present reflection.

If the beautiful is what gives us disinterested pleasure, the sublime prepares us "to esteem something highly even in opposition to our own sensible interests," i.e., even when we are afraid in front of the limitless "sublimity" of nature, or of God, and this thanks to imagination as well.

> In fact the feeling of the sublime in nature cannot well be thought without combining therewith a mental disposition which is akin to the moral. . . . In aesthetic judgment upon the sublime this dominion (of reason over sensibility) is represented as exercised by the imagination, regarded as an instrument of reason (§ 29).

If Kant has referred so far mainly to the sublime of Nature, he now turns his attention to the beautiful arts as representations of nature. Nature (as the "superhuman art") is the model of human art, but "beautiful arts must necessarily be considered as arts of genius" (§ 49). The standard of the aesthetic judgment of these beautiful arts is no longer related to a mere subjective sensation, but to a reflective judgment. Thus, Kant shifts from the be-

---

[282] M. W. Bundy, *The Theory of Imagination in Classical and Medieval Thought*, Urbana, University of Illinois, Studies in Language and Literature, XII, 1927, pp. 7-289.

[283] For Aristotle's concept of imagination as well as for that of subsequent philosophers, see Summers, op. cit., "Introduction; "Pleasure and imagination;" pp. 62-63; "Cogitation and human imagination", pp. 211 ff., and W. Duff, *Essay on Original Genius,* 1767, summarized by Barasch, *Modern Theories,* 1, pp. 285-289.

holder's feeling of beauty to the nature of the producer of beautiful art, the genius.[284] What are the prerequisites for producing beautiful arts that can only be those of a genius (§ 46 and § 47)?

Beautiful art must, first of all, have some purpose (*Absicht*), because otherwise it would be "a mere product of chance." For Kant, one does not have to know the purpose of natural beauty in order to be pleased by it. It is something that is simply given, whereas one must know and understand the purpose of beautiful art. We have thus moved away from the earlier statements of the *Analytic of the Beautiful*, in which Kant was taking into account only the formal beauty of an object that pleased the taste of the beholder and denying that it had any purpose at all. We will understand better what Kant means by "purpose" in § 49.

What are the prerequisites of genius?

The genius "who is a favourite of nature and must be regarded as a rare phenomenon" has, first of all, to understand the purpose of art, but in order to produce such art, he must have:

> artistic skill, imparted to every artist by the hand of nature, . . . a natural gift which must prescribe its rule to art, . . . a rule which cannot be reduced to a formula and serve as a precept, for then the judgement upon the beautiful would be determinable according to concepts.

There is therefore "something *scholastic* as an essential condition for any beautiful art." The rules are those that nature herself imparts to the artist who imitates her. Besides all

---

[284]At the end of the chapter on *Beauty and Creativity*, we mentioned how the concepts of genius, creativity, imagination and originality, in the sense of novelty, have been emphasized ever since the sixteenth century. These notions were to be developed further in the literature from the late sixteenth century onward. Thus, Lomazzo, in his *Idea del Tempio della Pittura*, 1590, ed. R. Klein, in 1974, or Roger De Piles in his *Abrège de la Vie des Peintres*, 1699, whose first sentence states that: "Genius is the first thing we must suppose in a painter, it is the part of him that cannot be acquired by study and labor," without making academic schooling superfluous, on the contrary. Major concern was given to these concepts throughout Europe in the late eigteenth century, for example in W. Duff's *Essay on the Original Genius*, 1767 or in J. G. Sulzer, in 1771-1777. (Barasch, *Modern Theories*, 1, pp. 285 ff); Summers, op. cit., pp. 122-124, where the author summarizes Lomazzo's ideas, which are very similar to those of Kant, namely that art is superior to nature, that genius is a natural disposition and inclination, that one cannot reach excellence without genius, etc. See also H. G. Tonelli, "Genius from the Renaissance to 1770," R. Wittkower, "Genius: Individualism in Art and Artists," and E. E. Lowinsky, "Musical Genius" in: *The Dictionary of the History of Ideas*, II, pp. 296-326.

these conditions, a genius must have "originality"[285] the talent (which) constitutes the essential (though not the only) element in the character of the genius. None of these elements can exist without the others (§ 47). For art to be beautiful, it has therefore to be produced by a genius.[286] The rule followed by a genius may become a model for his followers, even though it is hard to explain how that can be done without becoming a mere "aping" of his work, or a form of mannerism. In fact, his work cannot be imitated; it can only set an example for the awakening of another genius (§ 49).

Beautiful art shows a superiority to nature, not only because it can represent something that is ugly in nature (such as war or disease) as something beautiful, but because it can represent a concept which can be universally communicated thanks to the representation itself (§ 48). But how does this take place? Not as the result of some type of sudden inspiration, but as the result of a very long process of gradual improvement.

> The artist does not find this form as a thing of inspiration or as the result of a free swing of the mental powers, but of a slow and even painful process of improvement, by which he seeks to render it adequate to his thought, without detriment to the freedom of the play of his powers (§ 48).

The pleasing form which the artist gives to his work becomes only a means, a vehicle of communication:

> The pleasing form that is given to it is only the vehicle of communication and a mode, as it were, of presenting it . . . although it is combined with a definite purpose.

---

[285] Kant may use this term in the same way as William Duff uses it, for whom originality is a synonym for genius and of creativity. Thus by "the word *original* when applied to Genius, we mean that native and radical power which the mind possesses, of discovering something new and uncommon in every subject on which it employs its faculties. . . . The word *original*, considered in connection with Genius, indicates the Degree, not the Kind of this accomplishment and it always denotes its highest degree." Duff applies "original genius" to history painting for which there is only a short description, and "the Painter must imagine the rest." (Barasch, *Modern Theories,* 1, pp. 287, 289). Shaftesbury, who was also in Kant's Zeitgeist, wrote: "All is invention (the first part of painting), creation, divining, a sort of prophesying and inspiration, the poetical ecstatic and rapture . Things that were never seen; nor that ever were: yet feigned. Painter as poet, a second maker" (Hofstadter and Kuhns, p. 276).

[286] At the end of § 47, Kant comes back to the beholder's judgment, which could very well be that of our own time, and writes: "But it is quite ridiculous for a man to speak and decide like a genius in things which require the most careful investigation by reason. One does not know whether to laugh more at the impostor who spreads such a mist round him that we cannot clearly use our judgment, and so use our imagination the more, or at the public which naïvely imagines its inability to cognize (*erkennen*) clearly and to comprehend the masterpiece before it arises from new truths crowding in on it in such abundance . . . that details seem clumsy work."

                    The Path Toward Beauty

It would seem, then, that the formal beauty of any work becomes a symbol of what lies beyond it.

Still there is another essential "animating principle of the mind," which the genius must have for any art to be beautiful at all, and that is the Spirit (*Geist).*

> [Spirit] is the name given to the animating principle of the mind, . . . which animates the soul (*Seele*), . . . it is what puts the mental powers purposively (*zweckmässig*) into swing. . . . This principle is nothing other than the faculty of presenting aesthetical ideas. And by *aesthetical ideas,* I understand that representation of the imagination which occasions much thought, i.e., any concept, being capable of being adequate to it; it consequently cannot be . . . made intelligible by language. We easily see that it is the counterpart (*Pendant*) of a *rational idea,* which conversely is a concept to which no *intuition* (or representation of the imagination) can be adequate (§ 49).

If this Spirit is lacking there can be no beautiful art.[287] It is what puts the imagination itself "purposively" into motion. Through imagination, the genius can present, or rather re-present, ideas that cannot be made intelligible by language, and that thus become the counterpart of rational concepts .

> Imagination (as a productive faculty of cognition) is very powerful in creating another nature, as it were, out of the material that nature gives it, so that the material supplied to us by nature can be worked up . . . into something different which surpasses nature. . . . Such representations of the imagination we may call *ideas,* partly because they strive after something which lies beyond the bounds of experience and so seek to approximate a presentation of concepts of reason (intellectual ideas), but especially because no concept can fully be adequate to them as internal intuitions, thus giving to the latter the appearance of objective reality (§ 49).

These representations of the imagination

> stimulate more thought than can ever be comprehended in a definite concept, . . . and which consequently enlarge the concept itself in an unbounded fashion, because the imagination is here creative, and it brings the faculty of intellectual

---

[287] Summers, Chapter 6: "Spiritus," pp. 110 ff. The concept of the *Spirit,* like most other Kantian concepts, is not new in western Philosophy; it is the *pneuma* of the Stoics and of the Neo-Platonists, which is, furthermore, related to "genius" in Late Renaissance art theory, in Paolo Pino and in Lomazzo. It is the *Spiritus* of Saint Augustine, as the power of the soul, but also as the basis of the images that we form in our mind, etc.

Recall as well the *Ch'i*—the vital breath—of Chinese Painting, the *prana* of the Hindu, or the *ase*—the vital energy—of Yoruba sculpture. The essential and indefinable quality of a work of art is always determined by the Kantian *Geist.*

ideas (the reason), into movement; i.e., by a representation more thought (which indeed belongs to the concept of the object) is occasioned than can be grasped or made clear in it (§ 49).

Through the representations of the imagination, any given thought can thus be grasped much more easily than through words or rational concepts. Whereas Kant had stated earlier (§ 29) that the imagination is a mental disposition, a faculty that is suprasensible, or that could make us aware of the suprasensible (*das Übersinnliche*), here he calls it "a subjective state of the mind," or "a productive faculty of cognition that quickens our understanding as well as our cognitive faculties, but subjectively." It brings forth ideas that no science can teach. Those ideas accompany the concepts, while communicating them as well to others.

Thus, genius consists of "the happy relation" of understanding and imagination, which, thanks to the spirit, "the faculty of seizing the quickly passing play of imagination and of unifying it in a concept . . . can actually communicate universally an ineffable state of mind." Furthermore, it becomes free. It is through the presentation of *aesthetical ideas* in beautiful works of art, conceived of as vehicles of communication, that the genius actually quickens our cognitive faculties and makes the concept universally communicable. It is as if nature had supplied a new rule to the genius who imitates her. Hence, his work cannot be imitated, but only awaken another genius (§ 49).

In order to make a work of art pleasing for the beholder and transform it into a "vehicle of communication," the genius also needs to have taste, which consists of discipline and clarity, as well as the elimination of anything "prejudicial to the understanding," even if it is at the expense of imagination. "Beautiful art, therefore, requires imagination, understanding, spirit and taste" (§ 50). In short, the spirit of the genius sets his imagination in motion. Although it is a subjective state common to everyone, it allows him to re-present ideas and transform them into concepts that he can communicate universally to every beholder through the pleasing aspect of his works. This is precisely the purpose of beautiful art, or what makes beautiful art purposive. He finally evaluates the value of beautiful arts "by the culture they supply to the mind," by how much they stimulate our judgment for cognition. In so doing, he shifts back to the beholder (§ 53), who is now aware of the role of his own subjectivity and how much beautiful art can stimulate his mind and make him conscious of the suprasensible.

In the *Dialectic of the Aesthetical Judgment* (§ 55-§ 61), Kant calls the latter "the pure rational concept of the suprasensible which underlies the object and also the subject judging it, . . . which may be regarded as the suprasensible substrate of humanity" (§ 57). This is how art fulfils its purpose. At this point of his reflection, Kant declares that there is, in fact, no contradiction between his first thesis that a judgment of taste is not based on any concept, since it cannot be determined by proofs, and its final antithesis, that judgment is, on the contrary, based on concepts. Thus, Kant moves from mere sense experience to the in-

   The Path Toward Beauty

definite idea of the suprasensible which, though subjective, is within all human beings. For Kant, the suprasensible principle is "the sole key to the puzzle of this faculty whose sources are hidden from us; it can be made no further intelligible." This antinomy of the aesthetic judgment is what "forces us against our will to look beyond the sensible and to see in the suprasensible the point of union for all our a priori faculties, because no other expedient is left to make our reason harmonious with itself" (§ 57). Now we see why Kant chose to analyze beautiful art in his *Analytic of the Sublime* and not in the *Analytic of the Beautiful*.

At the end of his *Critique of the Aesthetical Judgment*, Kant states once again that there is no objective purposiveness in nature. Nature does not fashion beautiful forms for our satisfaction, rather this feeling of beauty is in ourselves; it is subjective but it is also purposive (*zweckmässig*). This feeling "depends upon the play of the imagination in its freedom, where it is we who receive nature with favor, not nature which shows us favor" (§ 58). Beautiful art is purposive because it is made by a genius who has understood that his art was purposive, although art "must receive its rules through aesthetical ideas (representations of the imagination), which are essentially different from rational ideas and definite purposes." He has understood the purposiveness of art thanks to his spirit, "the animating principle of the mind, which animates the soul and puts the mental powers of imagination *purposively* into swing," transforming images into universally communicable concepts. Through his imagination, which is "a subjective state of the mind," or "a productive faculty of cognition that quickens our understanding as well as our cognitive faculties, but subjectively," the genius can represent images that lead us far beyond any rational concept. This purposiveness of beautiful art can only be explained "on suprasensible grounds as necessary and universal, . . . as ideal." It is what Kant calls "the idealism of purposiveness," which he sees as the only hypothesis by which one can explain a judgment of taste, which demands a priori validity for everyone (§ 58).

Kant began his *Analytic of the Beautiful* by stating that every judgment of taste is subjective and relative to pleasure. By making this statement he was denying any validity to the judgment of taste because it was not determined by a universal, rational principle. In the *Analytic of the Sublime*, on the contrary, he validates this subjectivity itself, which is purposive, and which ultimately takes us much further than an objective concept could ever do. At the very end of this text, Kant attempts, through an analogy, to find an "accord" between the Beautiful and the Good, between the pleasure one feels when assuming a moral duty and the feeling of pleasure in the presence of the Beautiful; between free will and the freedom of the imagination and between reason and sensation, which leads him once again to the suprasensible ground:

> Now, I say the beautiful is the symbol of the morally good and that it is only in this respect (a reference which is natural to every man and which every man postulates in others as a duty) that it gives pleasure with a claim for the agreement of everyone else. [The Beautiful] makes the mind conscious of a certain ennoble-

ment and elevation above the mere sensibility to pleasure received through the senses. . . . That is the intelligible to which . . . taste looks, which accords with our higher facilities. . . . Hence, both on account of this inner possibility in the subject and of the external possibility of a nature that agrees with it, it finds itself to be referred to something within the subject as well as outside him, something which is neither nature nor freedom,[288] but which is yet connected with the suprasensible ground of the latter (§ 59).

Still, at the very end of his *Critique of the Aesthetical Judgment*, Kant recognizes once again that the judgment of taste cannot be determined by means of principle. Of course, there is *truth* as regards to the imitation of nature. There are universal rules taught by nature to the genius, by the master to his pupil, which are indispensable conditions for any beautiful art. But for beautiful art, there must also be "a certain ideal, which art must have before its eyes, although it cannot be completely attained in practice" (§ 60). Once again, Kant returns to the freedom of the imagination of the genius, by which he can represent ideas through images that no rational concept could ever convey. In so doing, the genius is also "stifled by its very conformity to law; and without these no beautiful art, and not even an accurately judging individual taste is possible"(§ 60).[289] Learning to judge beautiful art does not lie, however, in following precepts, "but in the cultivation of the mental powers," by means of a feeling of universal sympathy and the faculty of communication that have characterised human beings ever since they have learned to live in law-abiding society. This feeling of sympathy also "furnishes that true standard for taste as a sense universal to all men which no general rule can supply."

Kant concludes the entire *Critique of the Aesthetical Judgment* with yet another analogy between the Beautiful and the Good, between aesthetical and moral judgment, by affirming that taste must be educated through the development of moral feelings in order to assume an invariable form.

> Taste is primarily a faculty for judging the sensible illustration of moral ideas. . . . Pleasure is derived from what taste regards as valid for mankind in general, and not only for the private feeling of each person. Hence, it appears plain that the true foundation of taste is the development of moral feeling, because it is only when sensibility is brought into agreement with this that genuine taste can assume a definite, invariable form (§ 60).

---

[288] Freedom of the will in reference to the moral law, freedom of imagination in reference to the judgment of the beautiful.

[289] We might recall here that most art treatises of very different periods and civilizations have insisted on the necessity for all artists to follow rules and to master them in order to become free of the rules themselves, i.e., of their tyranny.

          The Path Toward Beauty

After validating the subjectivity of imagination, Kant also tries to justify once again the universal validity of taste, as if he could not fully accept his very first statement that:

> There can be no objective rule of taste to determine by means of concepts what is beautiful. . . . To seek for a principle of taste that might furnish, by means of definite concepts, a universal criterion of the beautiful is fruitless trouble, because what is sought is impossible and self-contradictory (§ 17).

To sum up: for Kant, there are no objective rules of taste; there is no rational concept of what beauty should be nor any precept that could teach one how to make or recognize beautiful art; there is no universal standard for beauty, but beautiful art made by a genius "quickens our understanding as well as our cognitive faculties," though through utterly subjective means. Through the representation of images, the genius leads us beyond any rational concept to the awareness "of the suprasensible which underlies the object and also the subject judging it . . . which may be regarded as the suprasensible substrate of humanity" (§ 57), while the "vehicle of communication" is the physical beauty itself of the work of art which pleases us.

This principle of subjectivity still holds today.

The Critique of Teleological Judgment (§ 79 - § 91) which follows, and which we will not analyze here, does not seem to be the second and last part of the *Critique of Judgment* alone, but rather a conclusion of the entire trilogy, raising at the very end the issue of the ultimate purposiveness (*telos, teleos,* the ultimate, the final, the end) of everything and concluding with an act of faith. It is, in fact, in this very last part of his trilogy that Kant comes back once more to God, whose existence cannot be proven by any rational, moral or empirical means (any more than that of beauty), but in whose existence Kant cannot not believe.

> If we expressed this proposition dogmatically as objectively valid, it would be: There is a God. But for us men, there is only permissible the limited formula: We cannot otherwise think and make comprehensible the purposiveness which must lie at the bottom of our cognition of the internal possibility of many natural things than by representing it and the world in general as the product of an intelligent cause, a God (§ 75).

And yet, at the very end of his trilogy, he writes: "I cannot know what God is, . . . " but at the same time he cannot envisage a world without ultimate purpose, which compels him to *think* a supreme cause for it, to think a suprasensible Being (God) as a supreme intelligence, without ever being able to demonstrate his existence.

Since only human beings perceive a purpose for things, would Kant not apply one to beauty as well? Can we not say that beautiful art partakes of the same great mystery as God's existence, which can neither be defined nor demonstrated by rational concepts or scientific means? They belong to what Kant calls the "suprasensible," which can be grasped only by human sensibility and imagination, based hence on a purely subjective but necessary presupposition.

Kant's view of the role of the genius recalls Eros and Diotima in Plato's *Symposium,* or the poet Stesichorus in the *Phaedrus.* By the eighteenth century, however, genius is no longer guided by love, nor inspired by a divinity, but led by the individual's spirit and the imagination, both striving towards something that lay beyond the bounds of experience, "that which no concept can define, the suprasensible." In Plato, it is through reason that we grasp the realm of the intelligible, in Kant, on the contrary, it is through sense experience and imagination. Kant reversed the path.

Kant's *Analytic of the Beautiful* begins where Hume left off. It is the first step in what we might call Kant's aesthetical education that leads us, through the *Analytic of the Sublime* and the definition of the genius as producer of beautiful art, to Kant's notion of the suprasensible, of which one can only say:

> We cannot otherwise think of . . . the purposiveness which must lie at the bottom
> of our cognition of the internal possibility of many natural things than by repre-
> senting it and the world in general as a product of an intelligent cause, God (§ 75).

For Kant, this proposition could only be a subjective one, whereas for Plato and earlier Western philosophers and artists, as well as other civilizations, truth and beauty were conceived of as objective.

Beauty and the Religion of Art

Unlike Kant, in his *Lectures on Aesthetics,*[290] Hegel once again linked the fine arts to beauty and beauty to truth. He gave these lectures twenty years after the publication of Kant's *Critique of Judgment,* in the wake of the European Enlightenment, but also during the period of passionate German Romanticism.

Romanticism contributed to the psychology of genius, stressing the creative imagination of the artist, considering art a vehicle for the expression of personal feelings, emotions and moods, and the projection of the artist's psychic life on his work and on his introspection and intuition. Among these feelings, however, one also finds religious fervor, a leaning towards the spiritual and an intuitive perception (*die dunkele Ahnung*) of the Divine, as well as a variety of subjective religious experiences, not necessarily related to institutionalized

---

[290] G. W. Friedrich Hegel, *Vorlesungen über Aesthetik* (1820-30), Berlin 1835-38, I-III, translated into English by T. M. Knox, *Aesthetics, Lectures on Fine Arts*, Oxford, 1975. All citations are taken from: "Hegel, The Philosophy of Fine Arts" in Hofstadter and in Kuhns, op. cit., pp. 382-445.

     The Path Toward Beauty

religion.[291] At the time, increasing importance was given to art criticism and to the empathy and experience of the beholder, which, in turn, influenced the artist and his feelings. Aesthetics gradually became a reflection on various arts, rather than on art or on beauty in general. While Hegel's *Lectures on Aesthetics* would seem to be opposed to these romantic tendencies, his religious fervour is not.

> The beauty of art stands *higher* than Nature. For the beauty of art is a beauty begotten, a new birth of the mind; and to the extent that Spirit and its creations stand higher than Nature and its phenomena, to that extent the beauty of art is more exalted than the beauty of Nature . . . which is neither essentially free nor self-aware.

Hegel affirmed that a work of art had necessarily to be beautiful. What was beautiful in art was the Idea which, like the work of art itself, originated in man's mind and spirit, in the fact that man was "a thinking consciousness," and not in Nature. It was beautiful when "it had received the baptism of the mind and the soul of man," and when the *Divine* was the focus of representation. He limited his inquiry to the beauty of fine art only insofar

> as it has established itself in a sphere which it shares with religion and philosophy, becoming thereby merely one mode and form through which the *Divine*, the profoundest interests of mankind and spiritual truths of widest range are brought home to consciousness and expressed.

In contrast to Kant, Hegel believed the feeling for beauty is not related to taste. Even when taste had been formed by abstract theory and highly cultivated, it remained external and one-sided, "lacking universality," and, in its superficiality, missed the essential depth of the work of art and of its meaning.

> The real depth of the subject matter remained, notwithstanding, a closed book to such a taste. Profundity of this kind demands not merely sensitive reception and abstract thought, but the reason in its concrete grasp and the most sterling qualities of soul-life. . . . Taste, on the contrary, is merely directed to the outside surfaces, which are the playground of the feelings, and upon one-sided principles may very well pass as currency. . . . For when great passions and the movements from a profound soul assert themselves, we do not bother ourselves anymore with the finer distinction of taste and its retail traffic of trifles. It is conscious that genius leaves such ground far behind; . . . and, shrinking before that power, feels

---

[291] See the writings of Herder (1778), Wackenroder (1792-98), Schelling (1802-1803), Solger (1815-29), Carus on Gaspar Friedrich (1831), Runge (about 1802), and Caspar Friedriech himself (about 1830), Solger (1815 and 1829) in: Barasch, *Modern Theories*, 1.

on its part far from comfortable, not knowing very well which way to turn.

Imagination, understanding, and *spirit* were, for Hegel, as for Kant (§ 50), the necessary requirements for beautiful art, along with talent and genius, but not *taste.* The function of the work of art was not to produce a feeling of pleasure through its beauty nor to arouse emotions. Its true function was "to satisfy exclusively spiritual interests."

For Hegel:

> Feeling is an undefined obscure region of spiritual life . . . a wholly empty form of subjective state. . . . For this reason, an inquiry into the nature of the emotions which art ought or ought not to arouse comes simply to a standstill in the undefined; it is an investigation which deliberately abstracts from genuine content. . . . Reflection upon feeling is satisfied with observation of the personal emotional state and its singularity, instead of penetrating and sounding the matter of study, in other words the work itself, and in doing so, bidding good-bye to the wholly subjective state and conditions. In feelings, however, it is just this subjective state, void of content, which is not merely accepted, but becomes the main thing; and this is precisely why people are so proud of having emotions.

The creative imagination of an artist "is the imagination of a great mind and a big heart."

> The creation of art is quite as much a spiritual as a self-cognized process. . . . For this reason, though almost anybody can reach a certain point in art, yet, in order to pass beyond this—and it is here that the art in question really begins—a talent for art which is inborn and of a higher order altogether is indispensable.

Hegel also insists on the need to incorporate "vital energy" into works of art, which is "in union with soul and emotions." He believed that the nineteenth-century artist "was (however) led astray from his art by critical opinions and judgments that infected his mind, losing thus its genuine truth and life." This last remark was made at a time when art criticism began to have increasing impact on viewers, collectors and artists, who aimed, on the contrary, at pleasing and at "arousing and giving life . . . to slumbering emotions . . . and filling the heart up to the brim." For Hegel, the true function of art was not to express personal emotions or to move the feelings of the spectator, but:

> to bring to consciousness the highest interests of the mind. An immediate consequence of this is that, so far as the content of fine art is concerned, it cannot range about in all wildness of an unbridled fancy. . . .

For him:
> The sensuous is spiritualized in art, or, in other words, the life of spirit comes to
> dwell in art under sensuous guise.

> The beautiful is the sensory manifestation of an idea.

Because, as we have seen, in Hegel's view the primary purpose of art is "to make the *Divine* the focus of representation," its function is "to reveal *truth* under the mode of art's sensuous or material configuration." Art aims essentially at beauty, which is one way truth is expressed. Truth and beauty were thus not relative or particular for Hegel, but universal, and they are represented by the idea of the Divine. According to Barasch,[292] the mythological tradition in Romantic scholarship[293] had placed art on a metaphysical level, paving the way for what was to be called "the religion of art." This tradition was also influenced by Neo-Platonism and Plotinus, leaving its imprint on the intellectual life of the nineteenth century. Hegel shared with his contemporaries the symbolic approach to art, whereby it mediates between the visible and the invisible.
> The show of art possesses the advantage that, in its own virtue, it points beyond
> itself. . . . Through it, the absolute is brought home to human consciousness.

He constantly distinguishes self-consciousness and consciousness from emotions and from feelings, objectivity from subjectivity. At the same time, he recognizes that sometimes they overlap.
> The human consciousness accepts God for its object in which the distinction
> between objectivity and subjectivity falls away.

Because "the beautiful was the sensuous manifestation of an idea," Hegel was essentially concerned with the idea itself, or with the content of fine art, with its meaning, and only insofar as it was spiritual. As Barasch points out: "Hegel tried to discover meanings within the unfolding historical process itself. The process was not only recorded, but interpreted."[294] Hegel created, in fact, an entire historical system, dividing the history of fine arts, as he knew it, into three major periods, or art forms, which were "the universal stages or phases

---

[292] Barasch, *Modern Theories*, 1, p. 233.
[293] See the work of a friend of Hegel such as F. Creuzer, *Symbolics and Mythology of the Ancient Nations*, 1810-12.
[294] Barasch, *Modern Theories*, 1, p. 182.

of the Idea of beauty itself:" the Pre-Classical, which he called "Symbolic,"[295] the Classical and the Post-Classical, which he called "Romantic." The "Romantic" art form refers mainly to Christian art as a whole and not to the Romanticism of the late eighteenth and early nineteenth century. It encompassed the entire post-classical world, covering several periods and very different styles.

Although Hegel recognized a few major differences of style within these art forms, occasionally linking form to content, he was mainly concerned with how the Idea of the Divine, the supreme subject of all art, "became embodied in the shape of art," and how the representation of the human form—"Spirit is only adequately presented to perception in its bodily form"—evolved in successive historical phases. Each of the three art forms was furthermore best represented by certain individual arts or media, rather than by art as a whole. Thus, the "symbolic" art form—that of Ancient Egypt—was best embodied by architecture, the building of the temple, a space for the divinity, for the concentration of "Spirit;" the "Classical" by sculpture; and the "Romantic" art form by painting, music and poetry. The Greek gods revealed themselves in their statues, hence sculpture became the best medium of religious revelation in Classical Greek art. On the other hand, the Christian God as pure Spirit was made visible and the subject of representation through His incarnation as Jesus Christ, while remaining essentially Spirit.[296]

> The Greek god is not abstract, but individual, and is in close association with the natural human form. The Christian God is also, no doubt, a concrete personality, but under the mode of pure spiritual actuality, who is recognized as Spirit and in Spirit. His medium of determinate existence is therefore essentially knowledge of the mind and not external shape, by means of which His representation can only be imperfect and not in the entire depth of His idea or notional concept.

Christian art "accepts Spirit for its object. . . . Its content is coincident with what Christianity affirms to be true of God as Spirit."

External appearance cannot any longer express the inner life, and if it is still called

---

[295] In this book, I have used the term "symbolic form of art" to characterize the non-naturalistic or conceptual styles of most visual arts that did not originate in Greece or did not belong to Greek heritage. Hegel called this pre-classical art form, especially Egyptian art, symbolic because in this form of art there is the meaning on one side, and the object or the shape symbolizing it on the other, and they do not coincide or overlap. For Hegel, the life of the spirit could only be perceived in sensory experience through the human figure. He therefore dismissed altogether any form of art that did not allow for the representation of the Divine in human form, such as Indian or Islamic art (which he called Turkish). He could not conceive of an abstract reference to the Divine.

[296] It is interesting to recall what we said about Medieval art and the revival of monumental figurative sculpture at the threshold of Romanesque churches. The abbots of Cluny had justified this revival using exactly the same arguments.

The Path Toward Beauty

to do so it merely has the task of proving that the external is an unsatisfying existence and must point back to the inner, to the mind and feeling, as the essential
element.

Hegel's "Romantic" art was an art of the inner life (*Innerlichkeit*). Because he considers it the most spiritual form of art, it also seemed to him the most beautiful. In this form of art, God was represented through his Son, both as Spirit and as man.[297]

> In such an object, art cannot merely work for sensuous perception. It must de-
> liver itself to the inward life, which coalesces with its object simply as though this
> were none other than itself, in other words, it must deliver itself to the intimacy of
> soul, to the heart, to the emotional life, which, as the medium of the Spirit itself,
> essentially strives after freedom and seeks and possesses its reconciliation only in
> the inner chamber of the spirit. It is this inward or ideal world that constitutes the
> content of the romantic sphere: it will, therefore, necessarily discover its repre-
> sentation as such an inner idea or feeling, and in the self-presentation or appear-
> ance of the same. The world of the soul and intelligence celebrates its triumph
> over the external world where the sensuous appearance sinks into worthlessness.

The "external vehicle of expression," or the individual arts best suited to the "Romantic" spiritual art were, therefore, also the most subjective, the least concrete and the most abstract: painting,[298] music and especially poetry.

> The content of this world is the beautiful, and the true beautiful, as we have seen,
> is spiritual being in concrete form, the Ideal; or, apprehended with still more
> intimacy, it is the absolute mind and truth itself. This region of divine truth, artisti-
> cally presented to sensuous vision and emotion, forms the center of the entire
> world of art.

At least up to the eighteenth century, most philosophers would have agreed with this last statement, but Hegel dealt with only one subject of representation, the Divine in a bodily form, and with no other. Since he was thinking as a philosopher, he never attempted to define or to describe how beauty of shape was obtained in order to reflect the beauty and truth of the Divine. Throughout his *Lectures*, he did stress that the creation of art requires

---

[297] For a very clear synthesis of Hegel's philosophy of art see: Barasch, *Modern Theories*, 1, pp. 178 ff.
[298] As Barasch emphasized (197-198), the specific medium of painting is color, which for Hegel is based on light and darkness. Light is an intrinsic component of the art itself, which has a close connection to the spiritual and the inner life. Painting not only shows us an object or figure in space, but is "a reflection of the spirit." The spiritual nature of painting makes it the art best suited to representing the spiritual nature of Christ and of the Christian saints. We are reminded of Plotinus and anticipate, *mutatis mutandis*, Kandinski's *Concerning the Spiritual in Art* of 1913.

the imagination of a great mind and a great heart as well as vital energy, and that art is a spiritual, self-conscious process through which the spirit of beauty "gradually comes to self-cognition," necessitating centuries-long evolution, to come to completion.

A century later, Heidegger[299] was to attempt, once again, to establish the link between art, beauty and truth, showing how the essence of truth (*das Wesen der Wahrheit*) could be revealed (*sich ereignen*) in a work of art, but only when that work of art had incorporated Being (*Sein*) itself. Thus, he asks, "What is truth itself, that it sometimes comes to pass in art?" This could not happen outside a struggle between what remained hidden and what was made visible through the work of art. The work of art is an allegory; it is a symbol: "the work makes public something other than itself." The artist creates—*schöpfen*—which in German also means to draw from a well. He draws truth from the well, that is Being: "Art-work opens up in its own way the Being of Beings. . . . This opening up, . . . this deconcealing the truth of being happens in the work. . . . Art is truth setting itself to work." Heidegger uses the example of a Greek temple, which simply stands in the middle of a rock-cleft valley.

> The temple-work, standing there, opens a world . . . as long as the god has not fled from it. It is the same with the sculpture of the god. . . . It is not a portrait whose purpose is to make it easier to realize how the god looks; rather it is a work that lets the god himself be present and, thus, is the god himself. . . . Towering up within itself, the work opens up a world and keeps it abidingly in force. To be a work means to set up a world. . . . That world is the ever non-objective to which we are subject as long as the paths of birth and death, blessing and curse, keep us transported into Being.

The artist brings truth into the light through the work of art, binding the temple to the earth of which it is made, and from which it emerges.

> The work moves the earth itself into the open of a world and keeps it there. The work lets the earth be an earth. . . . The earth, however as sheltering and concealing, tends always to draw the world into itself and keep it there. . . . In setting up a world and setting forth the earth, the work instigates this striving.

The work accomplishes this striving through a consecration (*Stiftung*). Only in such a way can truth be conserved and remain alive (*die schaffende Bewahrung der Wahrheit*).

> What is truth itself, that it sometimes comes to pass in art?

Heidegger refers to the Aegina pediments, now in the Munich museum, hence "with-

---

[299] M. Heidegger, *Der Ursprung des Kunstwerkes*, lectures given between 1935 and 1936. English trans. and ed. A. Hofstadter, "The Origin of the Work of Art," *Philosophies of Art and Beauty*, 1964, pp. 650 ff. In this summary, I have also followed George Steiner's *Martin Heidegger*, French trans., 1981, pp. 170 ff.

drawn from the temple and its world, . . . the world that stands there has perished." He also refers to Paestum or to the cathedral of Bamberg, still on their original sites, though belonging to a world which has vanished as well. Do these works, or, for that matter, all those works that are now exhibited in our museums, still open up a world and does truth still "come to pass" through them? If not, these works would remain only things, or objects (*Gegenstände*). They would be obtained through art, in the original sense of *techné*, and not yet qualify as *poiesis*, to paraphrase George Steiner: A work of art "that sets forth truth" is not based on the Greek concept of *mimesis*, but, on the contrary, is that which "discloses the hidden," manifests, or unconceals truth, Plato's *to on*, that which is, Being.

Beauty is one way in which truth occurs as unconcealedness.

Using different terms, under different influences, and especially in a totally different historical and artistic context, very similar concepts were to be developed by painters such as Kandinsky and Mondrian,[300] whose first abstract paintings aimed precisely at the spiritual in art and at universal beauty, but only insofar as it rejected all "bodily form." None were to refer any longer to the Divine, to God or to Christianity, or to any other institutionalized religion, but solely to the Spiritual.

Is the beauty of a work of art related to truth and to the spiritual, as Hegel and Heidegger stated? And if it is, how does this beauty arouse emotions and feelings? We will deal with these issues in the following two chapters, but from the point of view of the beholder.

---

[300] Wassily Kandinsky, *Concerning the Spiritual in Art*, 1912 and *Reminiscences*, 1913, in his *Complete Writings on Art*, ed. K.C. Lindsay and P. Vergo, 1982, 2 vols.; Piet Mondrian, *Collected Writing*, 1920-37, ed. and trans. H. Holtzmannn and M. James, Boston, 1986. Cf. also R. Lipsey, op. cit., 1988, pp. 40 ff, pp. 208 ff. and pp. 66 ff.; S. Ringborn, *The Sounding Cosmos. A Study of the Spiritualism of Kandisnky and the Genesis of Abstract Painting*, 1970; Barasch, *Modern Theories of Art, 2: From Impressionism to Kandinsky*, 1998.

PART III
The Artist and the Beholder

Beauty: Emotion and Feeling

How do artists deal with emotions? Why do some artworks overwhelm us and not others? Has beauty got something to do with it?

In architecture, any approach to space, form, light, scale, proportion, perspectives, types of materials and ornament, becomes a powerful means of guiding our emotions. These factors also carry meaning, and architects are perfectly aware of it. The beauty of a building depends on the successful interplay of all these elements: the harmony between the void and the solid and the play of light on both, the harmony between the building, its site and its use, and a balance between tradition and innovation, past and present.[301]

Each form of architecture must furthermore be understood in relation to its meaning. To speak only about sacred buildings, the meaning and function of a Greek temple (figs. 18 and 19) were different from those of an Egyptian or Indo-American one, just as a Cistercian abbey (fig. 36) was different from a contemporary urban Gothic cathedral (fig. 82), or a Byzantine domed church (figs. 49 and 50). Similarly, the meaning and ritual use of an Umayyad, Iranian or Ottoman Mosque (figs. 81, 83) were utterly different from those of an Early Renaissance church in Florence or a Baroque church in Rome (fig. 86). Rituals differed and the concept of the divinity itself differed from one civilization to the next, de-

---

[301] These observations have been reiterated by architects through the ages and, most recently, by I.M Pei and Renzo Piano. Gero von Boehm, *Conversations with I. M. Pei. Light Is the Key,* London, 2000; Renzo Piano, *Carnet de Travail*, Paris, 1997. See all the museums built by Renzo Piano and, for the balance between tradition and innovation, see especially his Cultural Center in Numea, New Caledonia, built between 1993 and 1997. See also the buildings and especially the museums designed by Tadao Ando and read his interviews.

pending on whether it was conceived as infinitely remote, absolutely invisible and transcendent, or, on the contrary, anthropomorphic, incarnated, symbolized by light, in terms of mathematical harmonies and geometrical shapes, or by means of figurative art. The architect of the Pantheon of Rome (fig. 80 a-b) and that of the Stupa of Sanchi in India(fig. 79) used the same circular form and the same ratios, but the buildings are totally different in

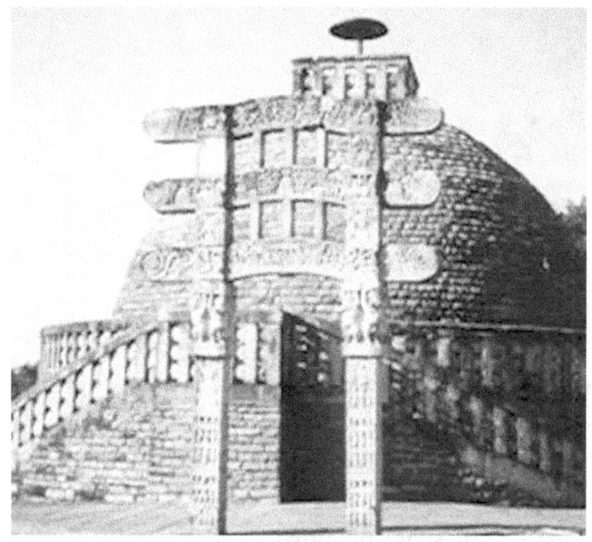

place, time, use and decoration, though equally beautiful. One remains outside and moves around the Stupa, whereas one is pulled inside the Pantheon(fig. 80 b) or the Hagia Sophia (fig. 80 d) or any Byzantine church of the eleventh century (fig. 50), irresistibly drawn up to the central cupola, which is the most important feature of the building, architecturally, liturgically and symbolically.

79 *Great Stupa*, begun in the 3rd century B.C.E., Sanchi, Madhya Pradesh, Central India

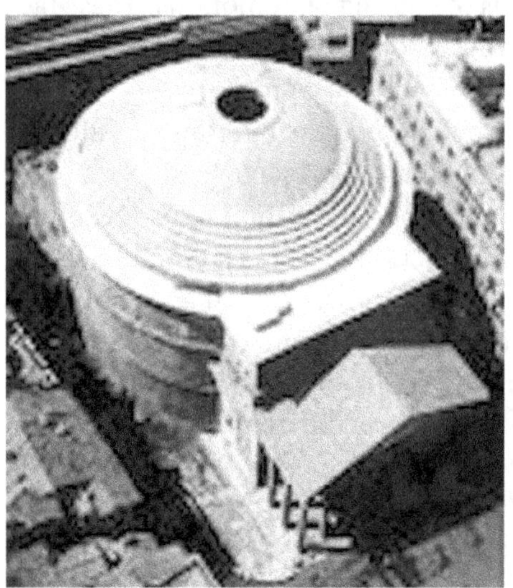

80 a Pantheon, Rome, 125-128

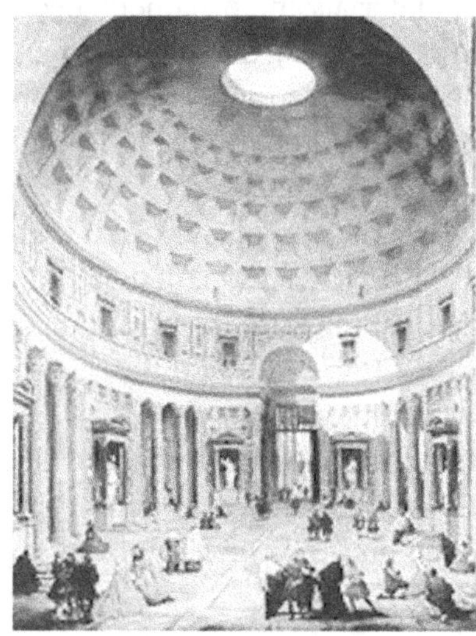

80 b Giovanni Paolo Panini, *Interior of the Pantheon, Rome*, c. 1734, Washington, D.C., National Gallery of Art

  The Path Toward Beauty

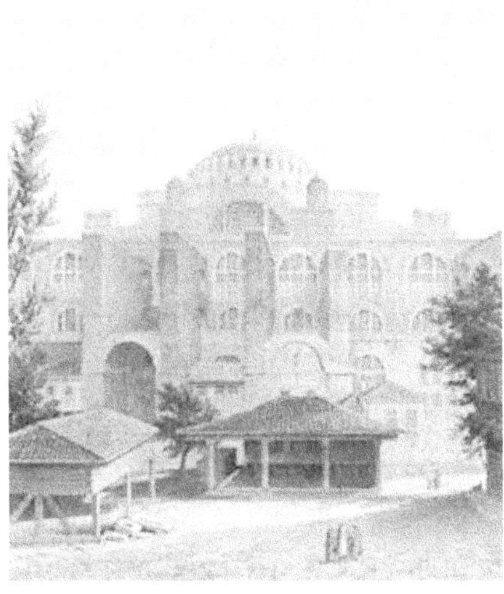

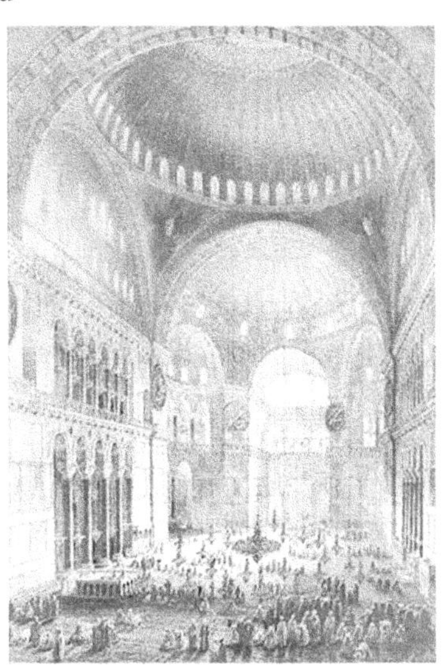

80 c Gaspare Trajano Fossati and Giuseppe Fossati, *Exterior of Haghia Sophia,* Istanbul (532-37), lithographs, c.1852 (detail)

80 d Gaspare Trajano Fossati and Giuseppe Fossati, *Interior of Haghia Sophia,* Istanbul (532-37), lithographs, c.1852

81 Sinan, Interior of the Mosque of Sultan Selim, 1568-75, Edirne, Turkey

The same ratios, such as 1/1 or 1/2, have, in fact, been used to totally different effect in very different types of buildings throughout the world, simply because they were recognized by the human mind as harmonious (figs. 39, 79, 80 a-d, 81, 85). Each of these buildings was built to allow the worshipper to enter into communication with a deity, but each one affects the beholder very differently. Some stop the worshipper outside (sacrifices and rituals took place outside a Greek temple; one does not enter into the stupa of Sanchi), or lead him inward or upward or around (Hagia Sophia in Constantinople/Istanbul, the Pantheon, the Ottoman mosques built by Sinan: figs. 80 a-d and 81), forcing him to stand still or to move as in a procession, through the centrality of a domed church, the frontality of a barrel-vaulted Romanesque church, or the diagonality of the crisscrossing ribs over oblong bays in a Gothic cathedral, producing an effect of unification in depth.[302]

Others bewilder the beholder through the use of multiple perspectives or by making him raise his eyes upward into a golden hemispherical vault and focus on a source of light or on the figure of the Pantocrator, the Omnipotent Christ. The oculus in the Pantheon is the only source of light, which moves within the building as the motion of the earth around the sun (fig. 80 b); in the Hagia Sophia of Istanbul, the builder concealed or revealed the central, most sacred space under the dome and towards the apse, forcing the beholder to look upward, following the light that becomes increasingly more intense, towards the huge, golden hemispherical vault (fig. 80 c); in Daphni, our eye moves towards the hemispherical vault where the Pantokrator takes the place of an oculus (fig. 50); in the Mosque of Edirne, built by Sinan, the gradual unfolding of quarter domes leads the eye towards the central hemispherical vault, so does the light and the decoration (fig. 81). Still others induce the be-

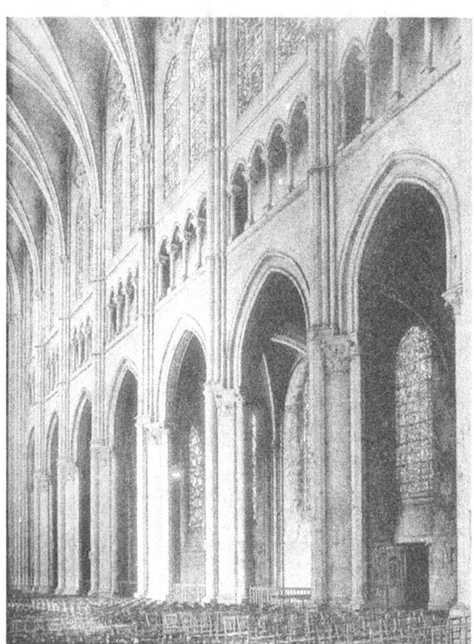

holder to contemplate the ever-changing light filtering through figurative stained glass windows, as in the Cathedrals of Bourges or of Chartres, leading the worshipper in a processional way, and through a straight-axis approach, towards the altar (fig. 82).

82 Nave, 1194-1220, Chartres Cathedral, France

In the Mosque of Córdoba (fig. 83 a), one penetrates the array of columns and superimposed arcades, moving, as in a forest, towards the most sacred *Mihrab*, guided by the increasingly rich decoration and light.

---

[302] Jean Bony, "Diagonality and Centrality in Early Rib-Vaulted Architecture," *Gesta*, 15, 1976, 1-2; Otto Demus, *Middle Byzantine Churches and their Decoration*, London, 1948 and idem, *Byzantine Mosaic Decoration*, 1955; Richard Krautheimer, *Early Christian and Byzantine Architecture*, Pelican Hisory of Art, 1975, chapter 9, pp. 215 ff.; Roland Mainstone, *Hagia Sophia; Architecturre, Structure and Liturgy of Justinian's Great Church*, Thames and Hudson, 1988; William MacDonald, *The Pantheon: Design, Meaning, and Progeny*, Harvard, 1981.

                    The Path Toward Beauty

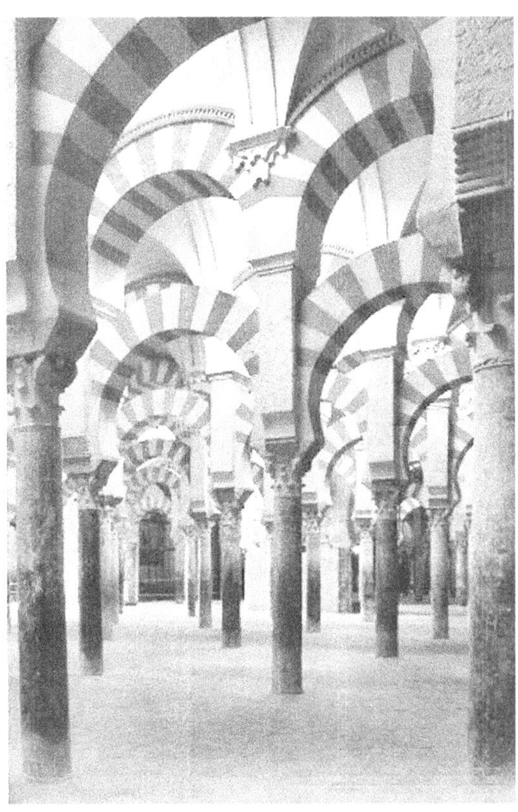

83 a   Prayer Hall, Great Mosque, begun 785-86, Córdoba, Spain

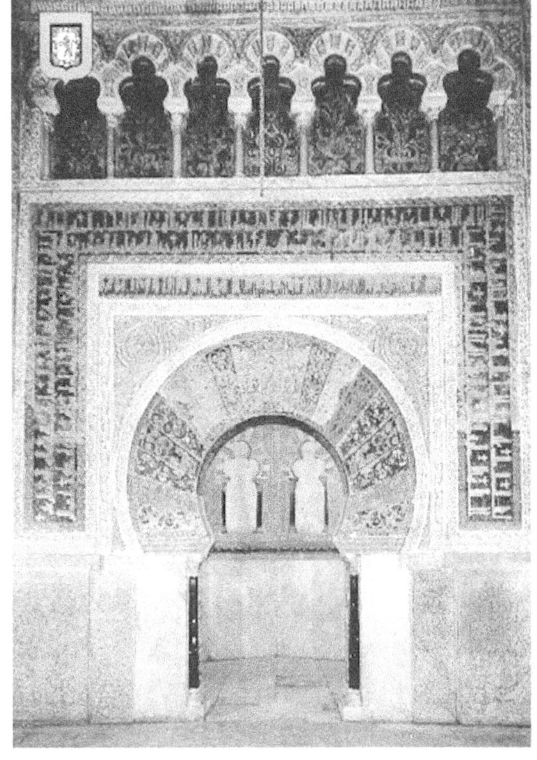

83 b   *Qibla* wall with view into the *Mihrab*, 965, Great Mosque, Córdoba, Spain

The light plays on the *muqarnas*[303] in the Lion's Court of the Alhambra in Granada (fig. 84) or outside and inside the mosques of Isfahan. It glides over the blue and golden mosaics of the Dome of the Rock in Jerusalem (fig. 85) and in San Vitale in Ravenna (fig. 34).

---

[303] Stalactites made of intricate geometrical stucco patterns, also called honeycomb vaults, but in fact highly decorated "squinches" with staggered rows of half niches, allowing for the transition between a square chamber, or bay, and the circular base of a covering cupola, and gradually used to decorate any curved surface.

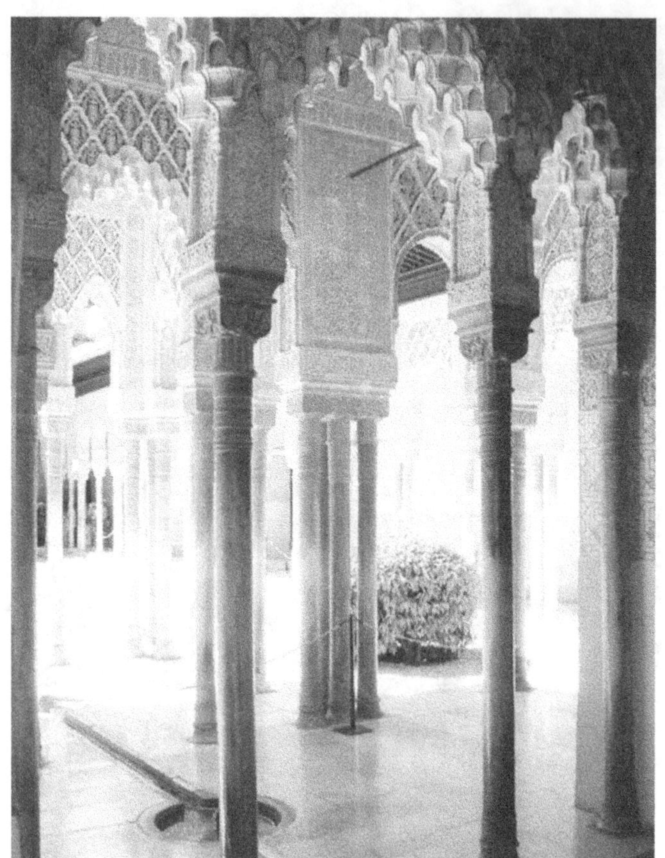

84   View into The Lion's Patio with its *muqarnas*, 1354-91, Alhambra, Granada, Spain

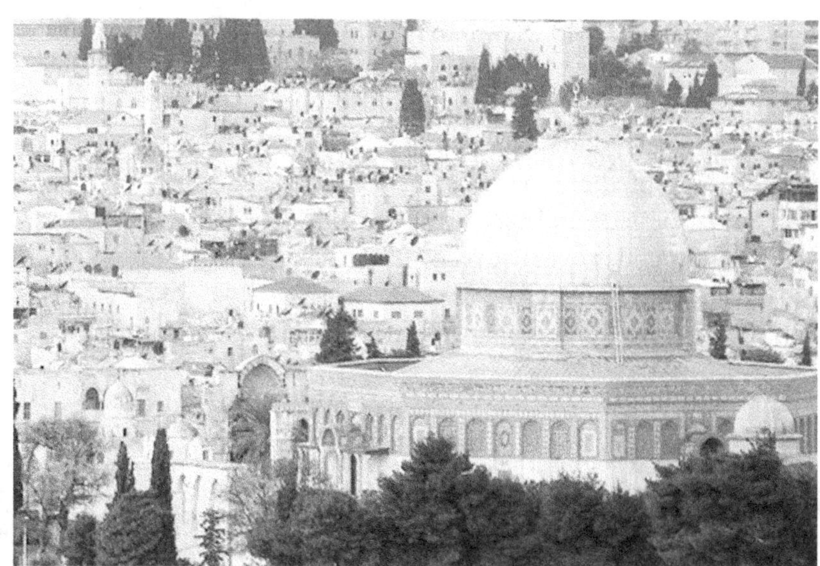

85   View of the exterior, Dome of the Rock, 7th century, Jerusalem

   The Path Toward Beauty

(fig. 34). Light could be made to glide on curved walls, as in Borromini's Church of San Carlo alle Quattro Fontane (fig. 86), and so on.

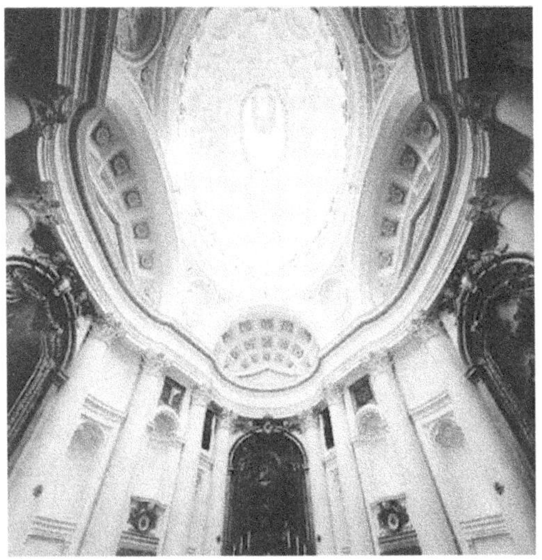

86   Borromini, Interior, San Carlo alle Quattro Fontane, 1638-1641, Rome

The builder could also choose to underline only the articulation of the space, as Brunelleschi did in his Early Renaissance buildings in Florence, such as in the Old Sacristy of San Lorenzo or in the Foundling Hospital (fig. 87), or as the builders did in the Cistercian abbeys of Fontenay (figs. 36, 98 and cover), Senanques (fig. 88), or Le Thoronet.

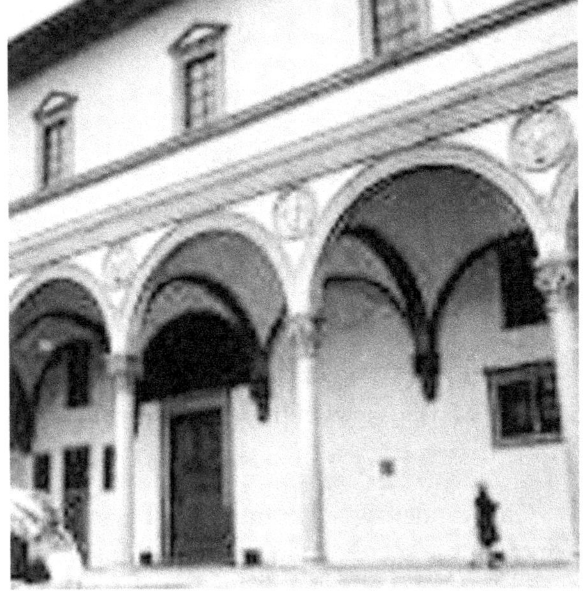

87 a   Brunelleschi, Foundling Hospital, begun 1419, Florence

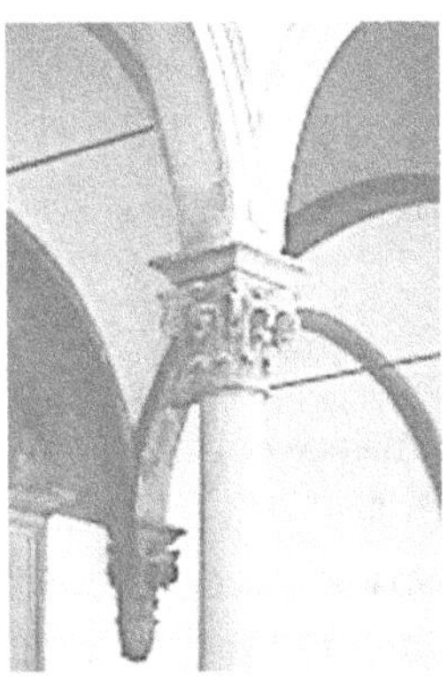

87 b   Detail of Fig. 87 a

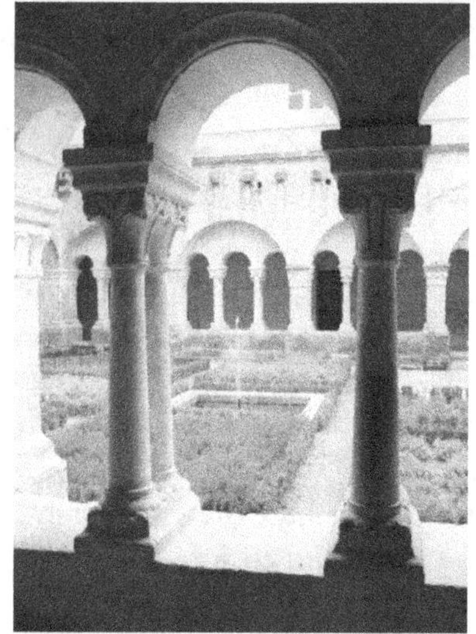

The same holds for contemporary buildings such as in I. M. Pei's Miho Museum near Tokyo (fig. 89) in which shafts of light enhance each part of the building.

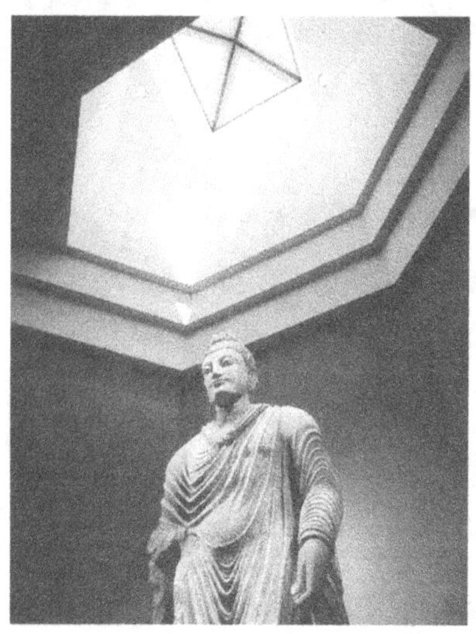

89 a

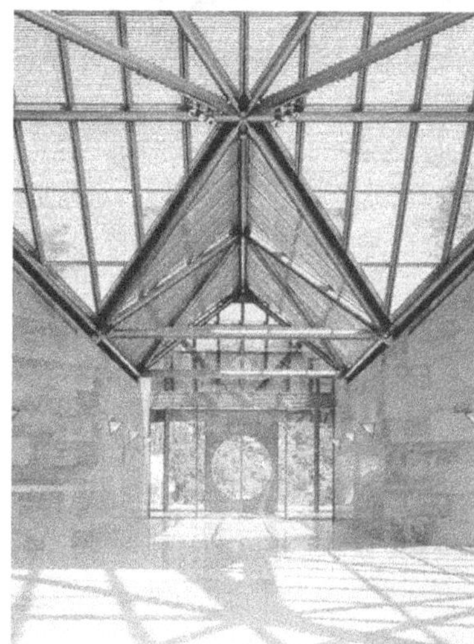

89 b

89 a-b I.M. Pei, Views of the Miho Museum, 1996, Shigaraki, Japan

One wonders whether museums have not perhaps become a late twentieth century substitute for the sacred buildings of old. Inside a sacred building, nevertheless, the beholder or worshipper is not only guided by the overall and specific articulation of space, but also through the meaningful absence or presence of different forms of ornamental or figurative art. In the same way, the Moorish sequence of patios like the Patio of the Lions at the Alhambra in Granada (fig. 84), conveys an ideal of life different from that of Francesco Laurana's courtyard in the Ducal Palace of Urbino (fig. 41) or the late twentieth century church of Tadao Ando in Osaka, but they are all equally beautiful (fig. 90).

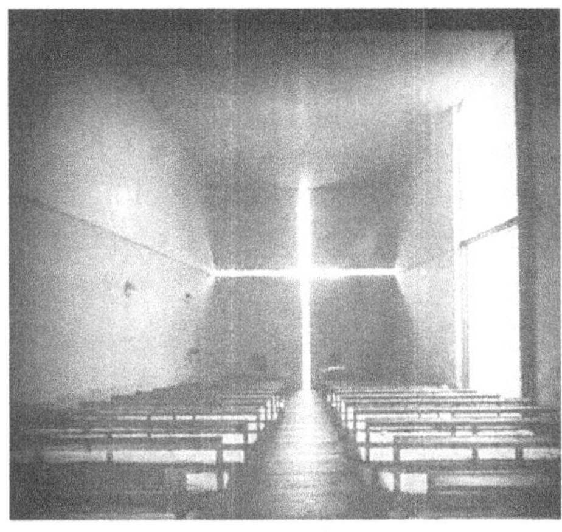

90 Tadao Ando, Church of the Light, 1989, Ibaraki, Osaka, Japan

Each builder had a different conception of beauty, and, therefore, combined the main architectural elements of space, volume and light differently. It would seem that Beauty is only achieved when we, as beholders or worshippers, are in fact overwhelmed by emotion.

For the figurative forms of art, we have touched on some of these issues in the third chapter of this book, when we discussed Yoruban, Chinese and Indian concepts of art. We saw, more specifically, how important it was in all three cultures to integrate into a work of art the vital energy, the breath of life (the Yoruban *ase,* the Indian *prâna,* the Chinese *ch'i*), in order for it to be fully shared or experienced by the beholder and considered as "good" or as "beautiful." We have seen to what extent the artist was compelled through a long apprenticeship to learn the technique of his craft, obeying traditional rules, subjecting himself to constraints and learning about myths and symbols in order to release that energy. All this required an incredible discipline, which gradually led him to freedom.

In the long history of art, art treatises and theory, little importance has been given to the personal emotion of the artist or of the beholder, for that matter. In the West, for example, it was not until the Romanticism[304] of the late eighteenth and nineteenth centuries that art was viewed as a means of expressing the artist's personal emotions, even though much earlier artists had become very keen to depict lifelike people in action and facial expressions

---

[304] The term *Romanticism* is used here in both, the broadest sense of non-or post-classical, was used by Hegel as well as in the sense of the specific historical period. Thus, between 1820 and 1830, Hegel wrote: "painting takes the heart as a content of its production" (Barasch, *Modern Theories,* 1, p. 189 ff, at p. 197). In 1857, Delacroix wrote: "The major source of interest comes from the soul of the artist, and it goes in a irresistible manner to the soul of the spectator" (George Mras, *Eugène Delacroix's Theories of Art,* Princeton, 1966, pp. 15 ff.); Casper David Friedrich, writing about landscape paintings, circa 1800, said: "It is not the faithful representation of air, water, rocks and trees that is the task of the painter, rather his soul and his emotions should be reflected in it" (Barasch, *Modern Theories,* 1, p. 318); in 1863, Baudelaire wrote: "A good picture, which is a faithful equivalent of a dream which has begotten it, should be brought into being like a world . . . and by this word (of dream) I mean the vision that comes from intense meditation" (*The Painter of Modern Life and Other Essays,* trans. J. Mayne, New York, 1986, p. 47).

and "the form of the body to express the various passions of the soul and to make visible what is in the mind" to move the beholder.[305]

In Eastern texts, the personal emotion of the artist is disregarded altogether. A sense of vitality has, however, been inherent since the very earliest figurine of a Hindu Valley dancing girl (c. 2300-1750 BC). We see the same vitality in later representations of the god Shiva as the Lord of the Dance (fig. 15), enacting the end of the world before it is re-created, and in the hand gestures, *mudràs,* of the Buddha, each one associated with various actions and events in his life (the earth-touching *mudrà,* for example, is identified with his enlightenment, the wheel-turning gesture stands for his First Sermon about the Law and so on).

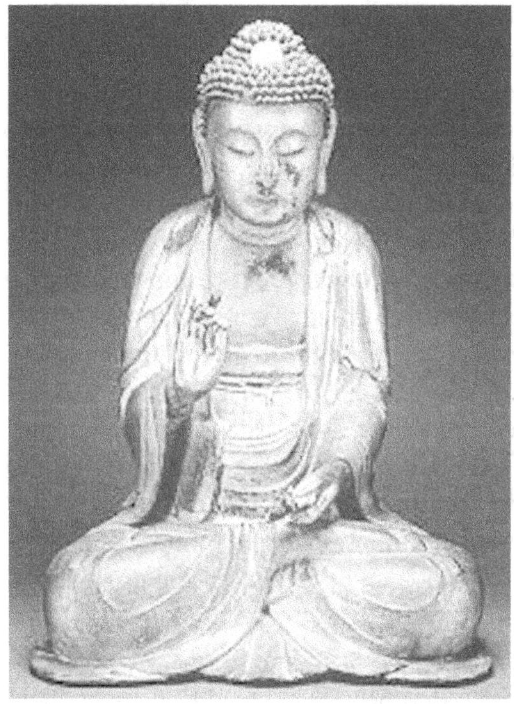

91 *Teaching Buddha*, 12th century, from Korea, Paris, Musée Guimet

In Hindu and Buddhist art, every position or movement of the body, every foot posture or hand gesture, every motion of the eyebrow, every erotic representation of loving couples—the *mithuna*—relates, in fact, to the life of a divinity in the Hindu pantheon, or to that of the Buddha or a Boddhisattva. All are highly codified within an equally codified art, especially when rendering sacred figures.[306]

---

[305] Nicolas Poussin to Félibien, 1647-48 in: Anthony Blunt, *Nicolas Poussin*, p. 220. About the emotional impact that a work of art should have on the beholder, see the previous chapter on the art theories of the Late Renaissance and of the seventeenth and eighteenth centuries.
[306] Benjamin Rowland, *The Art and Architecture of India: Buddhist, Hindu, Jain*, Harmondsworth, Pelican History of Art, reprint of 1985, pp. 51, 154, figs. 5, 259 etc.; and J. C. Harle, *The Art and Architecture of the Indian Subcontinent*, reprint of 1990, figs. 36, 99. 181.

                    The Path Toward Beauty

92 *Meditating Buddha*, c. 14th century, Anuradhapura, Sri Lanka

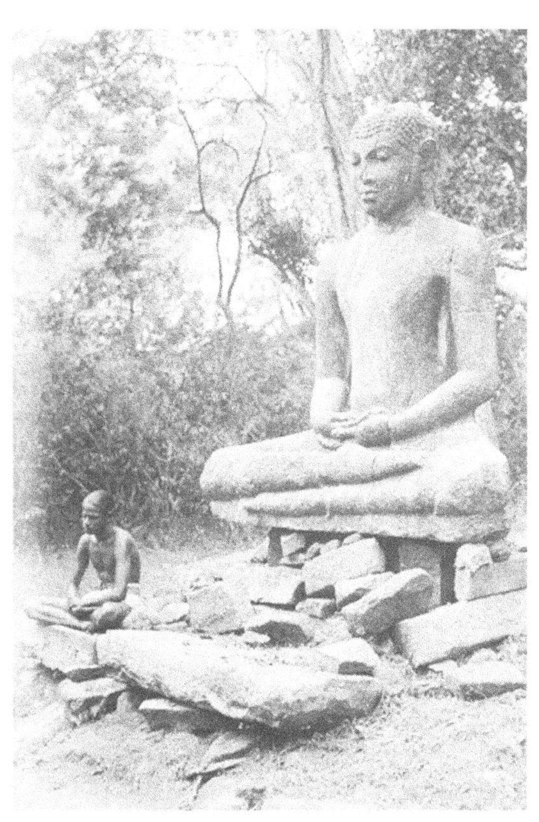

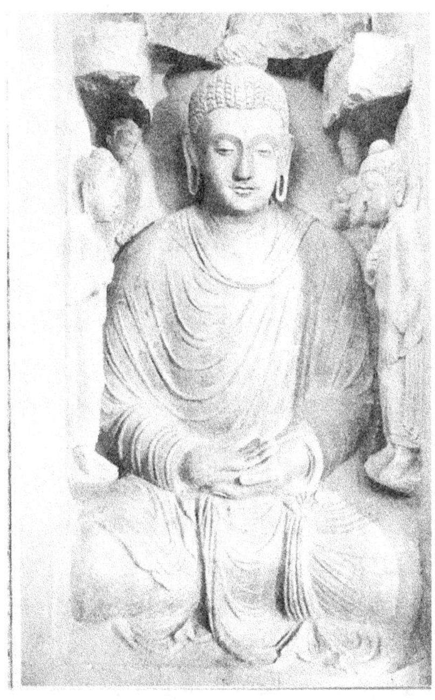

93 *Meditating Buddha*, from Taxila, Taxila Museum, Pakistan

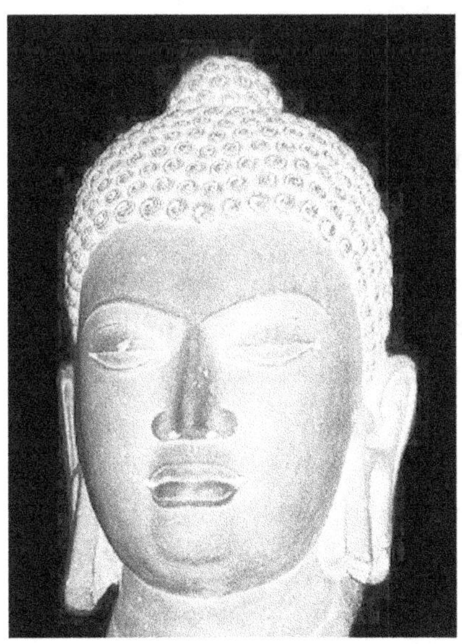

94 *Head of Buddha*, 4th-5th centuries

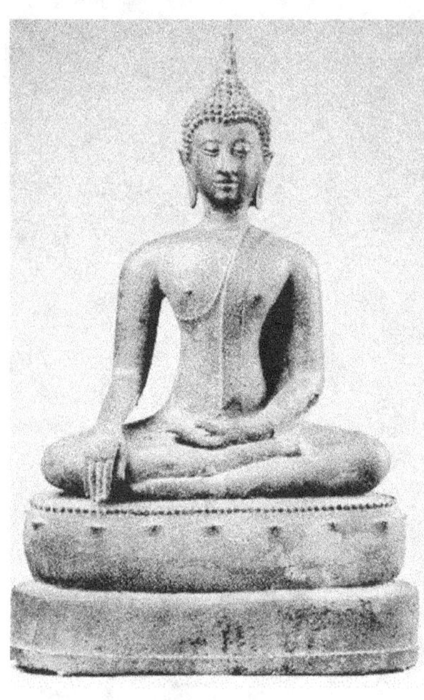

95 *Buddha "taking the earth as witness,"* Sukhothai period, 13th-14th centuries, from Thailand, London, British Museum

The *Nayta Shastras* by Bharata,[307] an Indian treatise of the first century, defines various types of emotions, especially how the spectator experiences them. This text, which all later Indian art treatises would cite, develops the concept of *rasa*, and the experience of *rasa*.[308] In everyday language, the term *rasa* was simply used in relation to the sensual pleasure given by something that tastes or smells good. In the aesthetic sense, in relation to art, one reads that a dance, a poem, a piece of music, or a painting have *rasa*, when the artist has become fully involved emotionally. At the same time the artist has to follow very precise codes to put the spectator into a similar state of *rasa*, defined as a state of spiritual bliss, ecstasy, enlightenment, or total communion with the work of art itself.

The *Nayta Shastra* mentions only eight feelings that are also called *rasa*: the erotic, the comic, the pathetic, the furious, the heroic, the terrible, the hateful, and the marvelous, to which was added a ninth of serenity or quietness. Each feeling has its particular subject matter or theme, with its corresponding attributes or settings. (The erotic feeling, for example, necessarily entailed a hero and a heroine, a lover and a beloved, to which might be added the moon, a garden, and so on.) Each feeling had its own conventional codes, such as certain hand gestures, body postures, movements of the eyebrows, direction of glances and embraces, as well as precise color codes, each one adapted to a specific theme. Furthermore, each of these major feelings was complemented by temporary or sudden emotions (the *vyabhichari bhavas* of which Bharata lists up to 32), including shame, boredom, amazement, etc., with all the corresponding, immediate physical reactions, such as an accelerated heartbeat, trembling hands, a change in facial colour or tone of voice, etc. Together, they were designed to lead to a state of a dominant, permanent feeling (*bhava*) such as love, joy, sadness, anger, energy, fear, disgust, wonder or equanimity, which correspond to the transformation of the nine initial *rasa*. Thus, erotic feeling, for example, would be transformed into love.

---

[307] See the authors mentioned in notes 76-83. The translation, from Sanskrit into English, at least in the Exhibition Catalogue of 1986, is by Manomohan Ghosh.
[308] B. Nath Goswamy, "Rasa: les délices de la raison," *Rasa, les neufs visages de l'art indien*, Paris, Galeries du Grand Palais, 1986, Exhibition Catalogue, pp. 19-30.

     The Path Toward Beauty

It was only with the emergence of the permanent, dominant feeling that the experience of *rasa* itself could take place and this could only occur within a receptive, cultivated audience. Both the artist and the spectator had to be not only highly receptive, but also very competent and fully knowledgeable about the codes themselves in order to experience *rasa*, which Coomaraswamy described as something

> simple, like the taste of a complex dish. . . . It compels an act of union between the actor (or poet or painter, or sculptor), the represented heroes and the audience. It does not exist beyond the perception of it. . . . We know it only by savouring it. . . . Amazement and expansion of the spirit, created by contact with a reality superior to this world, is the principle of all savor (*rasa*) and is found in all true poetry (music or visual art work). . . . The work of art itself serves as the stimulus to the release of the spirit from all inhibitions of vision and can only exist as a thing ordered to specific ends. Heaven and Earth are united in the analogy of art.[309]

Communication takes place through codes and symbols, but only insofar as both artist and beholder know their significance. If *rasa* is related to knowledge, is our apprehension of beauty not also related to it ?[310]

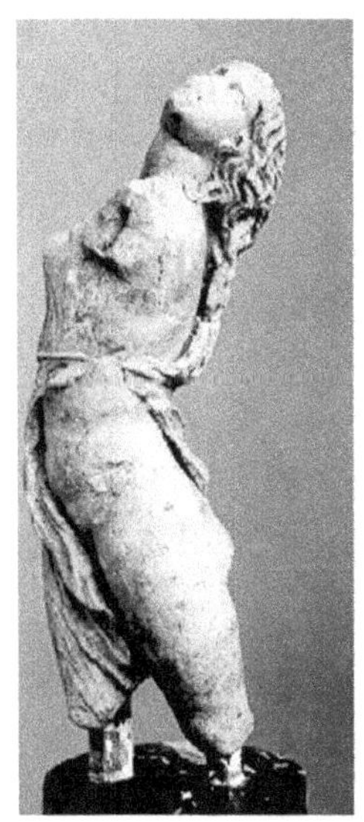

96   Skopas, *Maenad*, c. 350 B.C.E., Dresden, State
Art Collections: Sculpture Collection, Germany

In Greek naturalistic art, the emotional elements of *pathos* were not observed or represented until the fourth century B.C.E., when artists began to explore another aspect of the representation of life, with which they were already familiar through theater, introducing an entire range of what art historians were to call *pathos formulae*. These included heads thrown back, open lips, eyes rolled up, hair in wild curls, various body postures conveying a state of trance, fear, pain or other uncontrollable emotions, swollen muscles, deep facial wrinkles, flying drapery (figs. 96-98). Hence, observations taken at first from life, were transformed into conventional codes that were to become those of the entire Western world.

---

[309] *Transformation*, pp. 47 ff.

[310] In the West, around 1260, Thomas Aquinas wrote that "Beauty, on the other hand, has to do with knowledge, and we call beautiful a thing when it pleases the eye of the beholder (*visa placet*, and *visio*, for Thomas Aquinas, is always related to knowledge)." Thomas Aquinas, *Summa Theologica*, 1, 5, 4 ad 1. See also: Umberto Eco, *Art and Beauty in the Middle Ages*, trans. Hugh Bredin, Yale University Press, 1986, p. 70 ff.

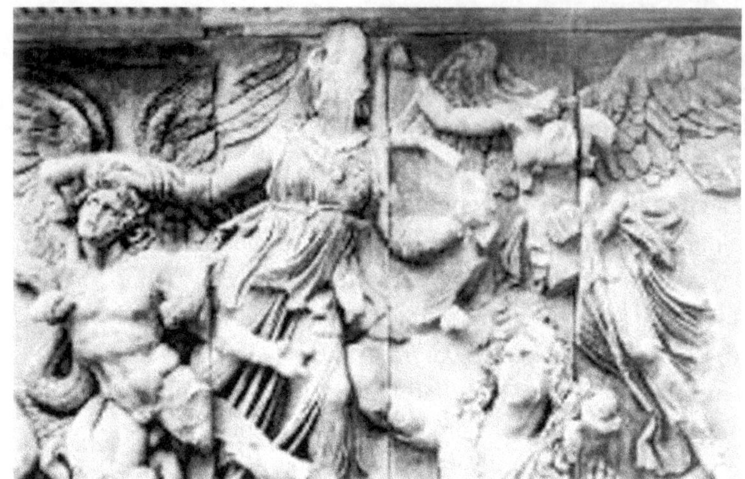

97 a *Athena Attacking the Giants*, detail of the Altar of Zeus from Pergamon, c. 175 B.C.E., Berlin, Staatliche Museen zu Berlin, Antiken Sammlungen, Pergamon-museum, Germany

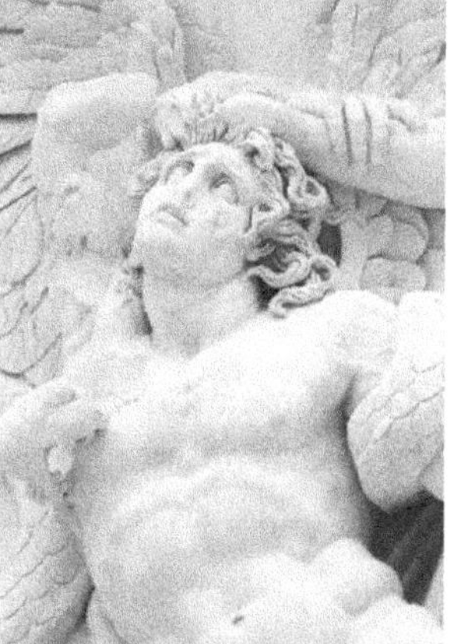

97 b Detail of Fig. 97 a

Pathos has been defined as the uncontrolled, immediate physical reaction to a very strong emotion or personal experience. It was no accident that the first representation of pain should have been introduced into sculpture in the Temple of Asklepios in Epidauros,[311] the Lourdes of Antiquity, where miraculous healings took place, and that it was developed during the Hellenistic period, a time of triumphant subjectivism. *Pathos* is opposed to or associated with *ethos*, defined as "character," which requires total self-control, as reflected in earlier classical antiquity, when works of art were still made in honor of the gods of the City and not as an instrument of personal and political propaganda (figs. 20-22, 26, 27, 28). The Latin term for *pathos* was *perturbatio* or *animum et sensus*.[312]

No Greek theoretical text of that period has survived. Aristotle's *Poetics* (c. 330 B.C.E.), which is more or less contemporaneous with the introduction of *pathos* into the visual arts, deals most specifically with the criteria for good tragedy, which ought to imitate actions arousing pity and fear, and thereby purge the spectator of these same emotions.

> A tragedy, then, is the imitation of an action that is serious, has magnitude, and is complete in itself, in language with pleasurable accessories, each kind brought separately in the various parts of the work; in a dramatic, not in a narrative form; with incidents arousing pity and fear, wherewith to accomplish its catharsis of such emotions (Poetics, 6, 1449 b).

---

[311] Pollitt, *Art and Experience in Classical Greece*, pp. 143 ff. and Figs. 59-61 and *idem, Art in the Hellenistic Age*, Cambridge, 1986.
[312] Pollitt, *The Ancient View of Greek Art*, pp. 30 ff. and pp. 194 ff.

          The Path Toward Beauty

Aristotle thus takes into account the reaction of the spectator. He devoted only five words to the subject of "catharsis," a non-discussion that later tradition vastly inflated.[313]

Emphasis on the personal feelings of the artist or of the beholder was rare in the West, at least up to Romanticism and the modern, rather vague concepts of intuition (*Ahnung*), and of empathy (*Einfühlung*).[314] Yet many texts of the late sixteenth and seventeenth centuries, in the aftermath of the Counter-Reformation, insist on the importance of depicting emotions, and thereby moving the beholder, and on "expression" in general. The portrayal of emotions became a central part of aesthetic thought in the Parisian Academy of Art (fig. 77).[315]

As beholders, however, we might not be moved at all by these expressive and codified means, and on the contrary, be overpowered by emotion before works of art that do not convey *pathos*, but lead us beyond the work itself into our deepest being. But what do we call emotion, after all, and how does emotion differ from feeling? For the sake of clarity and simplicity, we shall use the definitions of a contemporary neurologist, rather than the etymological, philosophical, psychological and psychoanalytical definitions.[316] According to the neurologist Antonio Damasio,[317] an emotion such as sorrow, fear, anguish, anger, strong attraction, amazement, scorn or empathy is stimulated by the view of an object and is immediate. It is activated by very different areas of the brain, all of them located outside those more specifically linked to vision. Vision, however, is the actual key that unlocks them all. It is, therefore, at the origin of emotions as well as of their mental elaboration, which Damasio calls feelings, which can, in turn, stimulate other emotions.

Both emotions and feelings are determined by the organization of our brain, and by the complexity and the depth of the convolutions of the cortex area, the neurons, and by development of the four lobes of the brain, each of them belonging to a different age on the evolutionary scale. Paul McLean has discovered that our brain consists, in fact, of three

---

[313] Aristotle, *Poétique*. Ed. J. Hardy, Paris, Belles Lettres, 1969, p. 16 ff.

[314] See especially Nicholas Poussin and Charles Le Brun according to Barasch, *Modern Theories* 1, Chapter 6.

[315] Ibid. p. 333. Le Brun wrote a *Traité de la passion* (1698), with practical advice on how to convey passions and emotions in paintings through facial expressions, illustrating his treatise with drawings. He does not deal only with the specific emotions of anger, laughter, weeping and despair already mentioned in Renaissance texts (Alberti, *Della Pittura*, II, 42, and Leonardo da Vinci, *Trattato*, McMahon, ns. 418 ff.), but borrows from, and goes beyond, Descartes' *Passions of the Soul* (1649), providing the artist with a range of codified models, rather than advising him to take only nature as a model, as Leonardo would have done more than a century earlier.

[316] See: André Lalande, *Vocabulaire technique et critique de la philosophie*, 5th ed., Paris, 1947, p. 29 (*Affection, Affectus*); p. 268 (*Emotion*), p. 964 (*Sentiment*).

[317] Antonio Damasio, *Looking for Spinoza: Joy, Sorrow, and the Feeling in the Brain*, 2003. (French trans. *Spinoza avait raison*, Paris, 2003. See also the updated bibliography and his previous books.

parts or of three cortices of very different ages that work together.[318] All three parts are interconnected, and each one determines a specific type of emotion, while only the most recent neo-cortex enables feelings, that is, the mental elaboration of emotions, which requires thought and self-consciousness.

Thus, the human brain is the result of a very long evolution, and emotion arises from the interaction of its various parts, some of them archaic, others more recent. The transformation of emotions into feelings, on the other hand, which occurs so quickly that analyzing the actual sequence of phenomena seems extremely difficult, is determined only by the neo-cortex, proper to *Homo Sapiens Sapiens*, which involves not only thought and self–awareness but also memory, education and culture.[319]

There are also different types of memory as well as different components, such as colors, light, composition, size, movement, relief, etc. Each one is apprehended by a specific hemisphere and area of the brain, which means that if one area is damaged, all our perceptions and our emotional responses to the event or to the object will be affected, and so will our feelings.[320]

Just as perception is never merely passive seeing; feelings are never static. The seat of human imagination,[321] hence, of our aptitude to use abstract and symbolic forms of communication, is situated in man's frontal lobe, which was not fully developed until *Homo Sapiens Sapiens,* around 100,000/50,000 years ago. At that point the neo-cortex was also in place, with its rows of neurons, that enabled the mental elaboration of emotions and the creation of the imaginary world of gods and of art, expressed by the earliest human entombment and works that did not fulfil any immediate utilitarian purpose (figs. 5-9).[322]

Since the very beginning of *Homo Sapiens Sapiens*, all forms of art have striven towards

---

[318] Paul McLean, "The triune brain, emotions and scientific bias," *The Neurosciences: Second Study Program*, ed., F. Schmitt, New York, Rockerfeller University, 1970. The three cortexes are: the arche-cortex which we inherited from the great reptiles of 250,000,000 years ago, which allows us to adapt ourselves to our environment; the paleo cortex, which dates from the earliest mammalians of 180,000,000 years ago and determines our primary emotions such as fear, joy, laughter, tears, but also some of our social emotions, such as empathy and certain forms of memory; and, finally, the most recent part of our brain, the neo-cortex, which developed from roughly 1,000,000 years ago—the time of the earliest symmetrical tools or bifacials—and was fully developed only with *Homo Sapiens Sapiens*, around 100,000 years ago—time of the earliest entombment—and, by c. 50/40,000, date of the earliest artifacts that did not fulfill an immediate utilitarian purpose and were symbolically charged. The neo-cortex forms 85% of our modern brain, and its neurons are aligned in perfect order, whereas those of the other two cortexes are in utter disorder.

[319] See also Damasio, op. cit.

[320] Roger Vigouroux, *La Fabrique du Beau,* Paris, 1992, 7-8.

[321] See above, p. 5.

[322] On the artistic level, this state was, however, prepared by two million years or so of making utilitarian artifacts or tools, progressively more specialized and more miniaturized.

                    The Path Toward Beauty

communication between man and man, and between man and the gods. This communication, as we saw earlier, always takes place through symbols perceived in signs and forms. In fact, as Deacon writes:

> With this new ability to create imaginary worlds, man may also have put order into the chaos of existence by giving it a meaning. Art fulfilled precisely this purpose, becoming a sign or a symbol of something else, acting as a means towards that end.[323]

The aesthetic stimulus also acts symbolically on the feeling or the apprehension of beauty, which is also a specifically human phenomenon (even though some animals may construct shelters and nests that seem to have been made deliberately to please a mate):

> The aesthetic stimulus is above all a symbol. The ability to symbolize is one of man's basic faculties. Man must grasp the meaning of things and construct out of fluctuating exterior signs invariants upon which he can carry out the mental operations required for relevant actions on the world.

> The aesthetic feeling is specifically human. While it is definitely rooted in archaic sub-cortical emotional behaviors, it also calls upon infinitely more elaborate functions. Indeed, it is not crude, rough, animal, visceral behavior, but rather something delicate, subtle, refined and intellectual. We are forced to admit the existence of an elaborate, hierarchical organization.

> Consequently, we can legitimately conclude that the frontal cortex ensures the hierarchical ordering of emotions and brings about a state of harmony between feelings and reason. The fact that it is closely connected to the temporal and frontal lobes as well as to the limbic system helps us to understand this ability.[324]

Emotions and feelings are totally interconnected, but symbolization is an integral part of the process, whereas feelings, are also determined by memory, education and culture and are, therefore, comparable to reasoning strategies. Damasio even speaks of the "rationality" of emotions and of feelings.[325]

Earlier in this text, we defined the term "symbol," a word which is often misused and carelessly employed. We saw how a symbolical act or artefact calls for the reunification of the visible and the known with the invisible and unknown, and how this process can fully take place only when the meaning of the work of art is disclosed. The symbol thus becomes

---

[323] Deacon, *The Symbolic Species*, p. 402.
[324] Vigouroux, op. cit., pp. 193 ff.; 233 ff.
[325] Damasio, op.cit., French trans, pp. 151-153.

a sign of the invisible, or of its presence, but only for those who are capable of perceiving it, who are aware of it and seek to understand its meaning.[326]

If a work of art becomes the symbol of something else and acts as a means towards that end, then symbolic knowledge, as M. M. Davy writes, is also comparable to a revelation, and the revelation, linked to the symbol, is always related to the level of awareness of the person who receives it. Could we not say the same about the feeling of beauty?

There is no such thing as a work of art without meaning, even when its maker affirms, more or less vehemently, that it has none, a statement which is significant in itself. At the same time, not all works of art are beautiful, and most artists never even aim at beauty.

While meaning and form intertwine in all works of art, our reactions to them differ according to our personal memories, education and culture. Yet it is puzzling to note that certain works of art have the same impact on many, very different, if not on all, beholders. Within the long perspective of time and with the widening of our cultural horizons, some works of art seem to have acquired an exceptional status and are universally recognized as being of the highest quality, as representing, in the most accomplished form, a moment of human civilization or of individual achievement. Each one of us could make his or her own list, and might well wonder if the same works would also appear on that of the others. Personally, when I think of the works of art on my imaginary list, they still evoke strong emotions. Do we all share a similar education and culture, are we all receptive to the same beauty?

All the works of art mentioned so far seem to have something essential and timeless in common, which is not determined by style, taste or fashion. Each work also belongs fully to its own civilization, yet is just as "alive" today as it must have been in its own time, transcending the limits of what Baudelaire called modernity: "Modernity is the transitory, fleeting, contingent half of art, while the other half is eternal and immutable."[327] However, many of these works would not have been considered either significant or beautiful by any of the art lovers or philosophers of eighteenth-century Europe, had they known about them, because they would not have conformed to the established concepts of beauty and art defined by the criteria inherited from Classical Greece and the High Renaissance and recognized in some of their highest achievements. The art of the Middle Ages or, for that matter, of virtually all the rest of the world was totally ignored, if not despised at the time.

---

[326] For the definition of *symbol* and some related references, I referred most specifically to: Marie-Madeleine Davy, *Initiation à la Symbolique romane. XIIe siècle*, Paris, Flammarion, 1964, pp. 98 ff. and Moshe Barasch, *Modern Theories*, 1, Chaps. 2, 3 and 4.

[327] Charles Baudelaire, *Le Peintre de la Vie Moderne*, IV, 1863:"La modernité c'est le transitoire, le fugitif, le contingent, la moitié de l'art, dont l'autre moitié est l'éternel et l'immuable."

     The Path Toward Beauty

It seems, therefore, that the criteria of beauty are in themselves meaningful and, as such, they too become signs and symbols. Why, during certain periods of Western art, was there such insistence on the lifelike quality of art and on the principle of *symmetria*, the beauty and "mystique" of certain mathematical proportions, the knowledge of perspective, and the quality of design or color, whereas in other periods and places, we find a similar insistence on conceptual, non-naturalistic forms of art that obey other canons and fulfil other purposes? What does that tell us about each culture as well as about Beauty?

If the criteria of beauty change, the concept of Beauty itself will also change, and that is equally meaningful. This concept is not, in fact, related to taste, but is instead determined by the changes that occur in art, by the diversity of form and meaning. This, in turn, has to be acknowledged in order to stimulate our emotions and awaken our feeling of beauty. Not to have recognized this may indeed be the touchstone of all aesthetic disputes since Hume and Kant.

Thus, we would like to reverse Malraux's words: "Why should art fail to undergo a mutation as vast as that of beauty?"[328] Why should beauty fail to undergo a mutation as vast as that of art? The meaning of beauty changes with every change in art, which never involves merely form, but also significance, thereby acting as a stimulus for our emotions and feelings, both of which also call for meaning.

When a work of art has such a powerful, emotional impact on us, beauty seems self-evident, although it cannot be defined by any rational argument or any particular rule that we have analyzed, even though the artists have followed one or another. Nevertheless, when an artwork has such power, it is not "obtained by the artist by aiming at pleasing the senses" alone, and still less made "to decorate," to borrow Henry Moore's expressions, nor is it, as Picasso puts it, merely "the application of a canon;" neither is it aiming at "Beauty in the Greek or Renaissance sense." Because the concept of beauty itself has changed its meaning, beauty in our own time may well participate in what Henry Moore calls "an expression of the significance of life," striking us at the deepest level and in the most mysterious part of our being with an unequivocal resonance.

Just as the concept of Beauty is meaningful in itself and its meaning has changed through the ages, we receive it differently depending on the degree of our own receptivity and knowledge, while some artworks are beautiful always and everywhere, as if there were also a universal and, hence, unchanging concept of beauty. Again, something seems to elude us, but could we not agree that the Beauty of an artwork is precisely that which Henry Moore called its "spiritual vitality," or what George Steiner calls "real presence" and

---

[328] André Malraux.

André Malraux "timeless presence,"[329] bringing to the fore that which would otherwise have remained hidden, making the invisible visible, summoning us with its presence? And has it not always been so, because of, or in spite of, canons and criteria, in even the Greek or Renaissance sense?

> Can we doubt that beauty is something more than symmetry, that symmetry itself owes its beauty to a remoter Principle? . . . Undoubtedly, this Principle exists, it is something that is perceived at the first glance, something which the soul names as from ancient knowledge and, recognizing, welcomes it, enters into unison with it (Plotinus, *Enneads*, I.6.2).

What do disparate works of art, such as the interior of the Cistercian church of Fontenay (figs. 36 and 98) and Rothko's Chapel in Houston (fig. 99) or some of his paintings (figs. 100, 103) have in common, and that makes them beautiful and confers such presence on them? Has it something to do with truthfulness, or with the search for truth? In his last public statement in 1958, Rothko said: "The dictum 'know thyself' is only valuable if the ego is removed from process in the search for truth."

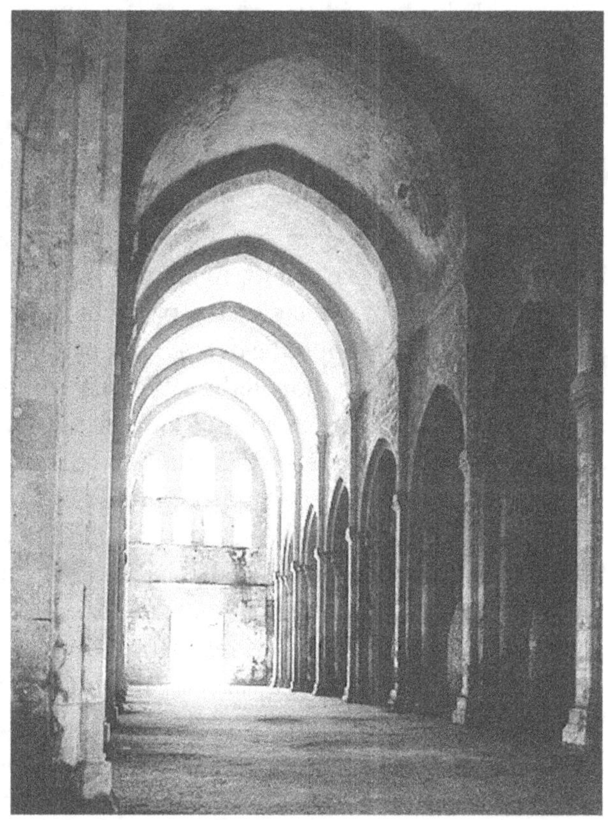

98 Interior view towards the west, 1139-41, Cistercian Abbey Church of Notre-Dame Fontenay

---

[329] Malraux, *The Voices of Silence*, *The Museum Without Walls*; idem, *The Metamorphosis of the Gods*. See also: Octavio Paz, *Quest for the Present*, about "the true time, that which we search for without knowing it: the present, the presence. . . . What do we know about the present? Nothing or nearly nothing. But the poets know one thing: the present is the living source of presences."

   The Path Toward Beauty

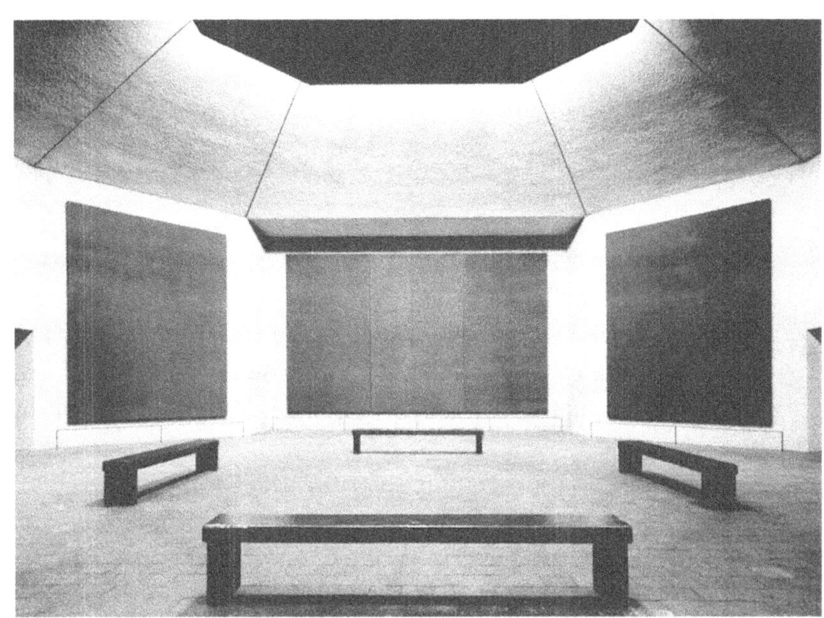

99 Interior, Rothko Chapel, dedicated in 1971, Houston, Texas

100 Mark Rothko, *Triptych*, Houston, Texas, for north wall of the Rothko Chapel, 1964-1967

Beauty in the Quest for Truth

"A man ought not to work for any why, not for God nor for his glory nor for anything at all that is outside him, but only for that which is his being, his very life within him."[330]
—Meister Eckhart, Sermon 65.

Beauty imposes itself, so does truth, and both baffle our rational understanding and defy definition. "Truth" is a word with so many implications and connotations that perhaps we might best begin by saying what it is not in the context of this chapter. By truth, we do not mean any form of dogmatic "truth," imposed by any church, religion or political ideology, nor for that matter, any notion of absolute "truth," except, insofar as it is explicitly sought by the artist.

In the context of the visual arts, "truth" does not refer to "a visible reality accurately represented" or "true to life" either, as Plato used the term *aletheia* in the *Sophist* (235^E ff.) or as Quintilian and Cicero the term *veritas*.[331] In this section, "truth" refers more particularly to the inner, personal truth of the artist, which he can only discover gradually through the long process of creation and which he cannot bring forth until his mind and hand are finally in full agreement. Along with artists in search of inner truth, we also find artists seeking to grasp the truth of life itself, the mystery of nature's beauty and harmony, attempting to understand its laws, to capture its essence and to be in unison with it.[332] Like Chinese painters and calligraphers, they try to be attuned to the *Ch'i*, the breath of life or the Vital Force of Heaven.[333] All these artists remind us of scientists who also want to understand and explain the beauty of the universe and hope to discover the truth when their theory is actually beautiful. Thus, the astrophysicist Trinh Xuan Thuan writes:

A theory is beautiful because of its inevitability. Just as when we listen to Bach,

---

[330] Coomaraswamy, "Meister Eckhart's View of Art," *Transformation*, p. 88.

[331] Pollitt, *The Ancient View of Greek Art*. pp. 170-182.

[332] Sometimes the artist searches for one form of truth through another, as was the case of Paul Cezanne when he drew and painted innumerable times the same Montagne Sainte-Victoire. As Matisse once said: "L'exactitude n'est pas la verité."

[333] Sze, op.cit., pp. 609 ff. ". . . virtually the entire contents of the Manual are aimed at developing the painter's spiritual resources (*Ch'i*) in order to express the Spirit (*Ch'i*), the Breath of the *Tao*." The authors of the Manual made no attempt, however, to formulate a definition of *Ch'i*. Like the Chinese philosophers, from whom the concept and the term were taken, they examined, discussed and revered the idea. As an aspect of *Tao*, *Ch'i* was recognized as something essentially indefinable, something perceptible only when man's *Ch'i* was exercised together with his intellectual faculties. Nevertheless, the constant references to the *Ch'i* are not merely rhapsodic; they are statements of a firm conviction of the existence of the *Ch'i*, the Breath or Vitalizing Force of the *Tao*, which was the belief underlying the whole of Chinese life in the order and harmony of nature, or, according to the familiar phrase, "the harmony of Heaven and Earth."

---

not a single note could have been changed without breaking the harmony, . . .
it is the same for a beautiful theory. . . . The most attractive aspect of Einstein's
theory resides in the fact that it is complete in itself. If only one of his conclusions were to be invalidated, the entire theory would have to be abandoned. It
is impossible to modify the theory without destroying the entire structure. . . .
The inevitability and necessity of a beautiful theory is such that, often when it
has been formulated, scientists wonder why it had not been evident before. The
second quality of a beautiful theory is that it must be simple: its ideas must rely
on a minimal number of hypotheses, no ornament.[334]

At the very end of the twentieth century, scientists are the only ones who are not afraid
to acknowledge the objectivity of beauty when it is related to truth. This correlation is made
again and again by mathematicians and astrophysicists. Let me give another example, that
of Andrew Wiles' 1995 solution to Fermat's theorem, which had remained unsolved since
1641. After seven or eight years of work, Wiles finally chose the most beautiful of his demonstrations as the one that had to be correct.[335]

Could we not define the formal beauty of any work of art in very similar terms?

Throughout this text, we have primarily talked about the beauty of works of art—anonymous or signed—that were in most cases made for ritual or religious purposes, hence by
artists who shared the beliefs of their commissioners and beholders, and who were rooted
in the same tradition. These works of art are recognized as beautiful, as being "of quality"
or "of compelling stature" when they make us aware of that which transcends them and
remains ultimately invisible and ineffable, something that, for lack of a better word, we have
called "the sacred," which is either present or not, independently of any particular religious
belief.

As Peter Brooke puts it:

All human impulses towards what we call in an imprecise and clumsy manner
"quality," come from a source whose true nature we entirely ignore but which
we are perfectly capable of recognizing when it appears either in ourselves or
in another person. It is not communicated through noise, but through silence.
Since one must use words, one calls it "sacred." . . . So, in thousands of very
unexpected forms, the invisible may appear, the quest for the sacred is thus a
search. The invisible may appear in the most everyday objects. . . . The sacred is
a transformation, in terms of quality, of that which is not sacred at the outset.[336]

---

[334] Trinh Xuan Thuan, *Le Chaos et l'Harmonie*, Paris, 1998, I, p. 26. The Science of Chaos defines beauty
in similar terms but through the non-Euclidian geometry of fractals. James Gleick, *Chaos, Making a New
Science,* 1987.

[335] A. Wiles, "Modular Eliptic—Curves and Fermat's last theorem," *Ann. Math.,* 141 (1995), 443-551.

[336] *Open Door,* pp. 69 ff. See also his *Empty Space,* pp. 42 ff.

Thus, we can unhesitatingly draw an analogy between beauty and "quality" when such a transformation takes place, when the referral to a transcendent dimension "underwrites" the work of art, whether the artist was aware of it or not.

We also discovered in previous chapters, as George Steiner underlines throughout all his texts, that:

> Everything we recognize as being of compelling stature in literature, art, music is of a religious inspiration or reference. . . . Referral and self-referral to a transcendent dimension, to that which is felt to reside either explicitly—this is to say ritually, theologically, by force of revelation—or implicitly, outside immanent or purely secular reach, does underwrite created forms from Homer and the *Oresteia* to the *Brothers Karamazov* and Kafka. It informs art from the cave of Lascaux to Rembrandt and to Kandinsky.[337]

In the twentieth century, artists rarely spoke of God or, for that matter, of beauty or of truth,[338] but they did refer to the notion of transcendence, outside any religious connotation. Braque told Picasso that if he believed in God, he would say of certain painters and their best paintings that they had been touched by grace, to which Picasso answered:

> Something sacred, that's it! We ought to be able to say that word, or something like it, but people would take it the wrong way, and give it a meaning it hasn't got. We ought to be able to say that such or such a painting is as it is, with its capacity for power, because it is "touched by God." But people would put a wrong interpretation on it. And yet it's the nearest we can get to the truth.[339]

When Matisse painted the Chapel of the Rosary for the Dominican nuns in Vence (France), finished in 1951, he was nearly eighty years old and he wrote:

> For me, the project is essentially a work of art. I meditate and let myself be penetrated by what I am undertaking. I do not know if I have faith or not. Perhaps I am a Buddhist. The essential thing is to work in a state of mind that approaches prayer. Modern art is certainly an art intended to delight, but this in no way implies that it has no religious or spiritual content. I didn't need to convert in order

---

[337] George Steiner, *Real Presences*, London, 1989, pp. 216 -217.

[338] In his *Aphorisms* of 1914-15, Franz Marc wrote: "The mysterious word truth always makes me think of this physical idea of a center of gravity. Truth is always on the move. It is always somewhere but never in the foreground, never on the surface. . . . Everything has appearance and essence, shell and kernel, mask and truth. What does it say against inward determination of things that we finger the shell without reaching the kernel, that we live the appearance instead of perceiving the essence, that the mask of things so blinds us that we cannot find the truth?"

[339] Cited in Roger Lipsey, *Art of Our Own.* p. 19. Malraux refers to Braques' quote in his *Tête d'Obsidienne.*

to execute the chapel of Vence. My inner attitude didn't change; it remained
what it was, what it is in front of a face, a chair, or a fruit. . . . My only religion is
that of love for the work to be created, love for creation and a great sincerity. I
made this chapel with a single feeling of expressing myself in depth.[340]

Max Beckmann wrote in 1939:
In my opinion, all important things in art since Ur of the Chaldees, since Tel Halaf
and Crete, have always originated from the deepest feeling about the mystery of
Being.[341]

Brancusi, whose writings and *Bird in Space* were already discussed in the prologue, did
not speak about truth, but about the essential and the spiritual:
Everything—animate or inanimate—has a spirit. At the turning point in the development of my métier, I said to myself: I must express the spirit of the subject.
The spirit will be alive forever, or, if you wish, the *idea* of the subject, that which
never dies. It grows in the viewer as life from life. Starting with this thought, you
naturally reach the conclusion that it is not the detail that creates the work, but
rather the essential. I worked hard to discover the means of more easily finding
for each subject the key form that would powerfully sum up the idea of the subject. Certainly that directed me to a non-figurative art; it is the result. But I never
proposed to astonish people through something odd. I reasoned simply, as you
can see, and I also reached something simple, terrible in its simplicity: a synthesis
that should suggest what I wanted to represent. I reached the point where I could
draw out of bronze, wood, or marble that hidden diamond, the essential.[342]

Brancusi wanted to decipher life, joining, as he said, with the universe and the elements,
by finding the inner proportion, which is the ultimate truth in all things, and by reaching
simplicity and "entering into the real sense of things." He summarized his whole approach
to art and to life by saying: "We cannot ever reach God, but the courage to travel towards
Him remains important."[343]

Dealing with such vast and intangible questions as those of Beauty and Truth, we are reminded of how Diotima initiated us to the mysteries of love in Plato's *Symposium*, and
more specifically to the love of beauty, leading us, step by step, to ever greater awareness

---

[340] Henry Matisse, *Écrits et Propos sur l'art* [*Matisse on Art*], ed. D. Fourcade, Paris, 1972, 264-265, 268n.
[341] Chipp, *Theories of Modern Art*, p. 189.
[342] Lipsey, op. cit., p. 225-246.
[342] Ibid.

of increasingly universal beauty and truth. Her speech begins, in fact, with the following statement.

> Having true convictions without being able to give reasons for them, surely you see that such a state of mind cannot be called understanding, because nothing irrational deserves the name, but it would be equally wrong to call it ignorance. How can one call ignorance a state of mind which hits upon the truth? The fact is that having true convictions is what I called it just now, a condition halfway between knowledge and ignorance (*Symposium*, 202).

Yet, in spite of Plato's insistence on the necessity of dialectical reasoning to distinguish the false from the true, once again he used a myth to express the truth. In the myth, Diotima compares Eros to a *daimon*, neither man nor god, but an intermediary between the two, inventing the philosophical myth of his conception on the day of the birth of Aphrodite, the goddess of beauty. His father was Plenty and his mother was Misery. For Plato, myth is, therefore, between knowledge and ignorance, an intermediate state in which we are made aware of a very deep truth, without, however, being able to define it by rational means. In short, the myth has the same function as the symbol.

As for the relationship between beauty and truth, we, too, have real convictions without being able to give reasons. At best, we can only try to shed light on that conviction through the texts of the artists themselves, limiting our inquiry to the twentieth century. The more twentieth century artists sought the essential, the more they seem to have chosen abstraction; the more abstract they became, the more isolated they felt and the more they had to explain their visual art in words.

The quest for truth, for honesty, for sincerity, for revealing the essential seems to have been at the origin of twentieth century abstract, non-figurative art, or art that no longer represented "things," such as that of Kandinsky, Brancusi, Malevich (figs. 65 and 101), Mondrian (fig. 102) as well as Klee, Rothko (figs. 99, 100 and 103) or Soulages. Each of these quests was different, but their common choice of abstraction reflects a common spiritual quest as if "art advanced where religion once led" (Mondrian).

The Path Toward Beauty

101   Kazimir Malevich, *White on White*, 1918, New York, Museum of Modern Art

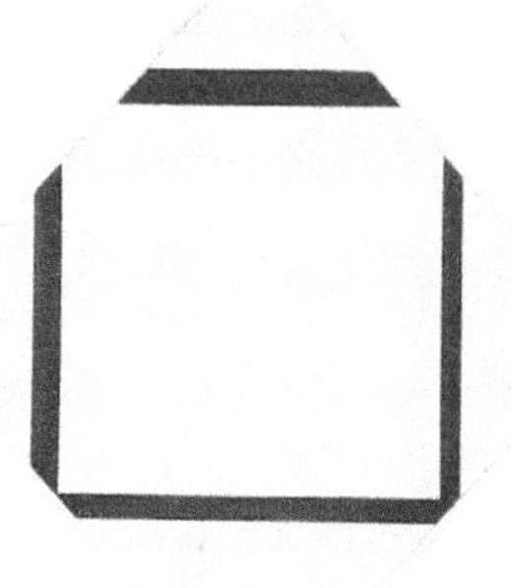

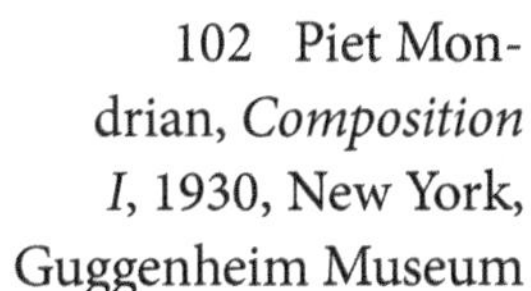

102   Piet Mondrian, *Composition I*, 1930, New York, Guggenheim Museum

103   Mark Rothko, *Untitled*, 1964

Kandinsky wrote *On the Spiritual in Art* in 1912, before the horrors of the First World War, that the "artist's eyes should always be directed to his inner life and his ear turned to the voice of internal necessity" which he could only do by abandoning any representational form of art. Continuing, he said:

> It must become possible to hear the whole world as it is without representational interpretation. . . . Abstract forms (lines, planes, dots, etc.) are not important in themselves, but only their inner sound, their life. . . . The world sounds. It is a cosmos of spiritually active beings. Even dead matter is living spirit.[344]

---

[344] Kandinsky and Mark, *The Blaue Reiter Almanac: Documentary Edition*, ed. K. Lankheit, New York, 1974, 164-165, 173.

In music, hearing is less linked to the material and outer world of objects, and the ear has access to what is invisible and which can only be translated into visual terms through abstract means.

Kandinsky's "living spirit" reminds us of the Chinese *ch'i-yün-sheng-tun* (breath of life-resonance-movement), the first and most important of the six canons of Chinese painting. The active, operative force in the universe is the *ch'i*,[345] it is the dynamic energy, the life breath, the movement that pervades everything, and without which any painting would be but a dead thing. Kandinsky concluded:

> In the final analysis every serious work is tranquil. Every serious work resembles in poise the quiet phrase "I am here." Like or dislike for the work evaporates, but the sound of that phrase is eternal.[346]

He was also influenced by Rudolf Steiner's *Anthroposophy*, just as Malevich was influenced by Ouspensky's mystic concept of the artist as one who could see what was hidden and penetrate into a higher order of reality.[347]

Malevich hung his *Black Square on a White Background* (fig. 65), the visual *Manifesto of Suprematism*, high across a corner of the exhibition room in Saint Petersburg, in the place usually reserved for an icon in an orthodox Russian house, thereby announcing his complete break from any form of figurative art, as well as the profound meaning of his abstract painting. In his *Manifesto of Suprematism*, of 1915, Malevich wrote:

> Art no longer cares to serve the state and religion; it no longer wishes to illustrate the history of manners; it wants to have nothing to do with objects, as such, and believes that it can exist in and for itself, without "things." . . . The square seemed incomprehensive and dangerous to the public and to the critics, . . . and this, of course, was to be expected. The ascent to non-objective art is arduous and painful . . . but is, nonetheless, rewarding. The familiar recedes farther and farther into the background. . . . No more likeness of reality, no idealistic images—nothing but a desert! But the desert is filled with the spirit. . . . To the suprematist, the visual phenomena of the objective world are in themselves meaningless, the significant thing is feeling as such, quite apart from the environment out of which it is called forth. Thus, art arrives at a non-objective representation, at Suprematism . . . . Suprematism is the rediscovery of pure art which, in the course of time, had

---

[345] Wen C. Fong, *Images of the Mind*, Princeton University Art Museum, 1984, pp. 4 and 28.

[346] Kandinsky, *Complete Writings on Art*, ed. Kenneth C. Lindsay and P. Vergo, Boston, 1982, 218.

[347] Rudolf Steiner, *Knowledge of the Higher Worlds and Its Attainment*, 1904 or *Christianity as Mystical Fact and the Mysteries of Antiquity*, 1902. See also S. Ringborn, *The Sounding Cosmos: a Study of Spiritualism of Kandinsky and the Genesis of Abstract Painting*, Acta Academiae Aboensis, ser. A, XXXVIII, Abo, Finland, 1970. P.D. Ouspensky, *Tertium Organum: the Third Canon of Thought, a Key to the Enigmas of the World*, New York, 1959.

become obscured by the accumulation of "things." . . . The form becomes an allusion to space, and the painting, an allusion to painting, revealing the essential,
the supreme or essential being, a world without objects.[348]

The *Black Square* of 1915 (fig. 65), or the *White Square on a White Background* of
1918 (fig. 101), in which Malevich seems to have arrived at his own truth, are impersonal,
geometric forms, impenetrable black or white surfaces. In Malevich's words:

> The keys of Suprematism are leading me to discover things still outside of cogni-
> tion. My new painting does not belong solely to the earth. The earth has been
> abandoned like a house. It has been decimated. Indeed man feels a great yearn-
> ing for space, a gravitation to break free from the globe of earth.

In answer to one of his critics, he wrote:

> In art one has the duty to represent the essential forms. Regardless of whether
> one likes them or not. Do you or don't you like it?—art does not ask you that, just
> as it didn't ask you when it created the stars in the sky.[349]

None of these painters ever mentioned beauty, but all of them strove towards what we
would call an inner truth, a quest for the "spiritual," the essential or the supreme. Mondrian
(fig. 102), who became a non-figurative abstract artist in the 1920s, was the first to connect
abstract art to the universal, the immutable and the absolute, the beautiful and the true.

> Thus, we must carefully distinguish between two forms of reality, one which has
> an individual and one which has a universal appearance. The latter, through neu-
> tral forms and colors. Pure abstract art aims at creating universal realities, pure
> and complete in its beauty, . . . it has always been only one struggle . . . to create
> universal beauty.[350]

For Mondrian, "the abstract in art is established by the most profound interiorization of the
outward and by the purest exteriorization of the inward." He used the simplest of square
shapes, pure colors and black horizontal and vertical bands of varying thickness, positioned
differently from one composition to another, thus creating interrelations of colored and
white rectangular shapes that differed according to the ratios he used. Yet none of his paintings look machine-made, despite his need for exactness to rid his work of individuality and

---

[348] K. Malevich, "Manifesto of Suprematism," *The Non-objective World*, trans. and ed. by Howard
Dearstyne, Chicago, 1959. Cf. also in: Robert L. Herbert ed., *Modern Artists on Art*, Englewood Cliffs,
1964, pp. 92-102.
[349] *Kasimir Malevich 1878-1935*, Exhibition Catalogue, Amsterdam, Stedelijk Museum, 1989, ill. 2 and 42,
pp. 70 and 165.
[350] Chipp, op. cit., pp. 349-364.

reach the universal. Mondrian was aware that "just as traditional aesthetic truths reappear in the new art but are expressed differently, so new life reveals traditional philosophic ideas and concepts, but practiced differently."[351] Mondrian's "Neo-platonic" texts as well as his paintings remind us of Plato's *Philebus*, where he speaks about the beauty of geometric figures and pure colors:

> I do not mean the beauty of human figures, or of paintings, I mean the straight line or the circle, the plane and solid figures, formed by means of compass, ruler and square . . . because I say that these figures are not, as the others, beautiful in some way, but they are always beautiful in themselves. They give us pleasure that belongs to them, and have nothing to do with the pleasure given by tickling. . . . There are also pure colors or unmixed colors that offer beauty and pleasure of the same kind, and pure notes that are not relatively beautiful, but absolutely beautiful (*Philebus*, 54).

For Paul Klee: "Everything passes, and what remains of former times, what remains of life, is the spiritual. The spiritual in art, or we might simply call it the artistic, in everything we do, the claim to the absolute is unchanging." [352]

What is the "spiritual"?[353] It is another way to name that which is neither strictly physical nor material, but forces us to question the world with our mind or spirit, to move inwardly and beyond immediate appearances in the quest for truth. It is another name for what Mircea Eliade called "the notion of the sacred," inherent and common to all men, independent of any religion, as opposed to the secular and to the profane, reflecting man's urge for transcendence, always in search of meaning.

In Hindu treatises we read about different degrees of perception, depending on whether the artist has used his carnal eye, his angelic eye, or his eye of wisdom. We are also told that there are three modes of contemplation, depending whether we stop at the material image, at the interior image or go beyond the image itself.[354] In a Sufi text, mentioned by Henry Corbin, we read about the eyes of flesh and the eyes of fire, the latter perceiving each thing as the outer sign of an inner fact, as if all things were part of a mysterious and divine whole, whereas the former perceives only the thing itself in its material evidence.[355]

---

[351] Ibid.

[352] Paul Klee, *Notebooks*, Vol. 2: *The Nature of Nature*, ed. J. Spiller, New York, 1973, 461.

[350] For Kant, "the spirit (*Geist*) is the animating principle of the mind . . . by means of which this principle animates the soul, . . . puts the mental powers purposively into swing" (*Analytic of the Sublime*, § 49). For Hegel, art "was the representation of *the Divine*, of spiritual truths of the widest range. Its function was "exclusively to satisfy spiritual interests."

[354] Coomaraswamy, "Paroksa and Abhasa," *Transformation of Nature into Art*, 4 and 5.

[355] Henry Corbin, "Eyes of Flesh and Eyes of Fire: Science and Gnosis," *Material for Thought*, 8, 1980, pp. 5-10. in R. Lipsey, *An Art of our Own*, Introduction.

Even if this quest for the "spiritual in art" is proper to the founders of twentieth century abstract art, there have been other periods of Western art in which the artists chose nonfigurative art, and very much for the same reasons. Though we cannot compare the abstract interlacing motifs of Irish Gospel Books of the eighth and ninth centuries or the arabesques and intricate geometric patterns of early Islamic art to the very different personal modes of twentieth century Western abstract art, nevertheless, in all these examples the individual artist refrains from telling a story or from representing his mental image of the natural world. His art becomes impersonal through the use of universal geometric forms. Thus, the monks who decorated the Irish *Book of Durrow* (fig. 104) or *Book of Kells* (fig. 31) obeyed the strictest geometrical principles and the complexity of the interlacing ornaments that cover those manuscripts are the result of an extremely subtle use of the compass on a scaffolding of squares. On some of the "carpet" pages, we see meanders of curvilinear and spiral lines, in constant metamorphosis, taking us into an endless wandering, in which we lose ourselves, although it apparently consists of a single ribbon motif which is convoluted to yield these patterns. When men and animals are intertwined within initials, they, too, become ribbon and ornament. To paint such pages required extraordinary concentration and discipline, as part of a spiritual initiation, and were intended as a means of meditation and prayer.

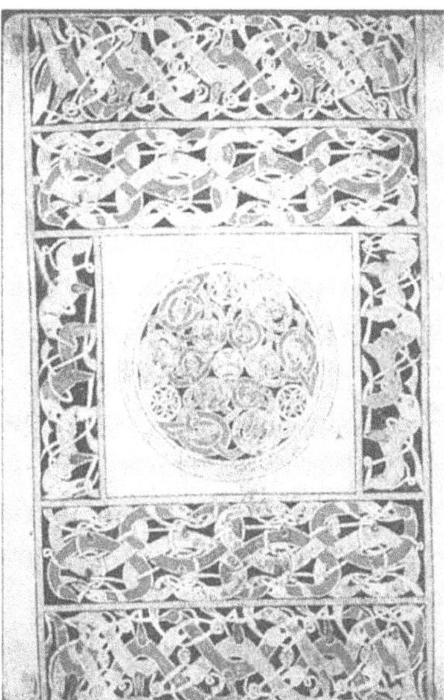

104 *Carpet Page with Animal Interlace,*
The Book of Durrow, c. 680, Dublin,
Trinity College Library (Ms. 57, fol. 192v)

At the end of *The Book of Durrow*, the scribe did not sign his name, but blessed his brethren and asked them to pray for him: "Pray for me brother, and may the Lord be with you."[356] He had no urge to explain his art either; his reasons were perfectly self-evident. We find the same concentration in the drawing of a Tibetan *mandala,* which is a very elaborate diagram of the cosmos, based on the square and the circle (fig. 105). Tibetan Buddhist monks draw it with a compass and ruler and use the four main primary colors. It implies an utter detachment from all worldly concerns and from the self; it is also a medium for meditation and proposes a path towards the center, or the heart of the world or, in Jungian terms, to the depth of man's soul.

---

[356] F. Henry, *L'Art Irlandais*, 2 vols, Édition Zodiaque, 1964, vol. 1, pp. 291 ff.

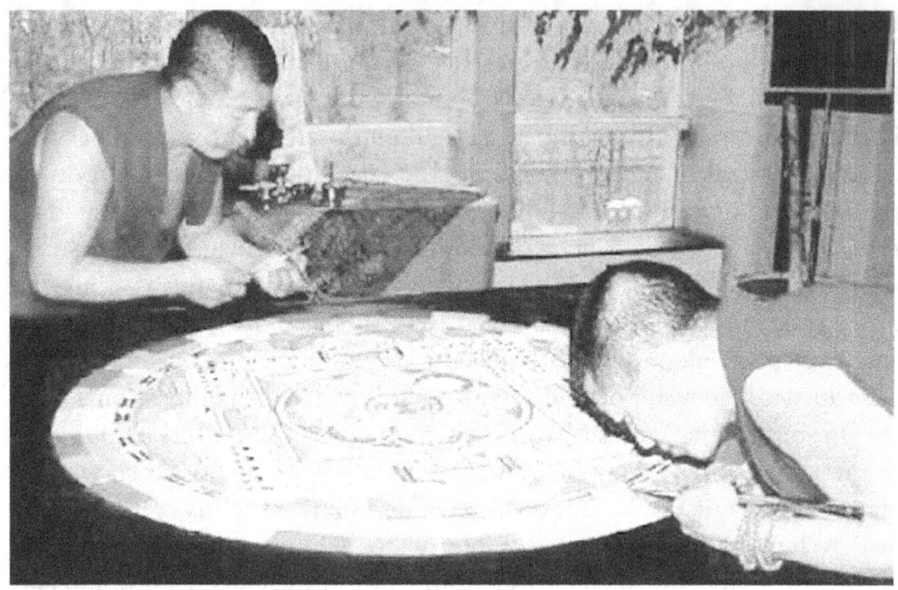

105
Tibetan
monks
working on a
Sand Mandala

In Islamic art, the interior wall surfaces of mosques and palaces, the prayer niches (*mihrabs*), domes and minarets, the bronze and ivory objects, textiles, ceramics, glass lamps, carpets and manuscripts, all are covered with purely ornamental motifs (figs. 2, 81, 83, 84). Figurative art is prohibited, or at least avoided, in public and religious buildings. Artists who would have attempted to imitate the living were condemned as if they had competed with God, who alone gives shape to figures and is the sole creator because he alone gives life.[357] The Islamic ornamental patterns are intertwined with calligraphy rendering Qur'anic verses in Arabic, which became part of the decorative motifs. Arabic was the language in which God spoke to Mohammed, hence, it is the sacred language common to all Muslims. Islamic ornament depends on an infinite number of variables in which

> the visible unit of design—vegetal, geometric, or others—has been totally subordinated to a number of abstract principles. Physical form has been constricted into a vehicle for expression of something else than itself. . . . The geometric units translated into lines and circles and rhumbs . . . with an infinite growth of a design in which the observer loses himself.[358]

This approach to decoration appears first in the decoration of the Dome of the Rock in Jerusalem (fig. 85), the Mosque of Damascus, the prayer niche (*mihrab*) of Ibn Tulun in

---

[357] R. Ettinghausen, "The Man-Made Setting," *The World of Islam*, London, 1992, chapter 2, p. 62; Oleg Grabar, *The Formation of Islamic Art*, New Haven, 1973, pp. 75-103.

[358] Oleg Grabar, *Formation*, pp. 202 ff.; idem, *The Mediation of Ornament*, Princeton University Press, 1992 and Idem, *Penser l'art islamique. Une esthétique de l'ornement*, Paris, 1996, pp. 172 ff .

                              The Path Toward Beauty

Cairo, the *quibla* wall and *mihrab* of the great mosque of Córdoba (fig. 83 b) and, above all, the manuscripts of the Quran itself. Color also plays an important role throughout this patterned ornamentation that we find in all media, especially in the interior world of mosques, houses and gardens.[359] Their variety and beauty may not be meaningful in themselves, although they seem to be addressed to God rather than to men, for whom the inscriptions themselves are unreadable. They become an affirmation of faith, hence no longer intended to be deciphered word for word by worshippers or passers-by.

While the inscriptions are, in fact, visible from every vantage point, the background design of scrolls, arabesques or geometric patterns appears or disappears, according to the point of view, as if the Word of God was forever enduring, while man and his handiwork had at best only a fleeting existence. This symbolic function of writing existed even when it challenged the best epigraphists or when Arabic was not even locally spoken, because it always conferred power or authority to whatever it decorated.

In these examples of non-figurative art, the artists have remained anonymous and left no explanatory texts behind, yet, like abstract painters of the twentieth century, they moved away from the sensible reality to the intelligible world of geometry or the transcendental realm of the word of God. On the other hand, when beauty is found in the figurative arts, it is not because it is a visual translation of a precise text or teaching, but rather because the artist has succeeded in creating a visual equivalence between them. Both of them arise within a shared spiritual and intellectual climate. The artist has followed strict iconographic and stylistic rules, which he was also able to transcend. Let us take the example of the central portal of the basilica of Vézelay in Burgundy (figs. 59 a and b).[360] In the sculptural field of the tympanum, the sculptor gives us the visual equivalence not only of various pages of the New Testament (Acts 1 and 2, Rev. 22) and of the description of the theophany itself (Ps. 46/47; Ez. 20:33; Rev. 4:2-9), but also of "the sound of the violent wind which filled the entire house in which the apostles were sitting, when the tongues as of fire came to rest on the head of each one of them and they were suddenly filled with the Holy Spirit and began to speak different languages" (Acts 1 and 2). Furthermore, the sculptor belongs to the same period in which one might have read, especially in the Cluniac, Benedictine monastery of Vézelay, John Scotus Erigena's description of God, in his commentaries on the *Heavenly Hierarchy* of Pseudo-Dionysius the Aeropagite,[361] who may have been a further source of inspiration. He used various means to make us partake of his own vision: the ideally beautiful features of the elongated face of Christ, the importance given to the hierarchy of sizes and location, hence the immensity of Christ, who fills the entire height of the tympanum,

---

[359] Ettinghausen, op. cit., p. 61, pp. 68-70.

[360] F. Salet, *La Madeleine de Vézelay,* Melun, 1948 and *Cluny et Vézelay, l'oeuvre des sculpteurs,* Paris, 1995; B. Rupprecht, *Romanische Skulptur in Frankreich,* Introduction, Munich, 1984, figs. 149 ff.; Focillon, *L'Art des sculpteurs romans,* Presses Univeritaires de France, Paris, 1964.

[361] Y. Christe, *Les Grands portails romans,* Geneva, 1969, especially pp. 176-178.

seated on his throne within the almond-shaped glory, with his knees bent sharply to his left, but confined to the immobility of the architectural frame, his arms outstretched, while the rays of the Holy Spirit come out of the enormous right hand to enlighten the apostles as well as the entire monastic community and the Church. The drapery of his gown, blown up by some invisible wind, spiralling around his hip and knees while the apostles, smaller, move frenetically towards him and each other. Such a portal and such beauty will lead any receptive beholder into the realm of the "spiritual," the "sacred," the transcendent, even though he might not be able to identify the iconography or may not believe in the doctrines of the Catholic Church. Yet the sculptor did believe in them. The same happens in front of other Romanesque portals, especially at the entrance to the abbey of Moissac (fig. 58).

> One can reach the absolute only through the faith implicit in the creative act . . . Artworks with the hieroglyphs of absolute truth. . . . He who cannot see truth, cannot see beauty.[362]

In his quest for truth, the artist is, once more, very close to the scientist, except that he has none of his instruments of verification. Thus, the biologist François Jacob, like so many other scientists, compares his work to that of the artist: neither of the two copies nature, both recreate it, both build up a vision of the universe, and the brain regulates, chooses the signals that come from the outside and puts them in order. Scientific work is linked to the idea of progress, which is not the case in art. A fully achieved work of art is never surpassed and it does not age, whereas, in science, everybody knows that, sooner or later, a theory will become obsolete. Beethoven did not surpass Bach nor did Picasso surpass Rembrandt, but Einstein surpassed Newton, and Victor Hugo was right in saying that Pascal, as scientist, was obsolete, but Pascal as writer was not.[363]

For Plato, on the other hand,

> the true essence of goodness searches his home in the nature of the beautiful. Measure and commensurability, as it turns out, are everywhere identifiable with beauty and excellence. . . . If you can comprehend goodness, let us search for it through three ideas, that of beauty, proportion and truth. . . . What is nearest to truth, pleasure or intelligence? Pleasure is deceitful; it is deprived of intelligence. Intelligence participates more fully in beauty than pleasure. . . . Pleasure is not the first of goods, and the first is measure. What is measurable partakes of the eternal nature. The second is proportion, the beautiful, the perfect. The third is intelligence and wisdom (*Philebus*, 64 e and 65 d).

---

[362] Tarkovsky, op.cit..
[363] François Jacob, *La Souris et l'Homme*, Paris, 1997.

      The Path Toward Beauty

Plato's insistence on measure and proportion, on the use of geometry and arithmetic to reach beauty and truth,[364] seems to confine us to a straitjacket and, therefore, annoys us, but we have to acknowledge that we find the same insistence in most texts of most civilizations. Even the Master sculptor of Vézelay's visionary tympanum (fig. 59 b) followed geometric principles,[365] and so did a Chardin and a Morandi (fig. 106) when painting their very private still lifes.

Thus, Morandi often refers to geometry.

> Remember Galileo: the true book of philosophy, the book of Nature, is written in letters foreign to our alphabet. These letters are square, circle, pyramid, cone and other geometric figures. I sense Galileo's thought in my long-standing conviction that the feelings and images aroused by the visible world, which is a formal world, are very different to express, or perhaps inexpressible through words. There are, in fact, feelings that have no relation, or a very indirect one, with daily emotions and interests, inasmuch as they have to do with forms, colors, space and light. . . . For me nothing is abstract; or rather I think nothing is more surreal and nothing is more abstract than the real. [366]

Morandi, however, was also to add that "with mathematics and geometry one does not explain everything, but nearly,"[367] and it is in this "nearly" that lies the living breath and the mystery of beauty. I have only shown the path towards it.

---

[364] For *Aletheia/Veritas* and *Teleios/Perfectus*, see Pollitt, *Ancient View of Greek Art*, 1974, pp. 170-182 and pp. 162 ff.

[365] J. Baltrusaitis, op.cit., especially pp. 181, 199 ff.

[366] L.Vitale, *Morandi, catalogo generale*, Milan, 2 vols. (trans. in R. Lipsey, op. cit., p. 365).

[367] "Dire qu'il (Pascal) n'était qu'un mathématicien. Il avait foi en la géometrie. Mais crois-tu que c'est peu de chose? Avec la mathématique, avec la géometrie, on explique presque tout. Presque tout." Cited by Philippe Jaccottet, *Le bol du pèlerin: Morandi*, Genève, 2201, p. 27. Galileo had said that "the great book of nature is written with the alphabet of geometry."

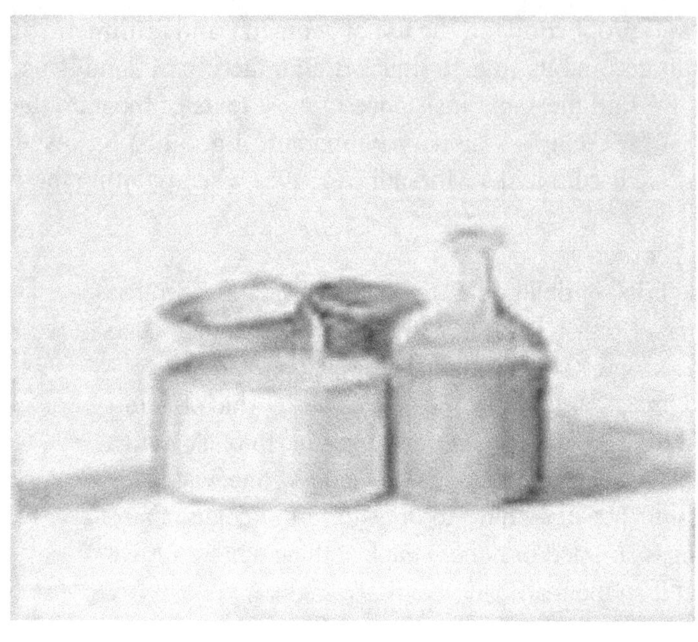

106 Giorgio Morandi,
Still Life, 1964

In this quest for truth, both artists and scientists discover the extent to which art and nature, as investigated by genetics, quantum and string physics, or astrophysics, are in unison. They agree on how man is, in fact, an integral part of the universe, obeying all its same rules.

The Chinese discovered that long ago, not through geometry or science, but rather through the Taoist ideas that everything is in constant transformation, and that the subjective and the objective are identical. To paint a bamboo, one must become a bamboo. For this process of identification to take place, however, the mind and the hand must cooperate. We conceive as beautiful that which underlies this unity, even though we may be unaware of it.[368]

At the end of this book, I can only agree, once again, with Roger Caillois, for whom beauty was not an invention, but a slow discovery:

> Man is not opposed to nature, he is nature, living matter, subject to the physical and biological laws that govern the universe. These laws penetrate him and organize him. Man coincides with these laws, or is, at least, inseparable from them. . . . These laws generate beauty and emanate beauty. . . . The eye belongs to the world that it reflects.[369]

---

[368] In the eleventh century, Su Shih wrote: "When Yü-ko painted bamboos, he was conscious only of the bamboos and not of himself as a man. Not only was he unconscious of his human form, but sick at heart, he left his own body, and it was transformed into bamboos of inexhaustible freshness and purity. As there is no more a Chuang-Tzù in the world, who can understand such concentration of the spirit?" (O. Siren, *Chinese on the Art of Painting*, New York, 1963, p. 54). Chuang-Tzu was an early Taoist philosopher and Yü-ko was a painter who died in 1079. For the Taoists, there was no concept for "being" or "truth," since everything was conceived in constant transformation. There was, thus, no conflict between *to on* (that which is) and *to phainomenon* (that which appears) of Plato, nor between his concepts of *doxa* (opinions) and of *aletheia* (truth).

[369] Roger Caillois, "Beauté," in *Cohérences adventureuses*, 1965, p. 197.

It is in this quest for truth that beauty may emerge and beauty in turn makes us aware of that truth, which cannot be imposed or dictated from the outside, but which is discovered, very gradually, through the long process of creation.[370]

<hr>

[370] "Truth is the truth of Being. Beauty does not occur alongside and apart from this truth. When truth sets itself into the work, it appears. . . . Thus, the beautiful belongs to the advent of truth." Heidegger, in *The Origin of the Work of Art,* 1938, A. Hofstadter and R. Kuhns, op. cit., p. 702. Keats, "Beauty is truth, truth is beauty—that is all/Ye know on earth, and all ye need to know." Keats, *Ode on a Grecian Urn.* "But what is beautiful, appears blissful within itself." (*Was aber schön ist, selig scheint es ihm selbst*). Mörike, *Auf eine Lamp* (On a lamp), last verse.

PART IV

Epilogue and Conclusion

A rt did not always aim at beauty; art no longer aims at beauty, and yet there are works of art in all periods and in all civilizations that are simply and undeniably beautiful.

Beauty does exist. It is alive. It is timeless. And it does not cheat. What makes a work of art beautiful is not the criteria in themselves, but the fact that those criteria—whatever they may be—are part of the living experience of the artist.

This statement might well conclude our long inquiry into beauty as it is, has been, and continues to be conveyed by works of art. With this epilogue, we thus close the circle we opened in the prologue, where all the issues were raised only partially by the four examples we chose.

The Little Prince was struck by wonder when he discovered the beauty of his rose, which he thought to be unique: "she" had tamed him, they had established links with each other, and he loved her. Once he came down to earth, he realized that she was not unique. She was beautiful because he knew and loved her. He also discovered that what makes something beautiful remains invisible. Scientists would have added that the beauty of the rose, her shape and color, were, furthermore, the result of millions of years of trial and error in Nature to ensure the survival of the species or even of life itself. In the Buddhist tradition, *the Kizaemon Tea-Bowl* (fig. 1) was beautiful as the result of an age-old tradition of pottery, whereby the potter made no distinction between "I" and "it" or between "ugly" and "beautiful." Centuries later, this "ordinary" rice bowl was recognized by the first Zen Tea Masters as the most beautiful ever made. It is now enshrined in a temple in Kyoto. In the Islamic tradition, the beauty of the Iranian bowl from Nishapur (fig. 2) was also the result of a long experience of potters, but was made as perfect as possible because it was an offering to God,

Who, according to the hadith, "is beautiful and He loves beauty." In the twentieth century, Brancusi sculpted his *Bird* (fig. 3) throughout his life, until he succeeded in transforming one of them into the essence of flight itself. In his texts, he takes us on the path of this slow, gradual transformation, which occurred through years of work that imperceptibly became years of spiritual initiation. *The Little Prince* gives us the point of view of a beholder, while the other examples reveal that of the maker.

In all the other examples we have given throughout this book and the texts we have analyzed, from prehistoric cave painting, through very different civilizations, to the abstract art of the beginning of the twentieth century, each work of art was, indeed, the result of a long process of formation, with the gradual mastering of a craft and of its rules until the artist finally felt free. From that point onward, the aims differ, and beauty would not always be one of them, but quality certainly was, along with the compelling need to move forward and inward.

We have understood that beauty is, in fact, synonymous with what, for lack of a better word, we also call "quality,"[371] or what "we recognize as being of compelling stature."[372] When quality is attained, something else happens, which Peter Brook calls a transformation of that which is not sacred at the outset into the sacred, when something heretofore invisible becomes visible through the work of art.

The various issues related to beauty have been defined, explained, or approached by philosophers, artists, theoreticians and critics. Art treatises were usually written by artists for artists, providing practical advice, defining the rules inherent in any form of art, period and civilization. The personal writings of artists made us aware of how each work of art is, above all, the result of an endless process of creation. Art critics or theoreticians reveal instead a Zeitgeist, and the ever-changing taste of the public, which was and still is frequently confused with a feeling for beauty. Over the centuries, poets and philosophers have led us from the beauty of the artwork to a metaphysical notion of beauty, or from the visible work of art to something that transcends it. This has been the general path we discovered in this inquiry.

First, we analyzed non-Western criteria of beauty, including those underlying Islamic art, Chinese Taoist painting, Yoruba African sculpture, Hindu art, Buddhist pottery, Japanese Zen art and Navajo sand painting. Then, we took a more specific look at Western criteria of beauty and the most important Greek, Medieval, Renaissance and eighteenth-century texts. Whenever possible, we have intertwined Western concepts with Eastern ones, and ancient or traditional ones with those of the twentieth century, to underline what all these criteria and texts have in common, or, on the contrary, what differentiates them.

Just as every living organism is particular and shares the same modules of the genetic

---

[371] Peter Brook, *Open Door*, pp. 69 ff.
[372] George Steiner, *Real Presences*, 1989, p. 216.

code in different arrangements, each work of art is also particular, and yet there are common denominators found in all beautiful works of art. This analogy is striking in itself, and we would not have been able to make it before the discovery of the double helix of DNA! This analogy between the macrocosm, or the laws that govern the universe, and the microcosm, or the laws that penetrate and organize life, man and human art, has nevertheless been made in various texts throughout time. These same laws were always thought to generate and emanate beauty.[373] This search and the discovery of beauty have always moved scientists and artists alike, and no doubt all human beings who are capable of wonder,[374] on their way towards meaning and truth: "He who does not seek truth, cannot see beauty either." [375] And yet, only the inexorable judgment of time selects that which is beautiful, or that which we recognize as being of compelling stature. Beauty is a slow discovery, even though, at least as beholders, we sometimes simply know when something is beautiful as soon as we encounter it, as if beauty imposed itself, unequivocally.

What lies behind this relationship between beauty and truth, what motivates the scientist and drives the artist is love.

> Neither the greatest intelligence, nor imagination, nor both together, make
> genius. Love, love, love, that is the soul of genius.
> —Mozart.[376]

Except for the more recent reference to "imagination" and "genius," these words could have been those of many philosophers, Plato and Plotinus, first and foremost. Centuries later, Kant would not have disagreed.

But what is love? Like beauty and truth, we are perfectly capable of recognizing it when it is present, but that does not mean that we are capable of defining it. It is the *daimon* of Plato's *Symposium*, driving both "procreator" and beholder to the awareness of beauty, and acting as an intermediary between men and gods, moving us from the discovery of the particular, relative beauty of one single beloved object to the final revelation of the absolute

---

[373]Roger Caillois, "Esthétique généralisée," in *Cohérences aventureuses,* 1965, but identical concepts can be found in Chinese, Yoruba, Hindu or Navajo texts, as well as in the writings of Leonardo da Vinci.
[374] M. M. Davy, *La Montagne et sa symbolique,* 1996, pp. 182-183: "Beauty establishes communication with the invisible that rushes into the gulf created by amazement. . . . Receptiveness is required. . . . Every part of our being is filled with wonder. Nothing sentimental. The emotion that is felt produces a thrill and takes us upwards, directs us towards new heights. ("La beauté établit une communication avec l'invisible qui s'engouffre dans la béance suscitée par l'étonnement. . . . Une disponibilité se trouve requise. L'émerveillement envahit l'être dans sa totalité. Rien de sentimental. L'émotion ressentie produit un tréssaillement et un changement de niveau . . . fait monter; oriente vers un sommet. . . .")
[375] Andrey Tarkovsky, op. cit.
[376] *Les Lumières*, Paris, BNF, 1 Spring 2006: on the wall of the opening room of the exhibition.

but invisible beauty of God.[377] Love can also be a god-sent madness, which inspires the poet (the *manike*, the *manìa Mousòn)* of Plato's *Phaedrus,* without which there can be no beautiful poetry. Kant was to state in his *Analytic of the Sublime* that a genius alone could produce beautiful art, only insofar as he was driven by the Spirit (*Geist*), a principle of the mind which, like a *daimon*, puts "the mental powers purposively into swing" and "the imagination into motion," making the beholder conscious of "the pure rational concept of the suprasensible. . . ." All philosophers, as well as all artists, have recognized, or implied, that skill, criteria, intelligence and imagination, no matter how great, could never alone suffice to make a beautiful work of art. Beauty always reveals the vital energy of the artist.

The beauty of a work of art is like a large tree with multiple branches around a common trunk growing out of a great number of invisible roots, each of which partakes in its life, growth as well as beauty, without forgetting the quality of the soil from which it springs:[378] formal aspects, iconographical components, various religious beliefs, motivations, purposes and rules, each contributing to the final beauty of any particular work. Similarly, the beauty of a work of art is the result of centuries of creation and of countless artists. We are back to the rose of *The Little Prince*, whose beauty was forged by Nature, with no other aim than the survival of the species.

The aim of art has only exceptionally been to be beautiful, according to the Greek or Renaissance criteria.[379] In the West, at least up to the sixteenth-eighteenth centuries, and everywhere else until the twentieth century, its aim was essentially to fulfil a religious or

---

[377] This interrelation between beauty and love is found in many mythologies. For example, in Hindu mythology: the goddess of Beauty, Shrî (Lakshmî) is the mother of Kâma. Kâma, like Eros, is the creative impulse of all forms of life, hence also of all artistic creation.

[378] Paul Klee also used the simile of a tree, but in relation to the artist. "May I use a simile, the simile of the tree? The artist has studied this world of variety and has, we may suppose, unobtrusively, found his way in. His sense of direction has brought him into the passing stream of image and experience. This sense of direction in nature and life, this branching and spreading array, I shall compare with the root of the tree. From the root the sap flows to the artist, flows though him, flows to the eye. Thus, he stands as the trunk of the tree. Battered and stirred by the strength of the flow, he molds his vision into his work. As, in full view of the world, the crown of the tree unfolds and spreads in time and space, so with his work. Nobody would affirm that the tree grows its crown in the image of its root. Between above and below can be no mirrored reflection. It is obvious that different functions expanding in different elements must produce vital divergences. But it is just the artist who, at times, is denied those departures from nature which his art demands. He has even been charged with incompetence and deliberate distortion. And yet, standing at his appointed place, the trunk of the tree, he does nothing other than gather and pass on what comes to him from the depths. He neither serves nor rules—he transmits. His position is humble. And the beauty at the crown is not his own. He is merely a channel." *On Modern Art*, 1945, in R. Herbert, op. cit., pp. 76-77.

[379] These same criteria of beauty were slowly to become academic stereotypes, which, therefore, had to be revitalized, overcome or overthrown. A work of art has to convey a vital energy, which is that of the artist himself. That observation, too, is found in most texts of most civilizations.

        The Path Toward Beauty

ritual function. Its task was also to awaken human consciousness, and to produce a work of quality, transforming something which was invisible into something visible, or becoming the medium of a vital power, acting as a mediator or as a symbol.

Western art was affected by the subjectivism of the eighteenth century, the individualism and relativism of the nineteenth, Nietzsche's "death of God," and the end of the heritage of Antiquity and the Italian Renaissance long before the Cubists began their deconstruction of objects and figures, and Dada signed its final death certificate. This took place, in fact, before the horrors of the First World War and continued afterwards. The inhumanity of various revolutions, the Second World War and the Shoah, as well as the upheavals that followed, were to have an effect on civilization as a whole, especially on artists. The latter were further influenced by the new technological revolution and major scientific discoveries. What emerged in the twentieth century was the tragic awareness of the impermanence of life and of all creation; consciousness of the absurdity of traditional values and rules, even of life itself; the absence and silence of God and the waning of faith; the growing impact of psychoanalysis with the notion of the unconscious; increasing political and social involvement or rebellion; and so on. All of this led to a sense of emptiness and of nothingness and to a total relativism. The artists' ego was inflated through happenings and psychodrama and the general need to shock in order to exhibit or sell one's art, in short, to create a parody of beauty. The art of our own time shows, in fact, a compelling need for destruction and a rejection of all traditions, as if a clean slate was necessary for any creation, as if creation *ex nihilo* were possible.[380]

In spite of this Big Bang of twentieth century art,[381] in which the essential components of beauty seem to have been totally overthrown, except for the recurrence, here and there, of the universal language of geometry, some works, nevertheless, convey a deep spiritual inward quality which we do associate with beauty. Beauty has survived.

A painting by Rothko from 1960 shares the same stillness and beauty as the interior space of the twelfth century Cistercian church of Fontenay (figs. 98 and 99). Both of them act as media for meditation. Why?

For thousands of years, the concept of beauty was linked to the belief in the existence of divine, invisible Beauty, within us or beyond us, of order and harmony, or of the vital energy and breath of life that pervaded the entire universe and all creation. The artist discovered that same beauty, harmony and vital energy through his own process of creation,

---

[380] Painting is a thundering collision of different worlds, intended to create a new world, which is the work of art. Each work originates just as the cosmos—through catastrophes which, out of the chaotic din of instruments, ultimately create a symphony, the music of the spheres. The creation of works of art is the creation of a world. R. Herbert, op. cit., p. 35.

[381] *Big Bang, Destruction and Creation in Twentieth-Century Art.* Paris, Pompidou Center, 2005-2006. See all the articles of the catalogue. Recall also how the fairly recent science of chaos has discovered its own beauty through the new fractal geometry .

and sought to reveal it, incorporate it, make it visible. This happened only when a work of art acquired the quality or compelling stature found to be synonymous with beauty.

The vitality of beauty can also be found in the *Bunch of Asparagus* by Manet, the late paintings of Cézanne, the *Salad Bowl* of Nicolas de Staël, in many African and Oceanic sculptures, in Chinese and Japanese paintings, in sketches and drawings, or, for that matter, in a single brush stroke of Titian, Velázquez, Rembrandt or Chardin.

Beauty, as Plotinus wrote,

> is something that is perceived at the first glance, something which the Soul names as from an ancient knowledge and, recognizing it, enters into unison with it. . . . Such vision is for those only who see with the Soul's sight. . . . To any vision must be brought an eye that sees the mighty beauty. If the eye that adventures the vision be dimmed by vice, impure or weak, . . . then it sees nothing. To any vision must be brought an eye adapted to what is to be seen, and having some likeness to it. Never did eye see the sun unless it had first become sun like, and never can the Soul have a vision of the First beauty unless itself be beautiful (*Enneads*, 1, 6, 9).

This holds true for both the artist and the beholder.

Outside natural and acquired skills and norms of all types, all beautiful works of art seem to have been made by artists and craftsmen, striving towards what has been called variously: the Intelligible, Being, Beauty in itself, the Divine, God, Archetypal Beauty, the Essence, the Living Breath of Life, Truth, the Transcendent, the Suprasensible, or, *in fine*, inner being, the Sacred, the Supreme or the Spiritual. The latter term, first used by Kant and Hegel in relation to the production of beautiful arts, was to be used again in the writings of the earliest abstract painters: Kandisnky, Malevich and Mondrian, as well as in those of many other twentieth century artists, such as Klee, Brancusi, Matisse, Rothko and Henry

Moore, to mention but a few,[382] and yet again in Bill Viola's description of his 2001 videos.[383] The same spiritual quality is present in some contemporary buildings, just as it is present in some Islamic, Buddhist, Medieval and Early Renaissance places of worship.

Neither the recognition of beauty or of this vital power has anything to do with what "we like," with what gives us pleasure, or with any "good taste." These approaches are not mutually exclusive, but they must never be confused. Some works of the twentieth century, e.g., certain paintings by Picasso or Francis Bacon, would not be considered beautiful by any conventional standards nor characterized as "spiritual," although they nevertheless possess amazing vitality and compelling stature.[384] Thus, a work of art does not need to have a religious content or be the medium of a "metaphysical message" in order to have this stature. Something else occurs in certain works, which we are perfectly capable of recognizing.

> There is a path towards beauty, just as there is a path towards that which transcends human beings, and there can be no beauty outside that path.

---

[382] See Roger Lipsey, op. cit., Introduction, 1988, pp. 6-18, where Lipsey gives his own definitions of the Spiritual, and, more specifically, of the Spiritual in Art. "The beginning of the spiritual must be this looking beyond or looking more deeply within . . . The spiritual makes itself be known slowly in the course of that work. . . . The spiritual is not an abstract knowledge of the cosmos or human nature; it is a renewed discovery, a beginning again and again. . . . It is an incursion from above or deep within to which the ordinary human being in each of us can only surrender. It is the *daimon* to which Socrates listened, to which he could not but listen when he spoke within him. . . . The spiritual in art offers a transient experience of intensity, of a larger world and larger self." Would these definitions not suit Picasso's and Bacon's work as well?

[383] Bill Viola's *Five Angels for the Millennium* were installed at the very end of the exhibition called *Big Bang, Creation and Destruction in Twentieth-Century Art* (Paris, Pompidou Center, 2005-2006) in order to create what he calls "a place of contemplation." These *Five Angels*—Creation, Ascending, Fire, Departing, Birth—act as "messengers between the spiritual world and the world of consciousness." In fact, Viola forces the spectator to stop in the dark for a very long time and to gradually immerse himself in the slow unfolding of the perpetual destruction and regeneration of the cosmos, from which self-conscious human beings emerge, plunge, ascend and disappear again in the same primordial ocean, fire or interstellar space.

[384] Picasso observed that there was "Something sacred, that's it!" in certain works of art. "We ought to say that word, or something like it, but people would take it the wrong way, and give it a meaning it hasn't got. We ought to be able to say that such and such a painting is as it is, with its capacity for power, because it is 'touched by God' (*touché par la Grace*). But people would put a wrong interpretation on it. And yet, it's the nearest we can get to truth" (Lipsey, op. cit., p. 19). Francis Bacon, on the contrary, hated any metaphysical explanation, any reference to a form of inspiration; everything proceeded, for him, from the work itself, emerging suddenly, by accident. The most important thing was to do something in one's life that made it meaningful (Francis Bacon, *Entretiens avec Michel Archimbaut*, 1992; ed. Folio, 1996, pp. 71 and 93).

BIBLIOGRAPHY

Abiodun, Rowland, Henry J. Drewal, and John Pemberton III, eds. *The Yoruba Artist*. Washington, D.C., 1994.

Alberti, Leon Battista. *On Painting and On Sculpture*. Ed. and trans. Cecil Grayson. London, 1972.

Aristotle. *Poetics*. Ed. and trans. Stephen Halliwell. Chicago, 1998.

Aryan, K.C. *The Basis of Decorative Element in Indian Art*. New Dehli, 1981.

Auerbach, Ernst. *Mimesis. The Description of Reality in Western Literature*. Zurich, 1945.

Baltrusaïtis, J. *Formation, déformation. La stylistique ornementale dans la scupture romane*. Paris, revised eition, 1986.

Barasch, Moshe. *Modern Theories of Art, 1: From Winkelmann to Baudelaire*. New York, 1990.

Barasch, Moshe. *Modern Theories of Art, 2: From Impressionism to Kandinsky*. New York, 1998.

Barasch, Moshe. *Theories of Art: From Plato to Winckelmann*. New York, 1985.

Barou, Jean-Pierre. *L'oeil pense, Essai sur les arts primitifs contemporains*. Paris, 1996.

Baudelaire, Charles. *The Painter of Modern Life and Other Essays*. Trans. J. Mayne. New York, 1986).

Baxandall, Michael. *Giotto and the Orators*. Oxford, 1971.

Baxandall, Michael. *Painting and the Experience in Fifteenth Century Italy*. Oxford, 1972.

Belting, Hans. *An Anthropology of Images: Picture, Medium, Body*. Trans. Thomas Dunlap. Princeton, 2011.

Belting, Hans. *Likeness and Presence*. Trans. Edmund Jephcott. Chicago, 1994.

Blunt, Anthony. *Art and Architecture in France, 1500 to 1700*. Pelican History of Art, 7, London, 1957.

Blunt, Anthony. *Artistic Theory in Italy, 1450-1600*. Oxford, 1975.

Brauen, M. *Mandala: Sacred Circle in Tibetan Buddhism*. New York, 2009.

Brook, Peter. *Empty Space*. New York, 1968.

Brook, Peter. *The Open Door*. New York, 1993.

Bruno, Giordano. *The Heroic Frenzies*. Trans. Paul Memmo, Jr. New York, 1966.

Bruyne, Edgar de. *The Esthetics of the Middle Ages*. New York, 1969.

Buonarroti, Michelangelo. *Sonnets*. Trans. John Addington Symonds. London, 1878.

Burkert, Walter. *Lore and Science in Ancient Pythagoreanism*. Cambridge, Mass. 1972.

Cahn, Walter. *Masterpieces. Chapters on the History of an Idea*. Princeton, NJ, 1979.

Caillois, Roger. *Cohérences aventureuses: Esthétique généralisée*. Paris, 1973.

Cassagne, Albert. *La théorie de l'art pour l'art en France*. Geneva, 1979.

Castiglione, Baldassarre. *The Book of the Courtier*. Ed. Daniel Javitch and Charles Singleton. New York, 2002.

Chandrasekhar, S. *Truth and Beauty: Aesthetics and Motivations in Science*. Chicago, 1987.

Cheng, François. *Empty and Full: the Language of Chinese Painting*. Boston, 1994.

Chipp, H.B., ed. *Theories of Modern Art. A Source Book by Artists and Critics*. Berkeley, 1968.

Christe, Yves. *Les Grands Portails Romans*. Geneva, 1969.

Chung-Yuan, Chang. *Creativity and Taoism, A Study of Chinese Philosophy, Art and Poetry*. New York, 1963.

Clark, Kenneth. *Leonardo da Vinci*. Rev. ed. London, 2005.

Clayton P. and M. Price. *The Seven Wonders of the Ancient World*. London, 1988.

Clemens, R.J. *Michelangelo's Theory of Art*. New York, 1961.

Coomaraswamy, Ananda. *Christian and Oriental Philosophy of Beauty*. New York, 1956.

Coomaraswamy, Ananda. *The Origin of the Buddha Image and Elements of Buddhist Iconography*. Louisville, KY, 2006.

Coomaraswamy, Ananda. *Transformation of Nature in Art*. New York, 1956.

Corbin, Henry. "Eyes of Flesh and Eyes of Fire: Science and Gnosis," *Material for Thought*, 8 (1980), 5-10.

Cousin, Victor. *Lectures on the True, the Beautiful and the Good*. Trans. Orlando Williams Wight. New York, 1890.

Damasio, Antonio. *Looking for Spinoza: Joy, Sorrow, and the Feeling Brain*. Orlando, FL, 2003.

Davy, M.M. *Initiation à la symbolique romane*. Paris, 1977.

Deacon, Terrence. *The Symbolic Species: The Co-evolution of Language and of the Human Brain*. London, 1997.

Demus, Otto. *Byzantine Mosaic Decoration*. Boston, 1955.

Descartes, René. *Passions of the Soul*. Trans. Stephen Voss. Indianapolis, 1989.

Diderot, Denis. *Encyclopedia: The Complete Illustrations, 1762-1777*. 5 vols. Milan, 1978.

Diderot, Denis. *Selected Writings*. Trans. Derek Coltman. New York and London, 1966.

Drewal, Henry John., John Pemberton, Rowland Abiodun, and Allen Wardwell. *Yoruba: Nine Centuries of African Art and Thought*. New York, 1989.

Duff, William. *An Essay on Original Genius* (1767). Gainesville FL, 1964.

Dupré, Louis. *Passage to Modernity: An Essay in the Hermeneutic of Nature and Culture*. New Haven, 1993.

Duval, René. *Rasa, or Knowledge of the Self*. Toronto, 1982.

Eco, Umberto. *Art and Beauty in the Middle Ages*. New Haven, 1987.

Eliade, Mircea. *A History of Religious Ideas*. 3 vols. Chicago, 1978-1985.

Eliade, Mircea. *The Sacred and the Profane: The Nature of Religion*. New York, 1968.

Evdokimov, Paul. *The Art of the Icon: a Theology of Beauty*, Trans. Steven Bigham, Redondo Beach, CA, 1990.

Focillon, Henry. *Romanesque Sculpture*. New York, 1981.

Fong, Wen C. *Images of the Mind*. Princeton, N.J., 1984.

Fong, Wen C. *Summer Mountains. The Timeless Landscape*. New York, 1975.

Frankfort, Henry. *The Art and Architecture of the Ancient Orient*. Pelican History of Art, 4th ed., Harmondsworth, Eng. 1970.

Friedländer, Walter. *Caravaggio Studies*. Princeton, 1974.

Gleick, James. *Chaos, Making a New Science*. New York, 1987.

Gombrich, Ernst. *Art and Illusion*. New York, 1960.

Gombrich, Ernst. *Norm and Form*. New York, 1971.

Gombrich, Ernst. *Sense of Order*. Ithaca, N.Y. 1979.

Grabar, Oleg. *The Formation of Islamic Art*. New Haven, 1973.

Grabar, Oleg. *The Mediation of Ornament*. Paris, 1996.

Granet, Marcel. *The Religion of the Chinese People*. New York, 1975

Green, Brian. *The Elegant Universe*. New York, 1999.

Grenier, Catherine. *Big Bang: Destruction and Creation in Twentieth-Century Art*. Paris, 2005.

Guitton, Jean. Brichka and Igor Bogdanoff. *Dieu et la science*. Paris, 1991.

Harle, J.C. *The Art and Architecture of the Indian Subcontinent*. Harmondsworth, Eng. 1990.

Hegel, Friedrich G.W. *Aesthetics: Lectures on Fine Arts*. Trans. T. M. Knox. Oxford, 1975.

Heidegger, Martin. *Der Ursprung des Kunstwerkes*. Stuttgart, 1960.

Heisenberg, Elisabeth. *Inner Exile: Recollections of a Life with Werner Heisenberg*. Boston, 1984.

Heisenberg, Werner. *Physics and Beyond: Encounters and Conversations*. New York, 1971.

Henry, Françoise. *Irish Art*. 2 vols. Ithaca, N.Y., 1965-70.

Herbert, Robert L., ed., *Modern Artists on Art*. Englewood Cliffs, NJ, 1964.

Herder, Johann Gottfried. *Selected Writings on Aesthetics*. Ed. and trans. Gregory Moore. Princeton, 2006.

Hofstadter, A. and R. Kuhn, eds. *Philosophies of Art and Beauty: Selected Readings in Aesthetics from Plato to Heidegger*. New York, 1964.

Hopkins, Jeffrey. *Kālachakra Tantra, Rite of Initiation*. London, 1985.

Kandinski, Wassily. *Concerning the Spiritual in Art*. New York, 1947.

Kandinsky, Wassily. *Kandinsky, Complete Writings on Art*. Ed. Kenneth C. Lindsay and Peter Vergo. Boston, 1982.

Kandinski, Wassily, Annegret Hoberg, and Gabriele Münter. *Wassily Kandinsky and Gabriele Münter: Letters and Reminiscences, 1902-1914*. Munich, 1994.

Kandinsky, Wassily, et al. *The Blaue Reiter Almanac: Documentary Edition*. Trans. Henning Falkenstein. London, 1974.

Kant, Immanuel. *Critique of the Power of Judgment*. Trans. Paul Guyer and Eric Matthews. Cambridge, 2000.

Kant. Immanuel. *Observations on the Feeling of the Beautiful and the Sublime and Other Writings*. Trans. Paul Guyer. Cambridge, 2011.

Kirkegaard, Søren and Friedrich Wilhelm Joseph von Schelling. *The Concept of Irony, With Continual Reference to Socrates: Together with Notes of Schelling's Berlin Lectures*. Ed. and trans. Howard V. Hong and Edna H. Hong. Princeton, 1989.

Keuls, Eve. *Plato and Greek Painting*. Leiden, 1978.

Kitzinger, Ernst. *Byzantine Art in the Making*. London, 1977.

Klee, Paul. *Notebooks*. Ed. Jürg Spiller. Vol. 1, Trans. Ralph Manheim; vol. 2, Trans. Heinz Norden. London, 1961-73.

Koyré, A. *From the Closed World to the Infinite Universe*. New York, 1958.

Krautheimer, Richard. *Early Christian and Byzantine Architecture*. Pelican Hisory of Art. Harmondsworth, Eng. 1975.

Kris, Ernst, and Otto Kurz. *Legend, Myth, and Magic in the Image of the Artist. A Historical Experiment*. New Haven, 1979.

Leiris, Michel, and Jacqueline Delange. *African Art*. Trans. Michael Ross. London, 1968.

Leonardo da Vinci. *Master Draftsman*. Ed. Carmen C. Bambach. New York, 2003.

Leonardo da Vinci. *On Painting*. Ed. and trans. A. P. McMahon. Princeton, 1956.

Leonardo da Vinci. *The Literary Works of Leonardo da Vinci*. Edited with commentary by Carlo Pedretti. 2 vols. Oxford, 1977.

Leonardo da Vinci. *The Literary Works*. 2nd ed. 2 vols. Ed. J. P. Richter, London, 1939.

Leonardo da Vinci. *The Literary Works*. Ed. J. P. Richter, 3rd ed., 2 vols. London, 1970.

Lewer, Debbie, ed. *Post-Impressionism to World War II*. Blackwell Anthologies in Art History, 1. Malden, MA, 2006.

Lipsey, Roger. *An Art of Our Own: The Spiritual in Twentieth-Century Art*. Boston, 1988.

Lubac, Henri de. *Medieval Exegesis: The Four Senses of Scripture*. Grand Rapids, MI, 1998-2009.

MacDonald, William. *The Pantheon: Design, Meaning, and Progeny*. Cambridge, MA, 1981.

Mainstone, Roland. *Hagia Sophia; Architecture, Structure and Liturgy of Justinian's Great Church*. London, 1988.

Malevich, Kasimir. *Kasimir Malevich, 1878-1935: an exhibition of paintings, drawings and studies organised in association with the Stedelijk Museum, Amsterdam and held at the Whitechapel Art Gallery, London, October-November, 1959*. London, 1959.

Malraux, André. *The Metamorphosis of the Gods*. Trans. Stuart Gilbert. Garden City, N.Y., 1960.

Malraux, André. *The Museum Without Walls*. Trans. Stuart Gilbert and Francis Price. Garden City, N.Y. 1967.

Malraux, André. *The Voices of Silence*. Trans. Stuart Gilbert. Garden City, N.Y., 1953.

Mango, Cyril. *Art in the Byzantine Empire, 312-1453. Sources and Documents*. Cambridge, MA, 1972.

Mathew, Gervase. *Byzantine Aesthetics*. London, 1963.

Matisse, Henry. *Écrits et propos sur l'art*. Ed. C. Fourcade. Paris, 1972.

Mascaró, Juan. *The Bhagavad Gita*, 1962.

McEvilley, Thomas. *The Shape of Ancient Thought, Comparative Studies in Greek and Indian Philosophies*. New York, 2002.

Meeks, Wayne. "Vision of God and Scripture Interpretation in a Fifth-Century Mosaic." In *In Search of the Early Christians. Selected Essays*. ed. A. Hilton and H. G. Snyder. 230-262. New Haven, 2002.

Mondrian, Piet. *The New Art-The New Life: The Collected Writings of Piet Mondrian*. Ed. and trans. Martin Holzman, Harry and Martin James. London, 1986.

Mouilleron, Véronique Rouchon. *Vézelay: the Great Romanesque Church*. New York, 1999.

Mras, George. *Eugène Delacroix's Theory of Art*. Princeton, 1966.

Nietzsche, Friedrich. *The Portable Nietzsche*. Trans. Walter Kaufmann. New York, 1976.

Nietzsche, Friedrich. *Twilight of the Idols*. Trans. R. J. Hollingdale. New York, 1990.

Otto, Rudolf. *The Idea of the Holy: An Inquiry into the Non-rational Factor in the idea of the divine, etc.* 2nd edition. New York, 1950.

Ouspensky, P.D. *Tertium Organum: the Third Canon of Thought, a Key to the Enigmas of the World.* New York, 1959.

Pacioli, Luca. *La Divina Proporzione.* Ed. C. Winterberg. Vienna, 1899.

Paine, Robert T. and Alexander S. Soper. *Art and Architecture of Japan.* Pelican History of Art, 3rd edition. Harmondsworth, Eng., 1981.

Panofsky, Erwin. *Abbot Suger. On the Abbey of Saint Denis and its Art Treasures.* 2nd ed. Princeton, 1979.

Panofsky, Erwin. *Idea. A Concept in Art Theory.* New York, 1968.

Panofsky, Erwin. *Meaning in the Visual Arts.* Garden City, N Y. 1955.

Pevsner, Nikolaus. *Academies of Art.* New York, 1973.

Piano, Renzo. *Carnet de Travail.* Paris, 1997.

Piano, Renzo and Gero von Boehm. *Conversations with I. M. Pei. Light is the Key.* London, 2000.

Picq, Pascal. *Les Origines de l'Homme.* Paris, 2000.

Plato. *The Complete Works.* Trans. John M. Cooper and D. S. Hutchinson. Indianapolis, 1997.

Plato. *Phaedrus,* London, Penguin, 1973.

Pliny, the Elder. *Natural History.* Trans. H. Rackham. The Loeb Classical Library. 10 vols. Cambridge, MA., 1942-62.

Plotinus. *The Six Enneads.* Trans. Stephen Mackenna and B.S. Page. Chicago, 1952.

Pollitt, J.J. *Art and Experience in Classical Greece.* Cambridge, 1972.

Pollitt, J.J. *Art in the Hellenistic Age.* Cambridge, 1986.

Pollitt, J.J. *The Ancient View of Greek Art: Criticism, History, and Terminology.* New Haven, 1974.

Popham, A.E. *The Drawings of Leonardo da Vinci.* New York, 1945.

Popper, Karl. *Logic of Scientific Discovery.* London, 1959.

Popper, Karl. *Objective Knowledge.* Oxford, 1979.

Poussin, Nicolas. *Lettres et propos sur l'art.* Ed. Anthony Blunt. Paris, 1964.

Pritchard, James. *Ancient Near Eastern Texts,* 2 vols. Princeton, N.J., 1955.

Pseudo-Dionysius, *The Complete Works.* Classics of Western Spirituality. Trans. Colm Luibheid. Mahwah, N.J. 1987.

Reynolds, Joshua. *Discourses.* London, 1992.

Ringborn, S. *The Sounding Cosmos: a Study of Spiritualism of Kandinsky and the Genesis of Abstract Painting.* Acta Academiae Aboensis, ser. A, XXXVIII. Abo, Finland, 1970.

Robb, Nesca A. *Neoplatonism of the Italian Renaissance.* London, 1935.

Rowland, Benjamin. *The Art and Architecture of India: Buddhist, Hindu, Jain.* Pelican History of Art, Harmondsworth, Eng. 1985.

Rowley, George. *Principles of Chinese Painting.* Princeton, 1974.

Saint-Exupéry, Antoine de. *The Little Prince.* Trans. Katherine Woods, New York, 1943.

Savage-Rumbaugh, Sue. *Ape Language: From Conditional Response to Symbol.* New York, 1986.

Schäfer, Heinrich. *Principles of Egyptian Art.* Ed. and trans. John Baines. Oxford, 1974.

Schama, Simon. *The Embarrassment of Riches.* London, 1987.

Semerano, Giovanni. *L'infinito: un equivoco millenario. Le antiche civiltà del Vicino Oriente e le origini del pensiero Greco.* Milan, 2001.

Shapiro, Meyer. "On perfection: Coherence and Unity of Form and Content." In *Uncontrollable Beauty: Toward a New Aesthetics,* Ed. Bill Beckley and David Shapiro. New York, 1998.

Shih-T'ao [Shitao]. *Enlightening Remarks on Painting.* Trans. Richard E. Strassberg. Pasadena, CA, 1989.

Sirén, Osvald. *The Chinese on the Art of Painting.* New York, 1963.

Spivey, Nigel. *Understanding Greek Sculpture. Ancient Meaning, Modern Reading.* London, 1997.

Steiner, George. *Grammars of Creation.* New Haven, 2001.

Steiner, George. *Martin Heidegger.* Chicago, 1981.

Steiner, George. *Real Presences.* London, 1989.

Steiner, Rudolf. *Christianity as Mystical Fact and the Mysteries of Antiquity,* 3rd. ed. London, 1938.

Steiner, Rudolf. *Knowledge of the Higher Worlds and its Attainment.* New York, 1947.

Stolnitz, Jerome, ed. *Aesthetics.* Sources in Philosophy. London, 1965.

Summers, David. *The Judgment of Sense, Renaissance Naturalism and the Rise of Aesthetics.* Cambridge, 1987.

Sze, Mai-mai. *The Tao of Painting: A Study of the Ritual Disposition of Chinese Painting: With a Translation of the Chien tzu yuan hua chuan, or Mustard Seed Garden Manual of Painting (1679-1701). 2 vols.,* Bollingen Series, 49. New York, 1956.

Tanizaki, Junichiro. *In Praise of Shadows.* New Haven, 1977.

Tarkovsky, Andrey. *Sculpting in Time.* Trans. Kitty Hunter-Blair, New York, 1987.

Todorov, Tzvetan. *Theories of the Symbol.* Trans. Catherine Porter. Ithaca, N.Y. 1982.

Vasari, Giorgio. *The Lives of the Painters, Sculptors and Architects (1568).* Trans. Gaston du C. de Vere. Introduction and Notes by David Ekserdjian. 2 vols. New York, 1996.

Vico, Giambattista. *Princples of New Science Concerning the Common Nature of the Nations.* Trans. Thomas G. Bergin and Max Harold Fisch. Ithaca, N.Y. 1968.

Vigouroux, Roger. *La Fabrique du Beau.* Paris, 1992.

Weinberg, Steven L. *Dreams of a Final Theory: The Scientist's Search for the Ultimate Laws of Nature.* New York, 1992.

Willett, Frank. *African Art.* Rev. ed. London, 1997.

Winckelmann, Johann Joachim. *History of Ancient Art.* New York, 1968.

Wittkower, Rudolf. "Genius: Individualism in Art and Artists." *Dictionary of the History of Ideas,* vol. 2 (1973), 297-312.

Xuan Thuan, Trinh. *Chaos and Harmony: Perspectives on Scientific Revolutions of the Twentieth Century.* Oxford, 2001.

Yanagi, Soëtsu. *The Unknown Craftsman: A Japanese Insight into Beauty.* London, 1972.

LIST OF ILLUSTRATIONS

1. *Kizaemon Tea-Bowl*, from Korea. Yi Dynasty, 16th century, Kyoto, Daitokuji
2. *Bowl with Kufic Inscription*, from Nishapur, 10th century. Image source: http://seco.glendale.edu/ceramics/nishapurbowl.html
3. Constantin Brancusi, *Bird in Space*, c. 1930, New York, Guggenheim Museum. © 2012 Artists Rights Society (ARS), New York / ADAGP, Paris
4. *Laurel Leaf, Feuille de laurier*, Solutrean stone tool, c. 19,000 B.P., Les Eyzies-de-Tayac, National Prehistoric Museum
5. *Lion-headed Figurine*, from Hohlenstein-Stadel, Germany, c. 35,000-30,000 B.P., Ulmer Museum, Ulm, Germany
6. *Female Figurine of Lespugue*, c. 20,000 B.P., Paris, Musée de l 'Homme
7. *Horses,* Wall painting, Chauvet Cave, c. 34,000 B.P., Vallon-Pont-d'Arc, Ardèche, France
8. *Lions,* Wall painting, Chauvet Cave, c. 34,000 B.P., Vallon-Pont-d'Arc, Ardèche, France
9. *Aurochs,* detail from the *Hall of Bulls*, Lascaux Cave, c. 15,000 B.P., Dordogne France
10. *Yoruba Dancing Staff*, Paris, Private Collection
11 a. *Figurine representing a divinity,* Caroline Archipelago, Nukuoro Atoll, Micronesia
11 b. *Spoon,* from the Fiji Islands, Geneva, Barbier-Mueller Museum
12. Wu Zhen (1280-1354), *Study of Bamboo*, detail, Taipei, National Palace Museum
13. Muqi, *Six Persimmons*, second half of 13th century, Kyoto Ryokoin, Daitokuji (detail)
14. Fan K'uan, (active late 10th to early 11th century), *Travelers amid Mountains and Gorges,* Taipei, *National Palace Museum*
15. *Sculpture of Shiva Dancing the Lalitam,* interior of Hindu Ravan ka khai Cave (Cave 14), Ellora. Photographer: Johnston, © The British Library Board
16. *Shiva as Lord of Dance (Nataraja)*, Chola period, (880-1279), late 12th early 13th century, New York, Metropolitan Museum of Art (detail)
17. Navajo Indians engaged in sand painting. Image source: www.artsology.com/navajo_sand_painting.php
18. *Doric Temple of Apollo,* Corinth, c. 550 B.C.E.

                      The Path Toward Beauty

47.   *Akhenaten, Nefertiti and their daughters under the protection of the rays of the Aten, the solar disk,* 18th Dynasty, Amarna Period, c. 1330 B.C.E. Berlin, Staatliche Museen zu Berlin – Preussischer Kulturbesitz, Agyptisches Museum

48.   *Kalachakra (Wheel of Time) Sand Mandala.* Created over three weeks by monks from the Namgyal Monastery in Dharamsala, India. Image source: www.buddhanet.net/kalimage.htm

49 a.   Floor plan, Daphni, Church of the Dormition, Daphni, Greece

49 b.   Model of a Byzantine cross-in-square church, 11th century

50.   *Christ Pantokrator,* mosaic c. 1100, central dome, Church of the Dormition, Daphni, Greece

51.   *Gudea of Lagash, with a floor-plan of a temple engraved on his lap,* Paris, Louvre, c. 2130 B.C.E.

52.   *The Cambrai Madonna,* c. 1340, New York, Metropolitan Museum of Art

53.   *Mandylion of Edessa (Portrait of Christ)* 6th century, Vatican, Rome

54.   *Christ as Ruler,* detail of the *Deesis* mosaic, 13th century, Istanbul, Hagia Sophia

55.   Canon of the ideal physical proportions of any representation of the Buddha. Image source: www.buddhanet.net/budart.htm

56.   *Miroku Bosatsu,* 7th century, Nara, Chuguji Temple

57.   *Portrait sculpture of the Monk Ganjin,* 8th century, Nara, Toshodaiji

58 a.   South Portal and Porch, priory church of Saint-Pierre, c. 1120, Moissac

58 b.   *Second Coming of Christ* (Revelation 4-5), c. 1120, detail of the tympanum showing *Christ in Majesty*

58 c.   Detail of 58 b

59 a.   *Christ Giving the Gift of the Spirit to the Apostles,* c. 1130, tympanum, central portal inside the narthex, Vézelay, Benedictine abbey church, Sainte-Marie Madeleine

59. b   Detail of the figure of Christ.

60.   Ornamental capital, c. 1100, cloister, Moissac, priory church, Saint-Pierre

61.   Gislebertus, *Eve,* c. 1130, fragment of a lintel from the church of Saint-Lazare, Autun. Now in the Musée Rolin, Autun

62 a.   *Apocalyptic Christ,* c. 1155, detail from the central tympanum, west façade, Chartres Cathedral.

62 b.   *Kings and Queens,* c. 1155, jamb statues, central portal, west façade, Chartres Cathedral

63.   *Christ in Majesty,* detail, apse painting, from Lerida, Church of Tahull, c.1123. Now in the National Museum of Catalonia, Barcelona, Spain

64.   *Guro Mask,* Ivory Coast, Private Collection

65.   Kazimir Malevich, *Black Square,* 1915, St. Petersburg, Russian Museum

66.   Leonardo da Vinci, *Star of Bethlehem,* c. 1506, Windsor Castle, Royal Library

67.   Leonardo da Vinci, *Anatomical studies of an old man,* 1510, Windsor, Royal Library

68.   *Dodecahedron* (after a drawing by Leonardo da Vinci), Woodcut, in Luca Pacioli's *De divina proportione,* 1509, Paris, Bibliothèque nationale de France.

69.   Leonardo da Vinci, *Facial Proportions of a Man in Profile; Study of Soldiers and Horses,* c. 1490-95, Venice, Gallerie dell'Accademia

70.   Leonardo da Vinci, *The Vitruvian Man (The Proportions of the Human Body According to Vitruvius),* 1492, Venice, Gallerie dell'Accademia

71.   Leonardo da Vinci, *Madonna and Child with St Anne and the Young St John,* Charcoal with white chalk heightening on paper, 1500-01, London, National Gallery

72.   Leonardo da Vinci, *Adoration of the Magi,* c. 1481, Florence, Uffizi Gallery

73.   Leonardo da Vinci, *Detail of arm, hand and sleeve drapery,* study for the painting of *The Virgin and Child, St. Anne and St. John the Baptist,* 1508-12, Windsor, Royal Library

74 a. Pablo Picasso, *Guernica*, 1937, Madrid, Museo Nacional Centro de Arte Reina Sofia. © 2012 Estate of Pablo Picasso / Artists Rights Society (ARS), New York

74 b. Pablo Picasso, study for *Guernica* © 2012 Estate of Pablo Picasso / Artists Rights Society (ARS), New York

75. Caravaggio, *Entombment*, 1602-03, Rome, Pinacoteca Vaticana

76. Nicholas Poussin, *Landscape with the Funeral of Phocion*, 1648, Paris, Musée du Louvre

77 a. Charles Le Brun, *Anger* from *Expressions of the Passions of the Soul* c. 1670, Paris, Musée du Louvre

77 b. *Terror*, 18th century, engraved by Gérard Audran, Paris, Bibliothèque nationale (ms. BnF, Est, Kc 21, pl. 17)

78. Peter Paul Rubens, *Descent from the Cross*, 1612, Antwerp, Cathedral

79. *Great Stupa*, begun in the 3rd century B.C.E., Sanchi, Madhya Pradesh, Central India

80 a. Pantheon, Rome, 125-128

80 b. Giovanni Paolo Panini, *Interior of the Pantheon, Rome*, c. 1734, Washington, D.C., National Gallery of Art

80 c. Gaspare Trajano Fossati and Giuseppe Fossati, *Exterior of Haghia Sophia*, Istanbul (532-37), lithographs, c.1852 (detail)

80 d. Gaspare Trajano Fossati and Giuseppe Fossati, *Interior of Haghia Sophia*, Istanbul (532-37), lithographs, c. 1852

81. Sinan, Interior of the Mosque of Sultan Selim, 1568-75, Edirne, Turkey

82. Nave, 1194-1220, Chartres Cathedral, France

83 a. Prayer Hall, Great Mosque, begun 785-86, Córdoba, Spain

83 b. *Quibla* wall with view into the *Mihrab*, 965, Great Mosque, Córdoba, Spain

84. View into The Lion's Patio with its *muqarnas*, 1354-91, Alhambra, Granada, Spain

85. View of the exterior, Dome of the Rock, 7th century, Jerusalem

86. Borromini, Interior, San Carlo alle Quattro Fontane, 1638-1641, Rome

87 a. Brunelleschi, Foundling Hospital, begun 1419, Florence

87 b. Detail of Fig. 87 a

88. Cloister, c. 1180, Senanques, Cistercian Abbey, France

89 a-b. I.M. Pei, Views of the Miho Museum, 1996, Shigaraki, Japan

90. Tadao Ando, Church of the Light, 1989, Ibaraki, Osaka, Japan

91. *Teaching Buddha*, 12th century, from Korea, Paris, Musée Guimet

92. *Meditating Buddha*, c. 14th century, Anuradhapura, Sri Lanka

93. *Meditating Buddha*, from Taxila, Taxila Museum, Pakistan

94. *Head of Buddha*, 4th-5th centuries

95. *Buddha "taking the earth as witness,"* Sukhothai period, 13th-14th centuries, from Thailand, London, British Museum

96. Skopas, *Maenad*, c. 350 B.C.E., Dresden, State Art Collections: Sculpture Collection, Germany

97 a. *Athena Attacking the Giants*, detail of the Altar of Zeus from Pergamon, c. 175 B.C.E., Berlin, Staatliche Museen zu Berlin, Antiken Sammlungen, Pergamonmuseum, Germany

97 b. Detail of Fig. 97 a

98. Interior view towards the west, 1139-41, Cistercian Abbey Church of Notre-Dame Fontenay

99. Mark Rothko, *Chapel*, dedicated in 1971, Houston, Texas. © 1998 Kate Rothko Prizel & Christopher Rothko / Artists Rights Society (ARS), New York

100. Mark Rothko, *Triptych*, Houston, Texas, for north wall of the Rothko Chapel, 1964-1967. © 1998

The Path Toward Beauty

INDEX

A

absolute, the 11, 12
abstract art
  before naturalism, 76
  essential and spiritual in, 170,
    171, 173
  Malevich on, 172, 173
  mathematical rules and
    geometric forms in, 46,
    47
  Mondrian on, 173, 174
  the spiritual in, 188, 189
  vision of the inaccessible, 85
aesthetic experience
  in Hindu art (*rasadana*), 32
  of art, 102
aesthetic judgment
  aesthetic values, grace and
    facility, 107
  in Hume, 12, 13
  in Kant, 12, 13, 123, 133, 134,
    135
  reflective judgment standard
    for, 128
aesthetics
  as form of knowledge, 10
  defined, 10, 11
  sense vs. intellectual

knowledge, 103
aesthetic values, grace and
    facility, 107
african art 19, 20, 21, 23
Alberti, Leon Battista
  art to please public, 104, 105
  physical vs. metaphysical
    beauty, 62, 63
  symmetry in, 63, 64
allegory, work of art as, 142
architecture
  form, meaning, and function
    in, 145, 146
  light in, 148, 151, 153*f*
  perspective in, 148
  Vitruvius, *Ten Books of*
    Architecture, 61
Aristotle
  form in, 48
  imagination in, 67
  law of fourfold causality in, 47
  symmetry in, 2
art. *see also* work of art
  aim of, 103, 108
    to embody and manifest
      beauty, 111, 112
    to express human emotion,
      110, 111, 112, 113
    to move emotion of

beholder, 106, 111, 112,
    115, 118
    to please, 106, 115, 116, 118
    to reveal truth, 139
    to satisfy spiritual interests,
      Hegel, 139
  allegorical meaning of, 61
  appeal to feelings *vs.* to reason,
    115
  as imitation
    of nature, 98, 99
    Plato 44
  as mediator between God and
    man, 11
  as sacred, xxii
  as spiritual process, 142
  as symbol, 7
  beauty of, Kant, 123
  defined, 3, 10*n*
  metaphysical significance of,
    15
  pure *vs.* philosophical, 14
  purpose of, 11, 133
  spiritual nature of, 14, 15
  to reveal the invisible, 9
  tradition *vs.* originality in, 87,
    88*n*
art and nature, science and, 17,

   The Path Toward Beauty

The Path Toward Beauty

The Path Toward Beauty

    The Path Toward Beauty

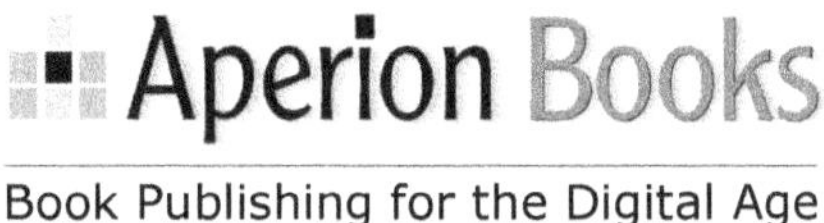

Book Publishing for the Digital Age

Aperion Books is dedicated to producing high quality publications that help people facilitate positive change in their lives. We specialize in publishing titles on spirituality, wellness, and personal growth.

Our unique Collaborative Publishing Program is specifically designed to help writers and authors expand their personal and professional horizons through creatively designed books that are distributed to national wholesalers and leading retailers.

www.ingramcontent.com/pod-product-compliance
Lightning Source LLC
Chambersburg PA
CBHW080253030726

47593CB00009B/2477